MongoDB in Action

MongoDB in Action

KYLE BANKER

MANNING

SHELTER ISLAND

Manning Publications Co.
20 Baldwin Road
PO Box 261
Shelter Island, NY 11964

Development editors: Jeff Bleiel, Sara Onstine
Copyeditor: Benjamin Berg
Proofreader: Katie Tennant
Typesetter: Dottie Marsico
Cover designer: Marija Tudor

ISBN 9781935182870
Printed in the United States of America
1 2 3 4 5 6 7 8 9 10 – MAL – 16 15 14 13 12 11

*This book is dedicated to peace and human dignity
and to all those who work for these ideals*

brief contents

contents

preface

Databases are the workhorses of the information age. Like Atlas, they go largely unnoticed in supporting the digital world we've come to inhabit. It's easy to forget that our digital interactions, from commenting and tweeting to searching and sorting, are in essence interactions with a database. Because of this fundamental yet hidden function, I always experience a certain sense of awe when thinking about databases, not unlike the awe one might feel when walking across a suspension bridge normally reserved for automobiles.

The database has taken many forms. The indexes of books and the card catalogs that once stood in libraries are both databases of a sort, as are the ad hoc structured text files of the Perl programmers of yore. Perhaps most recognizable now as databases proper are the sophisticated, fortune-making relational databases that underlie much of the world's software. These relational databases, with their idealized third-normal forms and expressive SQL interfaces, still command the respect of the old guard, and appropriately so.

But as a working web application developer a few years back, I was eager to sample the emerging alternatives to the reigning relational database. When I discovered MongoDB, the resonance was immediate. I liked the idea of using a JSON-like structure to represent data. JSON is simple, intuitive, human-friendly. That MongoDB also based its query language on JSON lent a high degree of comfort and harmony to the usage of this new database. The interface came first. Compelling features like easy replication and sharding made the package all the more intriguing. And by the time I'd built a few applications on MongoDB and beheld the ease of development it imparted, I'd become a convert.

Through an unlikely turn of events, I started working for 10gen, the company spearheading the development of this open source database. For two years, I've had the chance to improve various client drivers and work with numerous customers on their MongoDB deployments. The experience gained through this process has, I hope, been distilled faithfully into the book you're reading now.

As a piece of software and a work in progress, MongoDB is still far from perfection. But it's also successfully supporting thousands of applications atop database clusters small and large, and it's maturing daily. It's been known to bring out wonder, even happiness, in many a developer. My hope is that it can do the same for you.

acknowledgments

Thanks are due to folks at Manning for helping make this book a reality. Michael Stephens helped conceive the book, and my development editors, Sara Onstine and Jeff Bleiel, pushed the book to completion while being helpful along the way. My thanks goes to them.

Book writing is a time-consuming enterprise, and it's likely I wouldn't have found the time to finish this book had it not been for the generosity of Eliot Horowitz and Dwight Merriman. Eliot and Dwight, through their initiative and ingenuity, created MongoDB, and they trusted me to document the project. My thanks to them.

Many of the ideas in this book owe their origin to conversations I had with colleagues at 10gen. In this regard, special thanks are due to Mike Dirolf, Scott Hernandez, Alvin Richards, and Mathias Stearn. I'm especially indebted to Kristina Chowdorow, Richard Kreuter, and Aaron Staple for providing expert reviews of entire chapters.

The following reviewers read the manuscript at various stages during its development. I'd like to thank them for providing valuable feedback: Kevin Jackson, Hardy Ferentschik, David Sinclair, Chris Chandler, John Nunemaker, Robert Hanson, Alberto Lerner, Rick Wagner, Ryan Cox, Andy Brudtkuhl, Daniel Bretoi, Greg Donald, Sean Reilly, Curtis Miller, Sanchet Dighe, Philip Hallstrom, and Andy Dingley. Thanks also to Alvin Richards for his thorough technical review of the final manuscript shortly before it went to press.

Pride of place goes to my amazing wife, Dominika, for her patience and support, and my wonderful son, Oliver, just for being awesome.

about this book

This book is for application developers and DBAs wanting to learn MongoDB from the ground up. If you're new to MongoDB, you'll find in this book a tutorial that moves at a comfortable pace. If you're already a user, the more detailed reference sections in the book will come in handy and should fill any gaps in your knowledge. In terms of depth, the material should be suitable for all but the most advanced users.

The code examples are written in JavaScript, the language of the MongoDB shell, and Ruby, a popular scripting language. Every effort has been made to provide simple but useful examples, and only the plainest features of the JavaScript and Ruby languages are used. The main goal is to present the MongoDB API in the most accessible way possible. If you have experience with other programming languages, you should find the examples easy to follow.

One more note about languages. If you're wondering, "Why couldn't this book use language X?" you can take heart. The officially supported MongoDB drivers feature consistent and analogous APIs. This means that once you learn the basic API for one driver, you can pick up the others fairly easily. To assist you, this book provides an overview of the PHP, Java, and C++ drivers in appendix D.

How to use this book

This book is part tutorial, part reference. If you're brand new to MongoDB, then reading through the book in order makes a lot of sense. There are numerous code examples that you can run on your own to help solidify the concepts. At minimum, you'll need to install MongoDB and optionally the Ruby driver. Instructions for these installations can be found in appendix A.

If you've already used MongoDB, then you may be more interested in particular topics. Chapters 7–10 and all of the appendixes stand on their own and can safely be read in any order. Additionally, chapters 4–6 contain the so-called "nuts and bolts" sections, which focus on fundamentals. These also can be read outside the flow of the surrounding text.

Roadmap

This book is divided into three parts.

Part 1 is an end-to-end introduction to MongoDB. Chapter 1 gives an overview of MongoDB's history, features, and use cases. Chapter 2 teaches the database's core concepts through a tutorial on the MongoDB command shell. Chapter 3 walks through the design of a simple application that uses MongoDB on the back end.

Part 2 is an elaboration of the MongoDB API presented in part 1. With a specific focus on application development, the three chapters in part 2 progressively describe a schema and its operations for an e-commerce app. Chapter 4 delves into documents, the smallest unit of data in MongoDB, and puts forth a basic e-commerce schema design. Chapters 5 and 6 then teach you how to work with this schema by covering queries and updates. To augment the presentation, each of the chapters in part 2 contains a detailed breakdown of its subject matter.

Part 3 focuses on performance and operations. Chapter 7 is a thorough study of indexing and query optimization. Chapter 8 concentrates on replication, with strategies for deploying MongoDB for high availability and read scaling. Chapter 9 describes sharding, MongoDB's path to horizontal scalability. And chapter 10 provides a series of best practices for deploying, administering, and troubleshooting MongoDB installations.

The book ends with five appendixes. Appendix A covers installation of MongoDB and Ruby (for the driver examples) on Linux, Mac OS X, and Windows. Appendix B presents a series of schema and application design patterns, and it also includes a list of anti-patterns. Appendix C shows how to work with binary data in MongoDB and how to use GridFS, a spec implemented by all the drivers, to store especially large files in the database. Appendix D is a comparative study of the PHP, Java, and C++ drivers. Appendix E shows you how to use spatial indexing to query on geo-coordinates.

Code conventions and downloads

All source code in the listings and in the text is presented in a `fixed-width font`, which separates it from ordinary text.

Code annotations accompany some of the listings, highlighting important concepts. In some cases, numbered bullets link to explanations that follow in the text.

As an open source project, 10gen keeps MongoDB's bug tracker open to the community at large. At several points in the book, particularly in the footnotes, you'll see references to bug reports and planned improvements. For example, the ticket for adding full-text search to the database is SERVER-380. To view the status of any such ticket, point your browser to http://jira.mongodb.org, and enter the ticket ID in the search box.

 You can download the book's source code, with some sample data, from the book's site at http://mongodb-book.com as well as from the publisher's website at http://manning.com/MongoDBinAction.

Software requirements

To get the most out of this book, you'll need to have MongoDB installed on your system. Instructions for installing MongoDB can be found in appendix A and also on the official MongoDB website (http://mongodb.org).

 If you want to run the Ruby driver examples, you'll also need to install Ruby. Again, consult appendix A for instructions on this.

Author Online

The purchase of *MongoDB in Action* includes free access to a private forum run by Manning Publications where you can make comments about the book, ask technical questions, and receive help from the author and other users. To access and subscribe to the forum, point your browser to www.manning.com/MongoDBinAction. This page provides information on how to get on the forum once you are registered, what kind of help is available, and the rules of conduct in the forum.

 Manning's commitment to our readers is to provide a venue where a meaningful dialogue between individual readers and between readers and the author can take place. It's not a commitment to any specific amount of participation on the part of the author, whose contribution to the book's forum remains voluntary (and unpaid). We suggest you try asking him some challenging questions, lest his interest stray!

 The Author Online forum and the archives of previous discussions will be accessible from the publisher's website as long as the book is in print.

about the cover illustration

The figure on the cover of *MongoDB in Action* is captioned "Le Bourginion," or a resident of the Burgundy region in northeastern France. The illustration is taken from a nineteenth-century edition of Sylvain Maréchal's four-volume compendium of regional dress customs published in France. Each illustration is finely drawn and colored by hand. The rich variety of Maréchal's collection reminds us vividly of how culturally apart the world's towns and regions were just 200 years ago. Isolated from each other, people spoke different dialects and languages. In the streets or in the countryside, it was easy to identify where they lived and what their trade or station in life was just by their dress.

Dress codes have changed since then and the diversity by region, so rich at the time, has faded away. It is now hard to tell apart the inhabitants of different continents, let alone different towns or regions. Perhaps we have traded cultural diversity for a more varied personal life—certainly for a more varied and fast-paced technological life.

At a time when it is hard to tell one computer book from another, Manning celebrates the inventiveness and initiative of the computer business with book covers based on the rich diversity of regional life of two centuries ago, brought back to life by Maréchal's pictures.

Part 1

Getting started

This part of the book provides a broad, practical introduction to MongoDB. It also introduces the JavaScript shell and the Ruby driver, both of which are used in examples throughout the book.

In chapter 1, we'll look at MongoDB's history, design goals, and application use cases. We'll also see what makes MongoDB unique as we contrast it with other databases emerging in the "NoSQL" space.

In chapter 2, you'll become conversant in the language of MongoDB's shell. You'll learn the basics of MongoDB's query language, and you'll practice by creating, querying, updating, and deleting documents. We'll round out the chapter with some advanced shell tricks and MongoDB commands.

Chapter 3 introduces the MongoDB drivers and MongoDB's data format, BSON. Here you'll learn how to talk to the database through the Ruby programming language, and you'll build a simple application in Ruby demonstrating MongoDB's flexibility and query power.

A database for
the modern web

In this chapter

- MongoDB's history, design goals, and key features
- A brief introduction to the shell and the drivers
- Use cases and limitations

If you've built web applications in recent years, you've probably used a relational database as the primary data store, and it probably performed acceptably. Most developers are familiar with SQL, and most of us can appreciate the beauty of a well-normalized data model, the necessity of transactions, and the assurances provided by a durable storage engine. And even if we don't like working with relational databases directly, a host of tools, from administrative consoles to object-relational mappers, helps alleviate any unwieldy complexity. Simply put, the relational database is mature and well known. So when a small but vocal cadre of developers starts advocating alternative data stores, questions about the viability and utility of these new technologies arise. Are these new data stores replacements for relational database systems? Who's using them in production, and why? What are the trade-offs involved in moving to a nonrelational database? The answers to those questions rest on the answer to this one: why are developers interested in MongoDB?

MongoDB is a database management system designed for web applications and internet infrastructure. The data model and persistence strategies are built for high read and write throughput and the ability to scale easily with automatic failover. Whether an application requires just one database node or dozens of them, MongoDB can provide surprisingly good performance. If you've experienced difficulties scaling relational databases, this may be great news. But not everyone needs to operate at scale. Maybe all you've ever needed is a single database server. Why then would you use MongoDB?

It turns out that MongoDB is immediately attractive, not because of its scaling strategy, but rather because of its intuitive data model. Given that a document-based data model can represent rich, hierarchical data structures, it's often possible to do without the complicated multi-table joins imposed by relational databases. For example, suppose you're modeling products for an e-commerce site. With a fully normalized relational data model, the information for any one product might be divided among dozens of tables. If you want to get a product representation from the database shell, we'll need to write a complicated SQL query full of joins. As a consequence, most developers will need to rely on a secondary piece of software to assemble the data into something meaningful.

With a document model, by contrast, most of a product's information can be represented within a single document. When you open the MongoDB JavaScript shell, you can easily get a comprehensible representation of your product with all its information hierarchically organized in a JSON-like structure.[1] You can also query for it and manipulate it. MongoDB's query capabilities are designed specifically for manipulating structured documents, so users switching from relational databases experience a similar level of query power. In addition, most developers now work with object-oriented languages, and they want a data store that better maps to objects. With MongoDB, the object defined in the programming language can be persisted "as is," removing some of the complexity of object mappers.

If the distinction between a tabular and object representation of data is new to you, then you probably have a lot of questions. Rest assured that by the end of this chapter I'll have provided a thorough overview of MongoDB's features and design goals, making it increasingly clear why developers from companies like Geek.net (SourceForge.net) and The New York Times have adopted MongoDB for their projects. We'll see the history of MongoDB and lead into a tour of the database's main features. Next, we'll explore some alternative database solutions and the so-called NoSQL movement,[2] explaining how MongoDB fits in. Finally, I'll describe in general where MongoDB works best and where an alternative data store might be preferable.

---

[1] JSON is an acronym for *JavaScript Object Notation.* As we'll see shortly, JSON structures are comprised of keys and values, and they can nest arbitrarily deep. They're analogous to the dictionaries and hash maps of other programming languages.

[2] The umbrella term *NoSQL* was coined in 2009 to lump together the many nonrelational databases gaining in popularity at the time.

1.1 Born in the cloud

The history of MongoDB is brief but worth recounting, for it was born out of a much more ambitious project. In mid-2007, a startup called 10gen began work on a software platform-as-a-service, composed of an application server and a database, that would host web applications and scale them as needed. Like Google's AppEngine, 10gen's platform was designed to handle the scaling and management of hardware and software infrastructure automatically, freeing developers to focus solely on their application code. 10gen ultimately discovered that most developers didn't feel comfortable giving up so much control over their technology stacks, but users *did* want 10gen's new database technology. This led 10gen to concentrate its efforts solely on the database that became MongoDB.

With MongoDB's increasing adoption and production deployments large and small, 10gen continues to sponsor the database's development as an open source project. The code is publicly available and free to modify and use, subject to the terms of its license. And the community at large is encouraged to file bug reports and submit patches. Still, all of MongoDB's core developers are either founders or employees of 10gen, and the project's roadmap continues to be determined by the needs of its user community and the overarching goal of creating a database that combines the best features of relational databases and distributed key-value stores. Thus, 10gen's business model is not unlike that of other well-known open source companies: support the development of an open source product and provide subscription services to end users.

This history contains a couple of important ideas. First is that MongoDB was originally developed for a platform that, by definition, required its database to scale gracefully across multiple machines. The second is that MongoDB was designed as a data store for web applications. As we'll see, MongoDB's design as a horizontally scalable primary data store sets it apart from other modern database systems.

1.2 MongoDB's key features

A database is defined in large part by its data model. In this section, we'll look at the document data model, and then we'll see the features of MongoDB that allow us to operate effectively on that model. We'll also look at operations, focusing on MongoDB's flavor of replication and on its strategy for scaling horizontally.

1.2.1 The document data model

MongoDB's data model is document-oriented. If you're not familiar with documents in the context of databases, the concept can be most easily demonstrated by example.

Listing 1.1   A document representing an entry on a social news site

```
{ _id: ObjectID('4bd9e8e17cefd644108961bb'),        ◁─┐  _id field
  title: 'Adventures in Databases',                       is primary key
  url: 'http://example.com/databases.txt',
```

```
  author: 'msmith',
  vote_count: 20,
                                              ❶ Tags stored as
  tags: ['databases', 'mongodb', 'indexing'],  ↵    array of strings

  image: {                                    ↖ Attribute points to
    url: 'http://example.com/db.jpg',         ❷ another document
    caption: '',
    type: 'jpg',
    size: 75381,
    data: "Binary"
  },                                          ❸ Comments stored as
                                               ↵    array of comment objects
  comments: [
    { user: 'bjones',
      text: 'Interesting article!'
    },

    { user: 'blogger',
      text: 'Another related article is at http://example.com/db/db.txt'
    }
  ]
}
```

Listing 1.1 shows a sample document representing an article on a social news site (think Digg). As you can see, a document is essentially a set of property names and their values. The values can be simple data types, such as strings, numbers, and dates. But these values can also be arrays and even other documents ❷. These latter constructs permit documents to represent a variety of rich data structures. You'll see that our sample document has a property, tags ❶, which stores the article's tags in an array. But even more interesting is the comments property ❸, which references an array of comment documents.

Let's take a moment to contrast this with a standard relational database representation of the same data. Figure 1.1 shows a likely relational analogue. Since tables are essentially flat, representing the various one-to-many relationships in your post is going to require multiple tables. You start with a posts table containing the core information for each post. Then you create three other tables, each of which includes a field, post_id, referencing the original post. The technique of separating an object's data into multiple tables likes this is known as *normalization*. A normalized data set, among other things, ensures that each unit of data is represented in one place only.

But strict normalization isn't without its costs. Notably, some assembly is required. To display the post we just referenced, you'll need to perform a join between the post and tags tables. You'll also need to query separately for the comments or possibly include them in a join as well. Ultimately, the question of whether strict normalization is required depends on the kind of data you're modeling, and I'll have much more to say about the topic in chapter 4. What's important to note here is that a document-oriented data model naturally represents data in an aggregate form, allowing you to work with an object holistically: all the data representing a post, from comments to tags, can be fitted into a single database object.

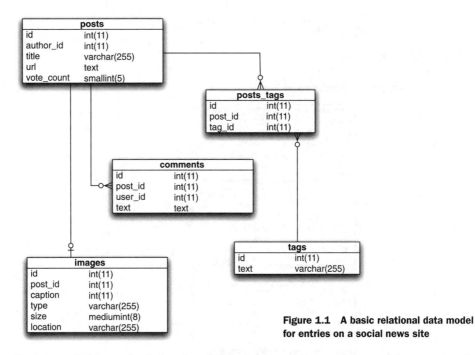

Figure 1.1 A basic relational data model for entries on a social news site

You've probably noticed that in addition to providing a richness of structure, documents need not conform to a prespecified schema. With a relational database, you store rows in a table. Each table has a strictly defined schema specifying which columns and types are permitted. If any row in a table needs an extra field, you have to alter the table explicitly. MongoDB groups documents into collections, containers that don't impose any sort of schema. In theory, each document in a collection can have a completely different structure; in practice, a collection's documents will be relatively uniform. For instance, every document in the posts collection will have fields for the title, tags, comments, and so forth.

But this lack of imposed schema confers some advantages. First, your application code, and not the database, enforces the data's structure. This can speed up initial application development when the schema is changing frequently. Second, and more significantly, a schemaless model allows you to represent data with truly variable properties. For example, imagine you're building an e-commerce product catalog. There's no way of knowing in advance what attributes a product will have, so the application will need to account for that variability. The traditional way of handling this in a fixed-schema database is to use the entity-attribute-value pattern,[3] shown in figure 1.2. What you're seeing is one section of the data model for Magento, an open source e-commerce framework. Note the series of tables that are all essentially the same, except for a single attribute, value, that varies only by data type. This structure allows

---

[3] http://en.wikipedia.org/wiki/Entity-attribute-value_model

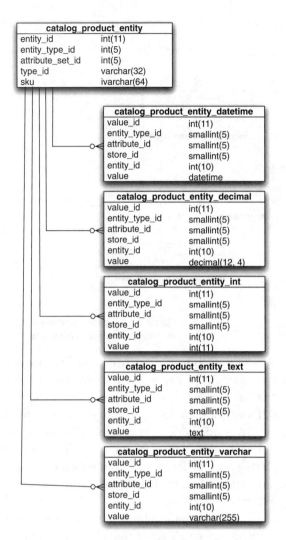

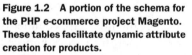

Figure 1.2 A portion of the schema for the PHP e-commerce project Magento. These tables facilitate dynamic attribute creation for products.

an administrator to define additional product types and their attributes, but the result is significant complexity. Think about firing up the MySQL shell to examine or update a product modeled in this way; the SQL joins required to assemble the product would be enormously complex. Modeled as a document, no join is required, and new attributes can be added dynamically.

1.2.2 *Ad hoc queries*

To say that a system supports ad hoc queries is to say that it's not necessary to define in advance what sorts of queries the system will accept. Relational databases have this property; they will faithfully execute any well-formed SQL query with any number of conditions. Ad hoc queries are easy to take for granted if the only databases you've ever used have been relational. But not all databases support dynamic queries. For instance, key-value stores are queryable on one axis only: the value's key. Like many other systems, key-value stores sacrifice rich query power in exchange for a simple scalability model. One of MongoDB's design goals is to preserve most of the query power that's been so fundamental to the relational database world.

To see how MongoDB's query language works, let's take a simple example involving posts and comments. Suppose you want to find all posts tagged with the term *politics* having greater than 10 votes. A SQL query would look like this:

```
SELECT * FROM posts
  INNER JOIN posts_tags ON posts.id = posts_tags.post_id
  INNER JOIN tags ON posts_tags.tag_id == tags.id
  WHERE tags.text = 'politics' AND posts.vote_count > 10;
```

The equivalent query in MongoDB is specified using a document as a matcher. The special $gt key indicates the greater-than condition.

```
db.posts.find({'tags': 'politics', 'vote_count': {'$gt': 10}});
```

Note that the two queries assume a different data model. The SQL query relies on a strictly normalized model, where posts and tags are stored in distinct tables, whereas the MongoDB query assumes that tags are stored within each post document. But both queries demonstrate an ability to query on arbitrary combinations of attributes, which is the essence of ad hoc queryability.

As mentioned earlier, some databases don't support ad hoc queries because the data model is too simple. For example, you can query a key-value store by primary key only. The values pointed to by those keys are opaque as far as the queries are concerned. The only way to query by a secondary attribute, such as this example's vote count, is to write custom code to manually build entries where the primary key indicates a given vote count and the value stores a list of the primary keys of the documents containing said vote count. If you took this approach with a key-value store, you'd be guilty of implementing a hack, and although it might work for smaller data sets, stuffing multiple indexes into what's physically a single index isn't a good idea. What's more, the hash-based index in a key-value store won't support range queries, which would probably be necessary for querying on an item like a vote count.

If you're coming from a relational database system where ad hoc queries are the norm, then it's sufficient to note that MongoDB features a similar level of queryability. If you've been evaluating a variety of database technologies, you'll want to keep in mind that not all of these technologies support ad hoc queries and that if you do need them, MongoDB could be a good choice. But ad hoc queries alone aren't enough. Once your data set grows to a certain size, indexes become necessary for query efficiency. Proper indexes will increase query and sort speeds by orders of magnitude; consequently, any system that supports ad hoc queries should also support secondary indexes.

1.2.3   Secondary indexes

The best way to understand database indexes is by analogy: many books have indexes mapping keywords to page numbers. Suppose you have a cookbook and want to find all recipes calling for pears (maybe you have a lot of pears and don't want them to go bad). The time-consuming approach would be to page through every recipe, checking each ingredient list for pears. Most people would prefer to check the book's index for the *pears* entry, which would give a list of all the recipes containing pears. Database indexes are data structures that provide this same service.

Secondary indexes in MongoDB are implemented as *B-trees*. B-tree indexes, also the default for most relational databases, are optimized for a variety of queries, including range scans and queries with sort clauses. By permitting multiple secondary indexes, MongoDB allows users to optimize for a wide variety of queries.

With MongoDB, you can create up to 64 indexes per collection. The kinds of indexes supported include all the ones you'd find in an RDMBS; ascending, descending, unique, compound-key, and even geospatial indexes are supported. Because MongoDB and most RDBMSs use the same data structure for their indexes, advice for managing indexes in both of these systems is compatible. We'll begin looking at indexes in the next chapter, and because an understanding of indexing is so crucial to efficiently operating a database, I devote all of chapter 7 to the topic.

1. A working replica set

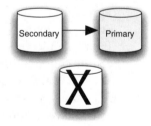

1.2.4   Replication

MongoDB provides database replication via a topology known as a *replica set*. Replica sets distribute data across machines for redundancy and automate failover in the event of server and network outages. Additionally, replication is used to scale database reads. If you have a read-intensive application, as is commonly the case on the web, it's possible to spread database reads across machines in the replica set cluster.

Replica sets consist of exactly one primary node and one or more secondary nodes. Like the master-slave replication that you may be familiar with from other databases, a replica set's primary node can accept both reads and writes, but the secondary nodes are read-only. What makes replica sets unique is their support for automated failover: if the primary node fails, the cluster will pick a secondary node and automatically promote it to primary. When the former primary comes back online, it'll do so as a secondary. An illustration of this process is provided in figure 1.3.

I discuss replication in chapter 8.

2. Original primary node fails and
   a secondary is promoted to primary

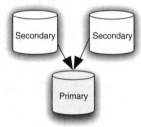

3. Original primary comes back online
   as a secondary

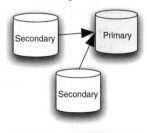

Figure 1.3   Automated failover with a replica set

1.2.5 *Speed and durability*

To understand MongoDB's approach to durability, it pays to consider a few ideas first. In the realm of database systems there exists an inverse relationship between write speed and durability. *Write speed* can be understood as the volume of inserts, updates, and deletes that a database can process in a given time frame. *Durability* refers to level of assurance that these write operations have been made permanent.

For instance, suppose you write 100 records of 50 KB each to a database and then immediately cut the power on the server. Will those records be recoverable when you bring the machine back online? The answer is, maybe, and it depends on both your database system and the hardware hosting it. The problem is that writing to a magnetic hard drive is orders of magnitude slower than writing to RAM. Certain databases, such as memcached, write exclusively to RAM, which makes them extremely fast but completely volatile. On the other hand, few databases write exclusively to disk because the low performance of such an operation is unacceptable. Therefore, database designers often need to make compromises to provide the best balance of speed and durability.

In MongoDB's case, users control the speed and durability trade-off by choosing write semantics and deciding whether to enable journaling. All writes, by default, are *fire-and-forget*, which means that these writes are sent across a TCP socket without requiring a database response. If users want a response, they can issue a write using a special *safe mode* provided by all drivers. This forces a response, ensuring that the write has been received by the server with no errors. Safe mode is configurable; it can also be used to block until a write has been replicated to some number of servers. For high-volume, low-value data (like clickstreams and logs), fire-and-forget-style writes can be ideal. For important data, a safe-mode setting is preferable.

In MongoDB v2.0, journaling is enabled by default. With journaling, every write is committed to an append-only log. If the server is ever shut down uncleanly (say, in a power outage), the journal will be used to ensure that MongoDB's data files are restored to a consistent state when you restart the server. This is the safest way to run MongoDB.

Transaction logging

One compromise between speed and durability can be seen in MySQL's InnoDB. InnoDB is a transactional storage engine, which by definition must guarantee durability. It accomplishes this by writing its updates in two places: once to a transaction log and again to an in-memory buffer pool. The transaction log is synced to disk immediately, whereas the buffer pool is only eventually synced by a background thread. The reason for this dual write is because, generally speaking, random I/O is much slower that sequential I/O. Since writes to the main data files constitute random I/O, it's faster to write these changes to RAM first, allowing the sync to disk to happen later. But since some sort of write to disk is necessary to guarantee durability, it's important that the write be sequential; this is what the transaction log provides. In the event of an unclean shutdown, InnoDB can replay its transaction log and update the main data files accordingly. This provides an acceptable level of performance while guaranteeing a high level of durability.

It's possible to run the server without journaling as a way of increasing performance for some write loads. The downside is that the data files may be corrupted after an unclean shutdown. As a consequence, anyone planning to disable journaling must run with replication, preferably to a second data center, to increase the likelihood that a pristine copy of the data will still exist even if there's a failure.

The topics of replication and durability are vast; you'll see a detailed exploration of them in chapter 8.

1.2.6   Scaling

The easiest way to scale most databases is to upgrade the hardware. If your application is running on a single node, it's usually possible to add some combination of disk IOPS, memory, and CPU to ease any database bottlenecks. The technique of augmenting a single node's hardware for scale is known as *vertical scaling* or *scaling up*. Vertical scaling has the advantages of being simple, reliable, and cost-effective up to a certain point. If you're running on virtualized hardware (such as Amazon's EC2), then you may find that a sufficiently large instance isn't available. If you're running on physical hardware, there may come a point where the cost of a more powerful server becomes prohibitive.

It then makes sense to consider scaling *horizontally*, or *scaling out*. Instead of beefing up a single node, scaling horizontally means distributing the database across multiple machines. Because a horizontally scaled architecture can use commodity hardware, the costs for hosting the total data set can be significantly reduced. What's more, the the distribution of data across machines mitigates the consequences of failure. Machines will unavoidably fail from time to time. If you've scaled vertically, and the machine fails, then you need to deal with the failure of a machine upon which most of your system depends. This may not be an issue if a copy of the data exists on a replicated slave, but it's still the case that only a single server need fail to bring down the entire system. Contrast that with failure inside a horizontally scaled architecture. This may be less catastrophic since a single machine represents a much smaller percentage of the system as a whole.

MongoDB has been designed to make horizontal scaling manageable. It does so via a range-based partitioning mechanism, known as *auto-sharding*, which automatically manages the distribution of data across nodes. The sharding system handles the addition of shard nodes, and it also facilitates automatic failover. Individual shards are made up of a replica set consisting of at least two nodes,[4] ensuring automatic recovery with no single point of failure. All this means that no application code has to handle these logistics; your application code communicates with a sharded cluster just as it speaks to a single node.

We've covered a lot of MongoDB's most compelling features; in chapter 2, we'll begin to see how some of these work in practice. But at this point, we're going to take

---

[4]   Technically, each replica set will have at least three nodes, but only two of these need carry a copy of the data.

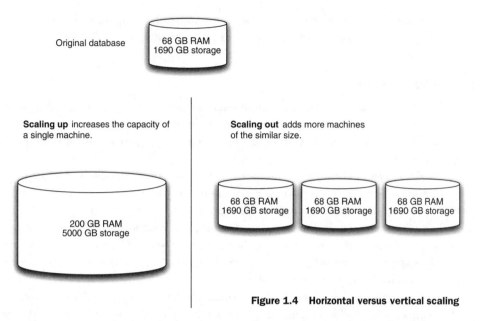

Original database — 68 GB RAM / 1690 GB storage

Scaling up increases the capacity of a single machine.

Scaling out adds more machines of the similar size.

200 GB RAM / 5000 GB storage

68 GB RAM / 1690 GB storage   68 GB RAM / 1690 GB storage   68 GB RAM / 1690 GB storage

Figure 1.4   Horizontal versus vertical scaling

a more pragmatic look at the database. In the next section, we'll look at MongoDB in its environment, the tools that ship with the core server, and a few ways of getting data in and out.

1.3 MongoDB's core server and tools

MongoDB is written in C++ and actively developed by 10gen. The project compiles on all major operating systems, including Mac OS X, Windows, and most flavors of Linux. Precompiled binaries are available for each of these platforms at mongodb.org. MongoDB is open source and licensed under the GNU-AGPL. The source code is freely available on GitHub, and contributions from the community are frequently accepted. But the project is guided by the 10gen core server team, and the overwhelming majority of commits come from this group.

> **ON THE GNU-AGPL** The GNU-AGPL is subject to some controversy. What this licensing means in practice is that the source code is freely available and that contributions from the community are encouraged. The primary limitation of the GNU-AGPL is that any modifications made to the source code must be published publicly for the benefit of the community. For companies wanting to safeguard their core server enhancements, 10gen provides special commercial licenses.

MongoDB v1.0 was released in November 2009. Major releases appear approximately once every three months, with even point numbers for stable branches and odd numbers for development. As of this writing, the latest stable release is v2.0.[5]

---

[5] You should always use the latest stable point release; for example, v2.0.1.

What follows is an overview of the components that ship with MongoDB along with a high-level description of the tools and language drivers for developing applications with the database.

1.3.1   *The core server*

The core database server runs via an executable called `mongod` (`mongodb.exe` on Windows). The `mongod` server process receives commands over a network socket using a custom binary protocol. All the data files for a `mongod` process are stored by default in /data/db.[6]

`mongod` can be run in several modes, the most common of which is as a member of a replica set. Since replication is recommended, you generally see replica set configurations consisting of two replicas, plus an arbiter process residing on a third server.[7] For MongoDB's auto-sharding architecture, the components consist of `mongod` processes configured as per-shard replica sets, with special metadata servers, known as *config servers*, on the side. A separate routing server called `mongos` is also used to send requests to the appropriate shard.

Configuring a `mongod` process is relatively simple compared with other database systems such as MySQL. Though it's possible to specify standard ports and data directories, there are few options for tuning the database. Database tuning, which in most RDBMSs means tinkering with a wide array of parameters controlling memory allocation and the like, has become something of a black art. MongoDB's design philosophy dictates that memory management is better handled by the operating system than by a DBA or application developer. Thus, data files are mapped to a system's virtual memory using the `mmap()` system call. This effectively offloads memory management responsibilities to the OS kernel. I'll have more to say about `mmap()` later in the book; for now it suffices to note that the lack of configuration parameters is a design feature, not a bug.

1.3.2   *The JavaScript shell*

The MongoDB command shell is a JavaScript-based tool for administering the database and manipulating data. The mongo executable loads the shell and connects to a specified `mongod` process. The shell has many of the same powers as the MySQL shell, the primary difference being that SQL isn't used. Instead, most commands are issued using JavaScript expressions. For instance, you can pick your database and then insert a simple document into the users collection like so:

```
> use mongodb-in-action
> db.users.insert({name: "Kyle"})
```

The first command, indicating which database you want to use, will be familiar to users of MySQL. The second command is a JavaScript expression that inserts a simple document. To see the results of your insert, you can issue a simple query:

---

[6] c:\data\db on Windows.

[7] These arbiter processes are lightweight and can easily be run on an app server, for instance.

```
> db.users.find()
{ _id: ObjectId("4ba667b0a90578631c9caea0"), name: "Kyle" }
```

The find method returns the inserted document, with the an object ID added. All documents require a primary key stored in the _id field. You're allowed to enter a custom _id as long as you can guarantee its uniqueness. But if you omit the _id altogether, then a MongoDB object ID will be inserted automatically.

In addition to allowing you to insert and query for data, the shell permits you to run administrative commands. Some examples include viewing the current database operation, checking the status of replication to a secondary node, and configuring a collection for sharding. As you'll see, the MongoDB shell is indeed a powerful tool that's worth getting to know well.

All that said, the bulk of your work with MongoDB will be done through an application written in a given programming language; to see how that's done, we must say a few things about MongoDB's language drivers.

1.3.3 Database drivers

If the notion of a database driver conjures up nightmares of low-level device hacking, don't fret. The MongoDB drivers are easy to use. Every effort has been made to provide an API that matches the idioms of the given language while also maintaining relatively uniform interfaces across languages. For instance, all of the drivers implement similar methods for saving a document to a collection, but the representation of the document itself will usually be whatever is most natural to each language. In Ruby, that means using a Ruby hash. In Python, a dictionary is appropriate. And in Java, which lacks any analogous language primitive, you represent documents using a special document builder class that implements LinkedHashMap.

Because the drivers provide a rich, language-centric interface to the database, little abstraction beyond the driver itself is required to build an application. This contrasts notably with the application design for an RDBMS, where a library is almost certainly necessary to mediate between the relational data model of the database and the object-oriented model of most modern programming languages. Still, even if the heft of an object-relational mapper isn't required, many developers like using a thin wrapper over the drivers to handle associations, validations, and type checking.[8]

At the time of this writing, 10gen officially supports drivers for C, C++, C#, Erlang, Haskell, Java, Perl, PHP, Python, Scala, and Ruby—and the list is always growing. If you need support for another language, there's probably a community-supported driver for it. If no community-supported driver exists for your language, specifications for building a new driver are documented at mongodb.org. Since all of the officially supported drivers are used heavily in production and provided under the Apache license, plenty of good examples are freely available for would-be driver authors.

Beginning in chapter 3, I describe how the drivers work and how to use them to write programs.

---

[8] A few popular wrappers at the time of this writing include Morphia for Java, Doctrine for PHP, and Mongo-Mapper for Ruby.

1.3.4   *Command-line tools*

MongoDB is bundled with several command-line utilities:

- `mongodump` *and* `mongorestore`—Standard utilities for backing up and restoring a database. `mongodump` saves the database's data in its native BSON format and thus is best used for backups only; this tool has the advantage of being usable for hot backups which can easily be restored with `mongorestore`.

- `mongoexport` *and* `mongoimport`—These utilities export and import JSON, CSV, and TSV data; this is useful if you need your data in widely supported formats. `mongoimport` can also be good for initial imports of large data sets, although you should note in passing that before importing, it's often desirable to adjust the data model to take best advantage of MongoDB. In those cases, it's easier to import the data through one of the drivers using a custom script.

- `mongosniff`—A wire-sniffing tool for viewing operations sent to the database. Essentially translates the BSON going over the wire to human-readable shell statements.

- `mongostat`—Similar to `iostat`; constantly polls MongoDB and the system to provide helpful stats, including the number of operations per second (inserts, queries, updates, deletes, and so on.), the amount of virtual memory allocated, and the number of connections to the server.

The remaining utilities, `bsondump` and `monfiles`, are discussed later in the book.

1.4   *Why MongoDB?*

I've already provided a few reasons why MongoDB might be a good choice for your projects. Here, I'll make this more explicit, first by considering the overall design objectives of the MongoDB project. According to its creators, MongoDB has been designed to combine the best features of key-value stores and relational databases. Key-value stores, because of their simplicity, are extremely fast and relatively easy to scale. Relational databases are more difficult to scale, at least horizontally, but admit a rich data model and a powerful query language. If MongoDB represents a mean between these two designs, then the reality is a database that scales easily, stores rich data structures, and provides sophisticated query mechanisms.

In terms of use cases, MongoDB is well suited as a primary data store for web applications, for analytics and logging applications, and for any application requiring a medium-grade cache. In addition, because it easily stores schemaless data, MongoDB is also good for capturing data whose structure can't be known in advance.

The preceding claims are bold. In order to substantiate them, we're going to take a broad look at the varieties of databases currently in use and contrast them with MongoDB. Next, I'll discuss some specific MongoDB use cases and provide examples of them in production. Finally, I'll discuss some important practical considerations for using MongoDB.

1.4.1 *MongoDB versus other databases*

The number of available databases has exploded, and weighing one against another can be difficult. Fortunately, most of these databases fall under one of a few categories. In the sections that follow, I describe simple and sophisticated key-value stores, relational databases, and document databases, and show how these compare and contrast with MongoDB.

Table 1.1 Database families

	Examples	Data model	Scalability model	Use cases
Simple key-value stores	Memcached	Key-value, where the value is a binary blob.	Variable. Memcached can scale across nodes, converting all available RAM into a single, monolithic data store.	Caching. Web ops.
Sophisticated key-value stores	Cassandra, Project Voldemort, Riak	Variable. Cassandra uses a key-value structure known as a *column*. Voldemort stores binary blobs.	Eventually consistent, multinode distribution for high availability and easy failover.	High throughput verticals (activity feeds, message queues). Caching. Web ops.
Relational databases	Oracle database, MySQL, PostgreSQL	Tables.	Vertical scaling. Limited support for clustering and manual partitioning.	System requiring transactions (banking, finance) or SQL. Normalized data model.

SIMPLE KEY-VALUE STORES

Simple key-value stores do what their name implies: they index values based on a supplied key. A common use case is caching. For instance, suppose you needed to cache an HTML page rendered by your app. The key in this case might be the page's URL, and the value would be the rendered HTML itself. Note that as far as a key-value store is concerned, the value is an opaque byte array. There's no enforced schema, as you'd find in a relational database, nor is there any concept of data types. This naturally limits the operations permitted by key-value stores: you can put a new value and then use its key either to retrieve that value or delete it. Systems with such simplicity are generally fast and scalable.

The best-known simple key-value store is memcached (pronounced *mem-cash-dee*). Memcached stores its data in memory only, so it trades persistence for speed. It's also distributed; memcached nodes running across multiple servers can act as a single data store, eliminating the complexity of maintaining cache state across machines.

Compared with MongoDB, a simple key-value store like memcached will often allow for faster reads and writes. But unlike MongoDB, these systems can rarely act as primary data stores. Simple key-value stores are best used as adjuncts, either as caching layers atop a more traditional database or as simple persistence layers for ephemeral services like job queues.

SOPHISTICATED KEY-VALUE STORES

It's possible to refine the simple key-value model to handle complicated read/write schemes or to provide a richer data model. In these cases, we end up with what we'll term a *sophisticated key-value store*. One example is Amazon's Dynamo, described in a widely studied white paper entitled *Dynamo: Amazon's Highly Available Key-value Store*. The aim of Dynamo is to be a database robust enough to continue functioning in the face of network failures, data center outages, and other similar disruptions. This requires that the system can always be read from and written to, which essentially requires that data be automatically replicated across multiple nodes. If a node fails, a user of the system, perhaps in this case a customer with an Amazon shopping cart, won't experience any interruptions in service. Dynamo provides ways of resolving the inevitable conflicts that arise when a system allows the same data to be written to multiple nodes. At the same time, Dynamo is easily scaled. Because it's masterless—all nodes are equal—it's easy to understand the system as a whole, and nodes can be added easily. Although Dynamo is a proprietary system, the ideas used to build it have inspired many systems falling under the NoSQL umbrella, including Cassandra, Project Voldemort, and Riak.

Looking at who developed these sophisticated key-value stores, and how they've been used in practice, you can see where these systems shine. Let's take Cassandra, which implements many of Dynamo's scaling properties while providing a column-oriented data model inspired by Google's BigTable. Cassandra is an open source version of a data store built by Facebook for its inbox search feature. The system scaled horizontally to index more than 50 TB of inbox data, allowing for searches on inbox keywords and recipients. Data was indexed by user ID, where each record consisted of an array of search terms for keyword searches and an array of recipient IDs for recipient searches.[9]

These sophisticated key-value stores were developed by major internet companies such as Amazon, Google, and Facebook to manage cross sections of systems with extraordinarily large amounts of data. In other words, sophisticated key-value stores manage a relatively self-contained domain that demands significant storage and availability. Because of their masterless architecture, these systems scale easily with the addition of nodes. They opt for eventual consistency, which means that reads don't necessarily reflect the latest write. But what users get in exchange for weaker consistency is the ability to write in the face of any one node's failure.

This contrasts with MongoDB, which provides strong consistency, a single master (per shard), a richer data model, and secondary indexes. The last two of these attributes go hand in hand; if a system allows for modeling multiple domains, as, for example, would be required to build a complete web application, then it's going to be necessary to query across the entire data model, thus requiring secondary indexes.

---

[9] http://mng.bz/5321

Because of the richer data model, MongoDB can be considered a more general solution to the problem of large, scalable web applications. MongoDB's scaling architecture is sometimes criticized because it's not inspired by Dynamo. But there are different scaling solutions for different domains. MongoDB's auto-sharding is inspired by Yahoo!'s PNUTS data store and Google's BigTable. Anyone who reads the white papers presenting these data stores will see that MongoDB's approach to scaling has already been implemented, and successfully so.

RELATIONAL DATABASES

Much has already been said of relational databases in this introduction, so in the interest of brevity, I need only discuss what RDBMSs have with common with MongoDB and where they diverge. MongoDB and MySQL[10] are both capable of representing a rich data model, although where MySQL uses fixed-schema tables, MongoDB has schema-free documents. MySQL and MongoDB both support B-tree indexes, and those accustomed to working with indexes in MySQL can expect similar behavior in MongoDB. MySQL supports both joins and transactions, so if you must use SQL or if you require transactions, then you'll need to use MySQL or another RDBMS. That said, MongoDB's document model is often rich enough to represent objects without requiring joins. And its updates can be applied atomically to individual documents, providing a subset of what's possible with traditional transactions. Both MongoDB and MySQL support replication. As for scalability, MongoDB has been designed to scale horizontally, with sharding and failover handled automatically. Any sharding on MySQL has to be managed manually, and given the complexity involved, it's more common to see a vertically scaled MySQL system.

DOCUMENT DATABASES

Few databases identify themselves as document databases. As of this writing, the only well-known document database apart from MongoDB is Apache's CouchDB. CouchDB's document model is similar, although data is stored in plain text as JSON, whereas MongoDB uses the BSON binary format. Like MongoDB, CouchDB supports secondary indexes; the difference is that the indexes in CouchDB are defined by writing map-reduce functions, which is more involved than the declarative syntax used by MySQL and MongoDB. They also scale differently. CouchDB doesn't partition data across machines; rather, each CouchDB node is a complete replica of every other.

1.4.2 Use cases and production deployments

Let's be honest. You're not going to choose a database solely on the basis of its features. You need to know that real businesses are using it successfully. Here I provide a few broadly defined use cases for MongoDB and give some examples of its use in production.[11]

---

[10] I'm using MySQL here generically, since the features I'm describing apply to most relational databases.

[11] For an up-to-date list of MongoDB production deployments, see http://mng.bz/z2CH.

WEB APPLICATIONS

MongoDB is well suited as a primary data store for web applications. Even a simple web application will require numerous data models for managing users, sessions, app-specific data, uploads, and permissions, to say nothing of the overarching domain. Just as this aligns well with the tabular approach provided by relational databases, so too does it benefit from MongoDB's collection and document model. And because documents can represent rich data structures, the number of collections needed will usually be less than the number of tables required to model the same data using a fully normalized relational model. In addition, dynamic queries and secondary indexes allow for the easy implementation of most queries familiar to SQL developers. Finally, as a web application grows, MongoDB provides a clear path for scale.

In production, MongoDB has proven capable of managing all aspects of an app, from the primary data domain to add-ons such as logging and real-time analytics. This is the case with *The Business Insider (TBE)*, which has used MongoDB as its primary data store since January 2008. TBE is a news site, although it gets substantial traffic, serving more than a million unique page views per day. What's interesting in this case is that in addition to handling the site's main content (posts, comments, users, and so on), MongoDB also processes and stores real-time analytics data. These analytics are used by TBE to generate dynamic heat maps indicating click-through rates for the various news stories. The site doesn't host enough data to warrant sharding yet, but it does use replica sets to ensure automatic failover in the event of an outage.

AGILE DEVELOPMENT

Regardless of what you may think about the agile development movement, it's hard to deny the desirability of building an application quickly. A number of development teams, including those from Shutterfly and The New York Times, have chosen MongoDB in part because they can develop applications much more quickly on it than on relational databases. One obvious reason for this is that MongoDB has no fixed schema, so all the time spent committing, communicating, and applying schema changes is saved.

In addition, less time need be spent shoehorning the relational representation of data into an object-oriented data model or dealing with the vagaries, and optimizing the SQL produced by, an ORM. Thus, MongoDB often complements projects with shorter development cycles and agile, mid-sized teams.

ANALYTICS AND LOGGING

I alluded earlier to the idea that MongoDB works well for analytics and logging, and the number of application using MongoDB for these is growing fast. Often, a well-established company will begin its forays into the MongoDB world with special apps dedicated to analytics. Some of these companies include GitHub, Disqus, Justin.tv, and Gilt Groupe, among others.

MongoDB's relevance to analytics derives from its speed and from two key features: targeted atomic updates and capped collections. Atomic updates let clients efficiently increment counters and push values onto arrays. Capped collections, often useful for logging, feature fixed allocation, which lets them age out automatically. Storing logging data in a database, as compared with the file system, provides easier organization and much greater query power. Now, instead of using `grep` or a custom log search utility, users can employ the MongoDB query language they know and love to examine log output.

CACHING

A data model that allows for a more holistic representation of objects, combined with faster average query speeds, frequently allows MongoDB to be run in place of the more traditional MySQL/memcached duo. For example, TBE, mentioned earlier, has been able to dispense with memcached, serving page requests directly from MongoDB.

VARIABLE SCHEMAS

Look at this code example:[12]

```
curl https://stream.twitter.com/1/statuses/sample.json -umongodb:secret
| mongoimport -c tweets
```

Here you're pulling down a small sample of the Twitter stream and piping that directly into a MongoDB collection. Since the stream produces JSON documents, there's no need to munge the data before sending it to database. The `mongoimport` tool directly translates the data to BSON. This means that each tweet is stored with its structure intact, as a separate document in the collection. So you can immediately operate on the data, whether you want to query, index, or perform a map-reduce aggregation on it. And there's no need to declare the structure of the data in advance.

If your application needs to consume a JSON API, then having a system that so easily translates JSON is invaluable. If you can't possibly know the structure of your data before you store it, then MongoDB's lack of schema constraints may greatly simply your data model.

1.5   Tips and limitations

For all these good features, it's worth keeping in mind a system's trade-offs and limitations. Some limitations should be noted before building a real-world application on MongoDB and running in production. Most of these are consequences of MongoDB's use of memory-mapped files.

First, MongoDB should usually be run on 64-bit machines. 32-bit systems are capable of addressing only 4 GB of memory. Acknowledging that typically half of this memory will be allocated by the operating system and program processes, this leaves just 2 GB of memory on which to map the data files. So if you're running 32-bit, and if you have even a modest number of indexes defined, you'll be strictly limited to as little as 1.5 GB of data. Most production systems will require more than this, and so a 64-bit system will be necessary.[13]

---

[12] This idea comes from http://mng.bz/52XI. If you want to run this code, you'll need to replace `-umongodb:secret` with your own Twitter username and password.

[13] 64-bit architectures can theoretically address up to 16 exabytes of memory, which is for all intents and purposes unlimited.

A second consequence of using virtual memory mapping is that memory for the data will be allocated automatically, as needed. This makes it trickier to run the database in a shared environment. As with database servers in general, MongoDB is best run on a dedicated server.

Finally, it's important to run MongoDB with replication, especially if you're not running with journaling enabled. Because MongoDB uses memory-mapped files, any unclean shutdown of a mongod not running with journaling may result in corruption. Therefore, it's necessary in this case to have a replicated backup available for failover. This is good advice for any database—it'd be imprudent not to do likewise with any serious MySQL deployment—but it's especially important with nonjournaled MongoDB.

1.6   Summary

We've covered a lot. To summarize, MongoDB is an open source, document-based database management system. Designed for the data and scalability requirements of modern internet applications, MongoDB features dynamic queries and secondary indexes; fast atomic updates and complex aggregations; and support for replication with automatic failover and sharding for scaling horizontally.

That's a mouthful; but if you've read this far, you should have a good feel for all these capabilities. You're probably itching to code. After all, it's one thing to talk about a database's features, but another to use the database in practice. Fortunately, that's what you'll be doing in the next two chapters. First, you'll get acquainted with the MongoDB JavaScript shell, which is incredibly useful for interacting with the database. Then, in chapter 3, you'll start experimenting with the driver, and you'll build a simple MongoDB-based application in Ruby.

MongoDB through
the JavaScript shell

In this chapter

- CRUD operations in the MongoDB shell
- Building indexes and using `explain()`
- Getting help

The previous chapter hinted at the experience of running MongoDB. If you're ready for a more hands-on introduction, this is it. Using the MongoDB shell, this chapter teaches the database's basic concepts through a series of exercises. You'll learn how to create, read, update, and delete (CRUD) documents and, in the process, get to know MongoDB's query language. In addition, we'll take a preliminary look at database indexes and how they're used to optimize queries. Then we'll end the chapter by exploring some basic administrative commands, and I'll suggest a few ways of getting help as you continue on. Think of this chapter as both an elaboration of the concepts already introduced and as a practical tour of the most common tasks performed from the MongoDB shell.

If you're completely new to MongoDB's shell, know that it provides all the features that you'd expect of such a tool; it allows you to examine and manipulate data and administer the database server itself. Where it differs from similar tools is in its query language. Instead of employing a standardized query language such as SQL, you interact with the server using the JavaScript programming language and a simple API. If you're not familiar with JavaScript, rest assured that only a superficial knowledge of the language is necessary to take advantage of the shell, and all examples in this chapter will be explained thoroughly.

You'll benefit most from this chapter if you follow along with the examples, but to do that, you'll need to have MongoDB installed on your system. Installation instructions can be found in appendix A.

2.1 Diving into the MongoDB shell

MongoDB's JavaScript shell makes it easy to play with data and get a tangible sense for documents, collections, and the database's particular query language. Think of the following walkthrough as a practical introduction to MongoDB.

We'll begin by getting the shell up and running. Then we'll look at how JavaScript represents documents, and you'll learn how to insert these documents into a MongoDB collection. To verify these inserts, you'll practice querying the collection. Then it's on to updates. Finally, you'll learn how to clear and drop collections.

2.1.1 Starting the shell

If you've followed the instructions in appendix A, you should have a working MongoDB installation on your computer. Make sure you have a running mongod instance; once you do, start the MongoDB shell by running the mongo executable:

```
./mongo
```

If the shell program starts successfully, your screen will look like the screenshot in figure 2.1. The shell heading displays the version of MongoDB you're running along with some additional information about the currently selected database.

If you know some JavaScript, you can start entering code and exploring the shell right away. Otherwise, read on to see how to insert your first datum.

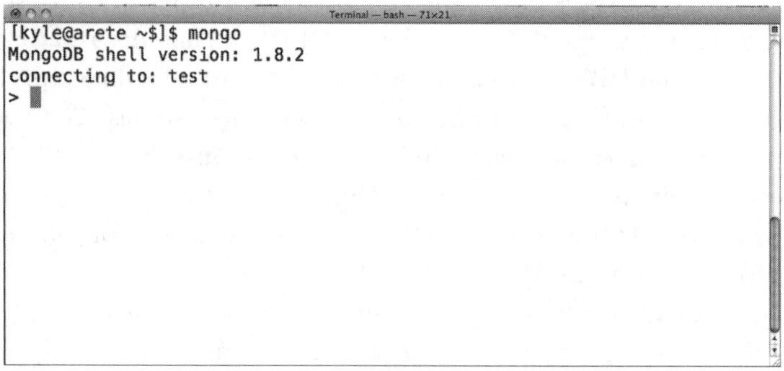

```
[kyle@arete ~$]$ mongo
MongoDB shell version: 1.8.2
connecting to: test
> █
```

Figure 2.1   The MongoDB JavaScript shell on startup

2.1.2 Inserts and queries

If no other database is specified on startup, the shell selects a default database called test. As a way of keeping all the subsequent tutorial exercises under the same namespace, let's start by switching to the tutorial database:

```
> use tutorial
switched to db tutorial
```

You'll see a message verifying that you've switched databases.

> **ON CREATING DATABASES AND COLLECTIONS** You may be wondering how we can switch to the tutorial database without explicitly creating it. In fact, creating the database isn't required. Databases and collections are created only when documents are first inserted. This behavior is consistent with MongoDB's dynamic approach to data; just as the structure of documents need not be defined in advance, individual collections and databases can be created at runtime. This can lead to a simplified and accelerated development process, and essentially facilitates dynamic namespace allocation, which can frequently be useful. That said, if you're concerned about databases or collections being created accidentally, most of the drivers let you enable a *strict mode* to prevent such careless errors.

It's time to create your first document. Since you're using a JavaScript shell, your documents will be specified in JSON (JavaScript Object Notation). For instance, the simplest imaginable document describing a user might look like this:

```
{username: "jones"}
```

The document contains a single key and value for storing Jones's username. To save this document, you need to choose a collection to save it to. Appropriately enough, you'll save it to the users collection. Here's how:

```
> db.users.insert({username: "smith"})
```

You may notice a slight delay after entering this code. At this point, neither the tutorial database nor the users collection has been created on disk. The delay is caused by the allocation of the initial data files for both.

If the insert succeeds, then you've just saved your first document. You can issue a simple query to verify that the document has been saved:

```
> db.users.find()
```

The response will look something like this:

```
{ _id : ObjectId("4bf9bec50e32f82523389314"), username : "smith" }
```

Note that an _id field has been added to the document. You can think of the _id value as the document's primary key. Every MongoDB document requires an _id, and if one isn't present when the document is created, then a special MongoDB object ID will be generated and added to the document at that time. The object ID that appears in your console won't be the same as the one in the code listing, but it

will be unique among all _id values in the collection, which is the only hard requirement for the field.

I'll have more to say about object IDs in the next chapter. Let's continue for now by
adding a second user to the collection:

```
> db.users.save({username: "jones"})
```

There should now be two documents in the collection. Go ahead and verify this by
running the count command:

```
> db.users.count()
2
```

Now that you have more than one document in the collection, we can look at some
slightly more sophisticated queries. Like before, you can still query for all the documents in the collection:

```
> db.users.find()
{ _id : ObjectId("4bf9bec50e32f82523389314"), username : "smith" }
{ _id : ObjectId("4bf9bec90e32f82523389315"), username : "jones" }
```

But you can also pass a simple query selector to the find method. A *query selector* is a
document that's used to match against all documents in the collection. To query for
all documents where the username is jones, you pass a simple document that acts as
your query selector like so:

```
> db.users.find({username: "jones"})
{ _id : ObjectId("4bf9bec90e32f82523389315"), username : "jones" }
```

The query selector {username: "jones"} returns all documents where the username
is jones—it literally matches against the existing documents.

I've just presented the basics of creating and reading data. Now it's time to look at
how to update that data.

2.1.3   *Updating documents*

All updates require at least two arguments. The first specifies which documents to
update, and the second defines how the selected documents should be modified.
There are two styles of modification; in this section we're going to focus on *targeted
modifications*, which are most representative of MongoDB's distinct features.

To take an example, suppose that user smith decides to add her country of resi-
dence. You can record this with the following update:

```
> db.users.update({username: "smith"}, {$set: {country: "Canada"}})
```

This update tells MongoDB to find a document where the username is smith, and
then to set the value of the country property to Canada. If you now issue a query,
you'll see that the document has been updated accordingly:

```
> db.users.find({username: "smith"})
{ "_id" : ObjectId("4bf9ec440e32f82523389316"),
  "country" : "Canada", username : "smith" }
```

If the user later decides that she no longer wants her country stored in her profile, she can remove the value just as easily using the $unset operator:

```
> db.users.update({username: "smith"}, {$unset: {country: 1}})
```

Let's enrich this example. You're representing your data with documents, which, as you saw in chapter 1, can contain complex data structures. So let's suppose that, in addition to storing profile information, your users can also store lists of their favorite things. A good document representation might look something like this:

```
{ username: "smith",
  favorites: {
    cities: ["Chicago", "Cheyenne"],
    movies: ["Casablanca", "For a Few Dollars More", "The Sting"]
  }
}
```

The favorites key points to an object containing two other keys which point to lists of favorite cities and movies. Given what you know already, can you think of a way to modify the original smith document to look like this? The $set operator should come to mind. Note in this example that you're practically rewriting the document and that this is a perfectly acceptable use of $set:

```
> db.users.update( {username: "smith"},
{ $set: {favorites:
    {
      cities: ["Chicago", "Cheyenne"],
      movies: ["Casablanca", "The Sting"]
    }
  }
})
```

Let's modify jones similarly, but in this case you'll add a couple of favorite movies:

```
db.users.update( {username: "jones"},
  {"$set": {favorites:
    {
      movies: ["Casablanca", "Rocky"]
    }
  }
})
```

Now query the users collection to make sure that both updates succeeded:

```
> db.users.find()
```

With a couple of example documents at your fingertips, you can now begin to see the power of MongoDB's query language. In particular, the query engine's ability to reach into nested inner objects and match against array elements proves useful in this situation. You can accomplish this kind query using a special dot notation. Suppose that you want to find all users who like the movie *Casablanca*. Such a query looks like this:

```
> db.users.find({"favorites.movies": "Casablanca"})
```

The dot between `favorites` and `movies` instructs the query engine to look for a key named `favorites` that points to an object with an inner key named `movies` and then to match the value of the inner key. Thus this query returns both user documents. To take a more involved example, suppose you know, a priori, that any user who likes *Casablanca* also like *The Maltese Falcon* and that you want to update your database to reflect this fact. How would you represent this as a MongoDB update?

You could conceivably use the `$set` operator again, but that would require you to rewrite and send the entire array of movies. Since all you want to do is add an element to the list, you're better off using either `$push` or `$addToSet`. Both operators add an item to an array, but the second does so uniquely, preventing a duplicate addition. This is the update you're looking for:

```
db.users.update( {"favorites.movies": "Casablanca"},
    {$addToSet: {"favorites.movies": "The Maltese Falcon"} },
        false,
        true )
```

Most of this should be decipherable. The first argument, a query selector, matches against users who have *Casablanca* in their movies list. The second argument adds *The Maltese Falcon* to that list using the `$addToSet` operator. The third argument, `false`, can be ignored for now. The fourth argument, `true`, indicates that this is a multi-update. By default, a MongoDB update operation will apply only to the first document matched by the query selector. If you want the operation to apply to all documents matched, then you must be explicit about that. Because you want your update to apply to both `smith` and `jones`, the multi-update is necessary.

We'll cover updates in more detail later, but do try these examples before moving on.

2.1.4   Deleting data

You now know the basics of creating, reading, and updating data through the MongoDB shell. We've saved the simplest operation, removing data, for last.

If given no parameters, a remove operation will clear a collection of all its documents. To get rid of, say, a `foo` collection, you enter

```
> db.foo.remove()
```

You often need to remove only a certain subset of a collection's documents, and for that, you can pass a query selector to the `remove()` method. If you want to remove all users whose favorite city is Cheyenne, the expression is pretty straightforward:

```
> db.users.remove({"favorites.cities": "Cheyenne"})
```

Note that the `remove()` operation doesn't actually delete the collection; it merely removes documents from a collection. You can think of it as being analogous to SQL's `DELETE` and `TRUNCATE TABLE` directives.

If your intent is to delete the collection along with all of its indexes, use the `drop()` method:

```
> db.users.drop()
```

Creating, reading, updating, and deleting are the basic operations of any database; if you've followed along, you should be in a position to continue practicing basic CRUD operations in MongoDB. In the next section, you'll learn how to enhance your queries, updates, and deletes by taking a brief look at secondary indexes.

2.2 *Creating and querying with indexes*

It's common to create indexes to enhance query performance. Fortunately, MongoDB's indexes can be created easily from the shell. If you're new to database indexes, this section should make clear the need for them; if you already have indexing experience, you'll see how easy it is to create indexes and then profile queries against them using the explain() method.

2.2.1 *Creating a large collection*

An indexing example only makes sense if you have a collection with many documents. So you'll add 200,000 simple documents to a numbers collection. Since the MongoDB shell is also a JavaScript interpreter, the code to accomplish this is simple:

```
for(i=0; i<200000; i++) {
  db.numbers.save({num: i});
}
```

This is a lot of documents, so don't be surprised if the insert takes a few seconds to complete. Once it returns, you can run a couple of queries to verify that all the documents are present:

```
> db.numbers.count()
200000

> db.numbers.find()
{ "_id" : ObjectId("4bfbf132dba1aa7c30ac830a"), "num" : 0 }
{ "_id" : ObjectId("4bfbf132dba1aa7c30ac830b"), "num" : 1 }
{ "_id" : ObjectId("4bfbf132dba1aa7c30ac830c"), "num" : 2 }
{ "_id" : ObjectId("4bfbf132dba1aa7c30ac830d"), "num" : 3 }
{ "_id" : ObjectId("4bfbf132dba1aa7c30ac830e"), "num" : 4 }
{ "_id" : ObjectId("4bfbf132dba1aa7c30ac830f"), "num" : 5 }
{ "_id" : ObjectId("4bfbf132dba1aa7c30ac8310"), "num" : 6 }
{ "_id" : ObjectId("4bfbf132dba1aa7c30ac8311"), "num" : 7 }
{ "_id" : ObjectId("4bfbf132dba1aa7c30ac8312"), "num" : 8 }
{ "_id" : ObjectId("4bfbf132dba1aa7c30ac8313"), "num" : 9 }
{ "_id" : ObjectId("4bfbf132dba1aa7c30ac8314"), "num" : 10 }
{ "_id" : ObjectId("4bfbf132dba1aa7c30ac8315"), "num" : 11 }
{ "_id" : ObjectId("4bfbf132dba1aa7c30ac8316"), "num" : 12 }
{ "_id" : ObjectId("4bfbf132dba1aa7c30ac8317"), "num" : 13 }
{ "_id" : ObjectId("4bfbf132dba1aa7c30ac8318"), "num" : 14 }
{ "_id" : ObjectId("4bfbf132dba1aa7c30ac8319"), "num" : 15 }
{ "_id" : ObjectId("4bfbf132dba1aa7c30ac831a"), "num" : 16 }
{ "_id" : ObjectId("4bfbf132dba1aa7c30ac831b"), "num" : 17 }
{ "_id" : ObjectId("4bfbf132dba1aa7c30ac831c"), "num" : 18 }
{ "_id" : ObjectId("4bfbf132dba1aa7c30ac831d"), "num" : 19 }
has more
```

The count() command shows that you've inserted 200,000 documents. The subsequent query displays the first 20 results. You can display additional results with the it command:

```
> it
{ "_id" : ObjectId("4bfbf132dba1aa7c30ac831e"), "num" : 20 }
{ "_id" : ObjectId("4bfbf132dba1aa7c30ac831f"), "num" : 21 }
{ "_id" : ObjectId("4bfbf132dba1aa7c30ac8320"), "num" : 22 }
...
```

The it command instructs the shell to return the next result set.[1]

With a sizeable set of documents available, let's try a few queries. Given what you know about MongoDB's query engine, a simple query matching a document on its num attribute makes sense:

```
> db.numbers.find({num: 500})
{ "_id" : ObjectId("4bfbf132dba1aa7c30ac84fe"), "num" : 500 }
```

But more interestingly, you can also issue range queries using the special $gt and $lt operators. You first saw these operators in chapter 1. (They stand for *greater than* and *less than*, respectively.) Here's how you query for all documents with a num value greater than 199,995:

```
> db.numbers.find( {num: {"$gt": 199995 }} )
{ "_id" : ObjectId("4bfbf1dedba1aa7c30afcade"), "num" : 199996 }
{ "_id" : ObjectId("4bfbf1dedba1aa7c30afcadf"), "num" : 199997 }
{ "_id" : ObjectId("4bfbf1dedba1aa7c30afcae0"), "num" : 199998 }
{ "_id" : ObjectId("4bfbf1dedba1aa7c30afcae1"), "num" : 199999 }
```

You can also combine the two operators to specify upper and lower boundaries:

```
> db.numbers.find( {num: {"$gt": 20, "$lt": 25 }} )
{ "_id" : ObjectId("4bfbf132dba1aa7c30ac831f"), "num" : 21 }
{ "_id" : ObjectId("4bfbf132dba1aa7c30ac8320"), "num" : 22 }
{ "_id" : ObjectId("4bfbf132dba1aa7c30ac8321"), "num" : 23 }
{ "_id" : ObjectId("4bfbf132dba1aa7c30ac8322"), "num" : 24 }
```

You can see that by using a simple JSON document, you're able to specify a sophisticated range query much in the way you might do in SQL. Because $gt and $lt are just two of a host of special keywords that comprise the MongoDB query language, you'll be seeing many more example queries in later chapters.

Of course, queries like this are of little value if they're not also efficient. In the next section, we'll start thinking about query efficiency by exploring MongoDB's indexing features.

---

[1] You may be wondering what's happening behind the scenes here. All queries create a cursor, which allows for iteration over a result set. This is somewhat hidden when using the shell, so it's not necessary to discuss in detail at the moment. If you can't wait to learn more about cursors and their idiosyncrasies, see chapters 3 and 4.

2.2.2　Indexing and explain()

If you've spent time working with relational databases, you're probably familiar with
SQL's EXPLAIN. EXPLAIN describes query paths and allows developers to diagnose slow
operations by determining which indexes a query has used. MongoDB has its own version of EXPLAIN that provides the same service. To get an idea of how it works, let's
apply it to one of the queries you just issued. Try running the following on your system:

```
> db.numbers.find( {num: {"$gt": 199995 }} ).explain()
```

The result should look something like what you see in the following listing.

Listing 2.1　Typical `explain()` output for an unindexed query

```
{
    "cursor" : "BasicCursor",
    "nscanned" : 200000,
    "nscannedObjects" : 200000,
    "n" : 4,
    "millis" : 171,
    "nYields" : 0,
    "nChunkSkips" : 0,
    "isMultiKey" : false,
    "indexOnly" : false,
    "indexBounds" : { }
}
```

Examining the explain() output, you may be surprised to see that the query engine
has to scan the entire collection, all 200,000 documents (nscanned), to return just
four results (n). The BasicCursor cursor type verifies that this query hasn't used an
index to return the result set. Such a large difference between the number of documents scanned and the number returned marks this as an inefficient query. In a real-
world situation, where the collection and the documents themselves would likely be
larger, the time needed to process the query would be substantially greater than the
171 milliseconds noted here.

　　What this collection needs is an index. You can create an index for the num key
using the ensureIndex() method. Try entering the following index creation code
yourself:

```
> db.numbers.ensureIndex({num: 1})
```

As with other MongoDB operations, such as queries and updates, you pass a document to the ensureIndex() method to define the index's keys. In this case, the {num:
1} document indicates that an ascending index should be built on the num key for all
documents in the numbers collection.

　　You can verify that the index has been created by calling the getIndexes()
method:

```
> db.numbers.getIndexes()
[
    {
```

```
      "name" : "_id_",
      "ns" : "tutorial.numbers",
      "key" : {
        "_id" : 1
      }
    },
    {
      "_id" : ObjectId("4bfc646b2f95a56b5581efd3"),
      "ns" : "tutorial.numbers",
      "key" : {
        "num" : 1
      },
      "name" : "num_1"
    }
]
```

The collection now has two indexes. The first is the standard _id index that's automatically built for every collection; the second is the index you just created on num.

If you run your query with the explain() method, you'll now see a dramatic difference in query response time, as shown in the next listing.

Listing 2.2   explain() output for an indexed query

```
> db.numbers.find({num: {"$gt": 199995 }}).explain()
{
  "cursor" : "BtreeCursor num_1",
  "indexBounds" : [
    [
      {
        "num" : 199995
      },
      {
        "num" : 1.7976931348623157e+308
      }
    ]
  ],
  "nscanned" : 5,
  "nscannedObjects" : 4,
  "n" : 4,
  "millis" : 0
}
```

Now that the query utilizes the index on num, it scans only the five documents pertaining to the query. This reduces the total time to serve the query from 171 ms to less than 1 ms.

If this example intrigues you, be sure to check out chapter 7, which is devoted to indexing and query optimization. Now we'll proceed now to look at the basic administrative commands required to get information about our MongoDB instance. You'll also learn some techniques for getting help from the shell, which will aid in mastering the various shell commands.

2.3   *Basic administration*

This chapter promised to be an introduction to MongoDB via the JavaScript shell. You've already learned the basics of data manipulation and indexing. Here I'll present some techniques for getting information about your `mongod` process. For instance, you'll probably want to know how much space your various collections are taking up or how many indexes you've defined on a given collection. The commands detailed here can take you a long way in helping you to diagnose performance issues and keep tabs on your data.

We'll also look at MongoDB's command interface. Most of the special, non-CRUD operations that can be performed on a MongoDB instance, from server status checks to data file integrity verification, are implemented using database commands. I'll explain what commands are in the MongoDB context and show how easy they are to use. Finally, it's always good to know where to look for help. To that end, I'll point out some places in the shell where you can turn for help to further your exploration of MongoDB.

2.3.1   *Getting database information*

You'll often want to know which collections and databases exist on a given installation. Fortunately, the MongoDB shell provides a number of commands, along with some syntactic sugar, for getting information about the system.

`show dbs` prints a list of all the databases on the system:

```
> show dbs
admin
local
test
tutorial
```

`show collections` displays a list of all the collections defined on the current database.[2] If the `tutorial` database is still selected, you'll see a list of the collections you worked with in the preceding tutorial:

```
> show collections
numbers
system.indexes
users
```

The one collection that you may not recognize is `system.indexes`. This is a special collection that exists for every database. Each entry in `system.indexes` defines an index for the database. You can query this collection directly, but its output is more easily viewed using the `getIndexes()` method, as we saw earlier.

For lower-level insight into databases and collections, the `stats()` method proves useful. When run on a database object, you'll get the following output:

```
> db.stats()
{
```

---

[2] You can also enter the more succinct `show tables`.

```
    "collections" : 4,
    "objects" : 200012,
    "dataSize" : 7200832,
    "storageSize" : 21258496,
    "numExtents" : 11,
    "indexes" : 3,
    "indexSize" : 27992064,
    "ok" : 1
}
```

You can also run the stats() command on an individual collection:

```
> db.numbers.stats()
{
    "ns" : "tutorial.numbers",
    "count" : 200000,
    "size" : 7200000,
    "storageSize" : 21250304,
    "numExtents" : 8,
    "nindexes" : 2,
    "lastExtentSize" : 10066176,
    "paddingFactor" : 1,
    "flags" : 1,
    "totalIndexSize" : 27983872,
    "indexSizes" : {
        "_id_" : 21307392,
        "num_1" : 6676480
    },
    "ok" : 1
}
```

Some of the values provided in these result documents are useful only in complicated debugging situations. But at the very least, you'll be able to find out how much space a given collection and its indexes are occupying.

2.3.2   *How commands work*

A certain set of MongoDB operations—distinct from the insert, update, delete, and query operations described so far in this chapter—are known as *database commands*. Database commands are generally administrative, as with the stats() methods just presented, but they may also control core MongoDB features, such as map-reduce.

Regardless of the functionality they provide, what all database commands have in common is their implementation as queries on a special virtual collection called $cmd. To show what this means, let's take a quick example. Recall how you invoked the stats() database command:

```
> db.stats()
```

The stats() method is a helper that wraps the shell's command invocation method. Try entering the following equivalent operation:

```
> db.runCommand( {dbstats: 1} )
```

The results are identical to what's provided by the stats() method. Note that the command is defined by the document {dbstats: 1}. In general, you can run any available command by passing its document definition to the runCommand method. Here's how you'd run the collection stats command:

```
> db.runCommand( {collstats: 'numbers'} )
```

The output should look familiar.

But to get to the heart of database commands, you need to see how the run-Command() method actually works. That's not hard to find out because the MongoDB shell will print the implementation of any method whose executing parentheses are omitted. So instead of running the command like this

```
> db.runCommand()
```

You can execute the parentheses-less version and see the internals:

```
> db.runCommand
  function (obj) {
    if (typeof obj == "string") {
      var n = {};
      n[obj] = 1;
      obj = n;
    }
    return this.getCollection("$cmd").findOne(obj);
  }
```

The last line in the function is nothing more than a query on the $cmd collection. To define it properly, then, a database command is a query on a special collection, $cmd, where the query selector defines the command itself. That's all there is to it. Can you think of a way to run the collection stats command manually? It's this simple:

```
db.$cmd.findOne( {collstats: 'numbers'} );
```

Using the runCommand helper is easier, but it's always good to know what's going on just beneath the surface.

2.4 Getting help

By now, the value of the MongoDB shell as a testing ground for experimenting with data and administering the database should be evident. But since you'll likely be spending a lot of time in the shell, it's worth knowing how to get help.

The built-in help commands are the first place to look. db.help() prints a list of commonly used methods for operating on database objects. You'll find a similar list of methods for operating on collections by running db.foo.help().

There's also built-in tab completion. Start typing the first characters of any method and then press the Tab key twice. You'll see a list of all matching methods. Here's the tab completion for collection methods beginning with get:

```
> db.foo.get
db.foo.getCollection(     db.foo.getIndexSpecs(     db.foo.getName(
```

```
db.foo.getDB(              db.foo.getIndexes(         db.foo.getShardVersion(
db.foo.getFullName(        db.foo.getIndices(
db.foo.getIndexKeys(       db.foo.getMongo(
```

If you're more ambitious, and comfortable with JavaScript, the shell makes it easy to examine the implementation of any given method. For instance, suppose you'd like to know exactly how the save() method works. Sure, you could go trolling through the MongoDB source code, but there's an easier way. Simply enter the method name without the executing parentheses. Here's how you'd normally execute save():

```
> db.numbers.save({num: 123123123});
```

And this is how you can check the implementation:

```
> db.numbers.save
function (obj) {
    if (obj == null || typeof obj == "undefined") {
        throw "can't save a null";
    }
    if (typeof obj._id == "undefined") {
        obj._id = new ObjectId;
        return this.insert(obj);
    } else {
        return this.update({_id:obj._id}, obj, true);
    }
}
```

Read the function definition closely, and you'll see that save() is merely a wrapper for insert() and update(). If the object you're trying to save doesn't have an _id field, then the field is added, and insert() is invoked; otherwise, an update is performed.

This trick for examining the shell's methods comes in handy; keep this technique at hand as you continue exploring the MongoDB shell.

2.5   *Summary*

You've now seen the document data model in practice, and we've demonstrated a variety of common MongoDB operations on that data model. You've learned how to create indexes, and seen a real-life example of index-based performance improvements through the use of explain(). In addition, you should be able to extract information about the collections and databases on your system, you now know all about the clever $cmd collection, and if you ever need help, you've picked up a few tricks for finding your way around.

You can learn a lot by working in the MongoDB shell, but there's no substitute for the experience of building a real application. That's why, in the next chapter, we're going from a carefree data playground to a real-world data workshop. You'll see how the drivers work, and then, using the Ruby driver, you'll build a simple application, hitting MongoDB with some real live data.

Writing programs
using MongoDB 3

In this chapter

- Introducing the MongoDB API through Ruby
- How the drivers work
- The BSON format and the MongoDB network protocol
- Building a complete sample application

It's time to get practical. Though there's much to learn from experimenting with the MongoDB shell, you can see the real value of this database only after you've built something with it. That means jumping into programming and taking a first look at the MongoDB drivers. As mentioned before, 10gen provides officially supported, Apache-licensed MongoDB drivers for all of the most popular programming languages. The driver examples in the book use Ruby, but the principles I'll illustrate are universal and easily transferable to other drivers. If you're curious, appendix D showcases driver APIs for PHP, Java, and C++.

We're going to explore programming in MongoDB in three stages. First, you'll install the MongoDB Ruby driver and introduce the basic CRUD operations. This should go quickly and feel familiar, since the driver API is similar to that of the shell. Next, we're going to delve deeper into the driver, explaining how it interfaces

> **New to Ruby?**
>
> Ruby is a popular and readable scripting language. The code examples have been designed to be as explicit as possible, so that even programmers unfamiliar with Ruby can benefit. Any Ruby idioms that may be hard to understand will be explained in the text. If you'd like to spend a few minutes getting up to speed with Ruby, start with the official 20-minute tutorial at http://mng.bz/THR3.

with MongoDB. Without getting too low-level, this section will show you what's going on behind the scenes with the drivers in general. Finally, you'll develop a simple Ruby application for monitoring Twitter. Working with a real-world data set, you'll begin to see how MongoDB works in the wild. This final section will also lay the groundwork for the more in-depth examples presented in part 2.

3.1 MongoDB through the Ruby lens

Normally when you think of drivers, what come to mind are low-level bit manipulations and obtuse interfaces. Thankfully, the MongoDB language drivers are nothing like that; instead, they've been designed with intuitive, language-sensitive APIs, so that many applications can sanely use a MongoDB driver as the sole interface to the database. The driver APIs are also fairly consistent across languages, which means that developers can easily move between languages as needed. If you're an application developer, you can expect to find yourself comfortable and productive with any of the MongoDB drivers without having to concern yourself with low-level implementation details.

In this first section, you'll install the MongoDB Ruby driver, connect to the database, and learn how to perform basic CRUD operations. This will lay the groundwork for the application you'll build at the end of the chapter.

3.1.1 Installing and connecting

You can install the MongoDB Ruby driver using RubyGems, Ruby's package management system.

> **NOTE**   If you don't have Ruby installed on your system, you can find detailed installation instructions at http://www.ruby-lang.org/en/downloads/. You'll also need Ruby's package manager, RubyGems. Instructions for installing RubyGems can be found at http://docs.rubygems.org/read/chapter/3.

```
gem install mongo
```

This should install both the mongo and bson[1] gems. You should see output like the following (the version numbers will likely be newer that what's shown here):

---

[1] BSON, which is explained in the next section, is the JSON-inspired binary format that MongoDB uses to represent documents. The bson Ruby gem serializes Ruby objects to and from BSON.

```
Successfully installed bson-1.4.0
Successfully installed mongo-1.4.0
2 gems installed
Installing ri documentation for bson-1.4.0...
Installing ri documentation for mongo-1.4.0...
Installing RDoc documentation for bson-1.4.0...
Installing RDoc documentation for mongo-1.4.0...
```

We'll start by connecting to MongoDB. First, make sure that mongod is running. Next, create a file called connect.rb and enter the following code:

```
require 'rubygems'
require 'mongo'

@con   = Mongo::Connection.new
@db    = @con['tutorial']
@users = @db['users']
```

The first two require statements ensure that you've loaded the driver. The next three lines instantiate a connection, assign the tutorial database to the @db variable, and store a reference to the users collection in the @users variable. Save the file and run it:

```
$ruby connect.rb
```

If no exceptions are raised, you've successfully connected to MongoDB from Ruby. That may not seem glamorous, but connecting is the first step in using MongoDB from any language. Next, you'll use that connection to insert some documents.

3.1.2 Inserting documents in Ruby

All of the MongoDB drivers are designed to use the most natural document representation for their language. In JavaScript, JSON objects are the obvious choice, since JSON is a document data structure; in Ruby, the hash data structure makes the most sense. The native Ruby hash differs from a JSON object only in a couple small ways; most notably, where JSON separates keys and values with a colon, Ruby uses a hash rocket (=>).[2]

If you're following along, go ahead and continue adding code to the connect.rb file. Alternatively, a nice approach is to use Ruby's interactive REPL, irb. You can launch irb and require connect.rb so that you'll immediately have access to the connection, database, and collection objects initialized therein. You can then run Ruby code and receive immediate feedback. Here's an example:

```
$ irb -r connect.rb
irb(main):001:0> id = @users.save({"lastname" => "knuth"})
=> BSON::ObjectId('4c2cfea0238d3b915a000004')
irb(main):002:0> @users.find_one({"_id" => id})
=> {"_id"=>BSON::ObjectId('4c2cfea0238d3b915a000004'), "lastname"=>"knuth"}
```

---

[2] In Ruby 1.9, you may optionally use a colon as the key-value separator, but we'll be sticking with the hash rocket in the interest of backward compatibility.

Let's build some documents for your *users* collection. You'll create two documents representing two users, smith and jones. Each document, expressed as a Ruby hash, is assigned to a variable:

```
smith = {"last_name" => "smith", "age" => 30}
jones = {"last_name" => "jones", "age" => 40}
```

To save the documents, you'll pass them to the collection's insert method. Each call to insert returns a unique ID, which you'll store in a variable to simplify later retrieval:

```
smith_id = @users.insert(smith)
jones_id = @users.insert(jones)
```

You can verify that the documents have been saved with some simple queries. As usual, each document's object ID will be stored in the _id key. So you can query with the user collection's find_one method like so:

```
@users.find_one({"_id" => smith_id})
@users.find_one({"_id" => jones_id})
```

If you're running the code in irb, the return values for these queries will appear at the prompt. If the code is being run from a Ruby file, prepend Ruby's p method to print the output to the screen:

```
p @users.find_one({"_id" => smith_id})
```

You've successfully inserted two documents from Ruby. Let's now take a closer look at queries.

3.1.3 *Queries and cursors*

You just used the driver's find_one method to retrieve a single result. It was simple, but that's because find_one hides some of the details of performing queries with MongoDB. You'll see how this is so by looking at the standard find method. Here are two possible find operations on your data set:

```
@users.find({"last_name" => "smith"})
```

```
@users.find({"age" => {"$gt" => 20}})
```

It should be clear that the first query searches for all user documents where the last_name is smith and that the second query matches all documents where the age is greater than 30. Try entering the second query in irb:

```
irb(main):008:0> @users.find({"age" => {"$gt" => 30}})
=> <#Mongo::Cursor:0x10109e118 ns="tutorial.users"
      @selector={"age" => "$gt" => 30}}>
```

The first thing you'll notice is that the find method doesn't return a result set, but rather a cursor object. Cursors, found in many database systems, return query result sets in batches for efficiency iteratively. Imagine that your users collection contained a million documents matching your query. Without a cursor, you'd need to return all those documents at once. Returning such a huge result right away would mean copying all that data into memory, transferring it over the wire, and then deserializing it on the client side. This would be unnecessarily resource intensive. To prevent this, queries instantiate a cursor, which is then used to retrieve a result set in manageable chunks. Of course, this is all opaque to the user; as you request more results from the cursor, successive calls to MongoDB occur as needed to fill the driver's cursor buffer.

Cursors are explained in more detail in the next section. Returning to the example, you'll now fetch the results of the $gt query:

```
cursor = @users.find({"age" => {"$gt" => 20}})

cursor.each do |doc|
  puts doc["last_name"]
end
```

Here you use Ruby's each iterator, which passes each result to a code block. Here, the last_name attribute is then printed to the console. If you're not familiar with Ruby iterators, here's a more language-neutral equivalent:

```
cursor = @users.find({"age" => {"$gt" => 20}})

while doc = cursor.next
  puts doc["last_name"]
end
```

In this case, you use a simple while loop that iterates over the cursor by assigning successive calls to the cursor's next method to a local variable, doc.

The fact that you even have to think about cursors here may come as a surprise given the shell examples from the previous chapter. But the shell uses cursors the same way every driver does; the difference is that the shell automatically iterates over the first 20 cursor results when you call find(). To get the remaining results, you can continue iterating manually by entering the it command.

3.1.4 Updates and deletes

Recall from the previous chapter that updates require at least two arguments: a query selector and an update document. Here's a simple example using the Ruby driver:

```
@users.update({"last_name" => "smith"}, {"$set" => {"city" => "Chicago"}})
```

This update finds the first user with a last_name of smith and, if found, sets the value of city to Chicago. This update uses the $set operator.

By default, MongoDB updates apply to a single document only. In this case, even if you have multiple users with the last name of smith, only one document will be updated. To apply the update to a particular smith, you'd need to add more conditions to your query selector. But if you actually want to apply the update to all smith documents, you must issue a *multi-update*. You can do this by passing :multi => true as the third argument to the update method:

```
@users.update({"last_name" => "smith"},
  {"$set" => {"city" => "New York"}}, :multi => true)
```

Deleting data is much simpler. You simply use the remove method. This method takes an optional query selector which will remove only those documents matching the selector. If no selector is provided, all documents in the collection will be removed. Here, you're removing all user documents where the age attribute is greater than or equal to 40:

```
@users.remove({"age" => {"$gte" => 40}})
```

With no arguments, the remove method deletes all remaining documents:

```
@users.remove
```

You may recall from the previous chapter that remove doesn't actually drop the collection. To drop a collection and all its indexes, use the drop_collection method:

```
connection = Mongo::Connection.new
db = connection['tutorial']
db.drop_collection('users')
```

3.1.5 Database commands

You saw in the last chapter the centrality of database commands. There, we looked at the two stats commands. Here, we'll look at how you can run commands from the driver using the listDatabases command as an example. This is one of a number of commands that must be run on the admin database, which is treated specially when authentication is enabled. For details on the authentication and the admin database, see chapter 10.

First, you instantiate a Ruby database object referencing the admin database. You then pass the command's query specification to the command method:

```
@admin_db = @con['admin']
@admin_db.command({"listDatabases" => 1})
```

The response is a Ruby hash listing all the existing databases and their sizes on disk:

```
{
    "databases" => [
        {
            "name" => "tutorial",
            "sizeOnDisk" => 218103808,
            "empty" => false
        },
        {
            "name" => "admin",
            "sizeOnDisk" => 1,
            "empty" => true
        },
        {
            "name" => "local",
            "sizeOnDisk" => 1,
            "empty" => true
        }
    ],
```

```
        "totalSize" => 218103808,
        "ok" => true
}
```

Once you get used to representing documents as Ruby hashes, the transition from the shell API is almost seamless. It's okay if you're still feeling shaky about using MongoDB with Ruby; you'll get more practice in section 3.3. But for now we're going to take a brief intermission to see how the MongoDB drivers work. This will shed more light on some of MongoDB's design and better prepare you to use the drivers effectively.

3.2 How the drivers work

At this point it's natural to wonder what's going on behind the scenes when you issue commands through a driver or via the MongoDB shell. In this section, we'll peel away the curtain to see how the drivers serialize data and communicate it to the database.

All MongoDB drivers perform three major functions. First, they generate MongoDB object IDs. These are the default values stored in the _id field of all documents. Next, the drivers convert any language-specific representation of documents to and from BSON, the binary data format used by MongoDB. In the foregoing examples, the driver serializes all the Ruby hashes into BSON and then deserializes the BSON that's returned from the database back to Ruby hashes.

The drivers' final function is to communicate with the database over a TCP socket using the MongoDB wire protocol. The details of the protocol are beyond our scope. But the style of socket communication, in particular whether writes on the socket wait for a response, is important, and we'll explore the topic in this section.

3.2.1 Object ID generation

Every MongoDB document requires a primary key. That key, which must be unique for all documents in each collection, is referenced by a document's _id field. Developers are free to use their own custom values as the _id, but when not provided, a MongoDB object ID will be used. Before sending a document to the server, the driver checks whether the _id field is present. If the field is missing, an object ID proper will be generated and stored as _id.

Because a MongoDB object ID is a globally unique identifier, it's safe to assign the ID to a document at the client without having to worry about creating a duplicate ID. Now, you've certainly seen object IDs in the wild, but you may not have noticed that they're made up of 12 bytes. These bytes have a specific structure which is illustrated in figure 3.1.

The most significant four bytes carry a standard Unix timestamp that encodes the number of seconds since the epoch. The next three bytes store the machine id, which is followed by a two-byte process id. The final three bytes store a process-local counter that's incremented each time an object ID is generated.

4c291856 238d3b 19b2 000001

4-byte timestamp   machine id   process id   counter   **Figure 3.1   MongoDB object ID format**

One of the incidental benefits of using MongoDB object IDs is that they include a timestamp. Most of the drivers allow you to extract the timestamp, thus providing the document creation time, with resolution to the nearest second, for free. Using the Ruby driver, you can call an object ID's generation_time method to get that ID's creation time as a Ruby Time object:

```
irb(main):002:0> id = BSON::ObjectId.new
=> BSON::ObjectId('4c41e78f238d3b9090000001')
irb(main):003:0> id.generation_time
=> Sat Jul 17 17:25:35 UTC 2010
```

Naturally, you can also use object IDs to issue range queries on object creation time. For instance, if you wanted to query for all documents created between October 2010 and November 2010, you could create two object IDs whose timestamps encode those dates and then issue a range query on _id. Since Ruby provides methods for generating object IDs from any Time object, the code for doing this is trivial:

```
oct_id = BSON::ObjectId.from_time(Time.utc(2010, 10, 1))
nov_id = BSON::ObjectId.from_time(Time.utc(2010, 11, 1))

@users.find({'_id' => {'$gte' => oct_id, '$lt' => nov_id}})
```

I've explained the rationale for MongoDB object IDs and the meaning behind the bytes. All that remains is to see how they're encoded. That's the subject of the next section, where we discuss BSON.

3.2.2   *BSON*

BSON is the binary format used to represent documents in MongoDB. BSON acts as both a storage and command format: all documents are stored on disk as BSON, and all queries and commands are specified using BSON documents. Consequently, all MongoDB drivers must be able to translate between some language-specific document representation and BSON.

BSON defines the data types you can use with MongoDB. Knowing which types BSON comprises, as well as a bit about their encoding, will take you a long way in using MongoDB effectively and diagnosing certain performance issues when they occur.

At the time of this writing, the BSON specification includes 19 data types. What this means is that each value within a document must be convertible into one of these types in order to be stored in MongoDB. The BSON types include many that you'd expect: UTF-8 string, 32- and 64-bit integer, double, Boolean, timestamp, and UTC datetime. But a number of types are specific to MongoDB. For instance, the object ID format described in the previous section gets its own type; there's a binary type for opaque blobs; and there's even a symbol type for languages that support it.

Figure 3.2 illustrates how you serialize a Ruby hash into a bona fide BSON document. The Ruby document contains an object ID and a string. When translated to a BSON document, what comes first is a 4-byte header indicating the document's size (you can see that this one is 38 bytes). Next are the two key-value pairs. Each pair begins with a byte denoting its type, followed by a null-terminated string for the key

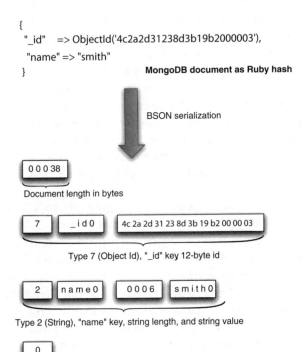

```
{
  "_id"   => ObjectId('4c2a2d31238d3b19b2000003'),
  "name" => "smith"
}
```
MongoDB document as Ruby hash

BSON serialization

`0 0 0 38`

Document length in bytes

`7` `_ i d 0` `4c 2a 2d 31 23 8d 3b 19 b2 00 00 03`

Type 7 (Object Id), "_id" key 12-byte id

`2` `n a m e 0` `0 0 0 6` `s m i t h 0`

Type 2 (String), "name" key, string length, and string value

`0`

Document null terminator

MongoDB document as BSON

Figure 3.2 Translating from Ruby to BSON

name, which is then followed by the value being stored. Finally, a null byte terminates the document.

Though knowing the ins and outs of BSON isn't a strict requirement, experience shows that some familiarity benefits the MongoDB developer. To take just one example, it's possible to represent an object ID as a string or as a BSON object ID proper. As a consequence, these two shell queries aren't equivalent:

```
db.users.find({_id : ObjectId('4c41e78f238d3b9090000001')});
db.users.find({_id : '4c41e78f238d3b9090000001'})
```

Only one of these two queries can match the _id field, and that's entirely dependent on whether the documents in the users collection are stored as BSON object IDs or as BSON strings that indicate the hex values of the ID.[3] What all of this goes to show is that knowing even a bit about BSON can go a long way in diagnosing simple code issues.

3.2.3 Over the network

In addition to creating object IDs and serializing to BSON, the MongoDB drivers have one more obvious core function: to communicate with the database server. As mentioned, this communication occurs over a TCP socket using a custom wire

---

[3] Incidentally, if you're storing MongoDB object IDs, you should store them as BSON object IDs, not as strings. Apart from being the object ID storage convention, BSON object IDs take up less than half the space of strings.

protocol.[4] This TCP business is fairly low-level and not so germane to the concerns of most application developers. What's relevant here is an understanding of when the drivers wait for responses from the server and when they "fire and forget" instead.

I've already spoken about how queries work, and obviously, every query requires a response. To recap, a query is initiated when a cursor object's next method is invoked. At that point, the query is sent to the server, and the response is a batch of documents. If that batch satisfies the query, no further round trips to the server will be necessary. But if there happen to be more query results than can fit in the first server response, a so-called getmore directive will be sent to the server to fetch the next set of query results. As the cursor is iterated, successive getmore calls will be made until the query is complete.

There's nothing surprising about the network behavior for queries just described, but when it comes to database writes (inserts, updates, and removes), the default behavior may seem unorthodox. That's because, by default, the drivers don't wait for a response from the server when writing to the server. So when you insert a document, the driver writes to the socket and assumes that the write has succeeded. One tactic that makes this possible is client-side object ID generation: since you already have the document's primary key, there's no need to wait for the server to return it.

This fire-and-forget write strategy puts a lot of users on edge; fortunately, this behavior is configurable. All of the drivers implement a write safety mode that can be enabled for any write (insert, update, or delete). In Ruby, you can issue a safe insert like so:

```
@users.insert({"last_name" => "james"}, :safe => true)
```

When writing in safe mode, the driver appends a special command called getlasterror to the insert message. This accomplishes two things. First, because getlasterror is a command, and thus requires a round trip to the server, it ensures that the write has arrived. Second, the command verifies that the server hasn't thrown any errors on the current connection. If an error has been thrown, the drivers will raise an exception, which can be handled gracefully. You can use safe mode to guarantee that application-critical writes reach the server, but you might also employ safe mode when you expect an explicit error. For instance, you'll often want to enforce the uniqueness of a value. If you're storing user data, you'll maintain a unique index on the username field. The unique index will cause the insert of a document with a duplicate username to fail, but the only way to know that it has failed at insert time is to use safe mode.

For most purposes, it's prudent to enable safe mode by default. You may then opt to disable safe mode for the parts of an application that write lower-value data requiring higher throughput. Weighing this trade-off isn't always easy, and there are several more safe mode options to consider. We'll discuss these in much more detail in chapter 8.

By now, you should be feeling more comfortable with how the drivers work, and you're probably itching to build a real application. In the next section, we'll put it all together, using the Ruby driver to construct a basic Twitter monitoring app.

---

[4] A few drivers also support communication over Unix domain sockets.

3.3 *Building a simple application*

We'll build a simple application for archiving and displaying tweets. You can imagine this being a component in a larger application that allows users to keep tabs on search terms relevant to their businesses. This example will demonstrate how easy it is to consume JSON from an API like Twitter's and convert that to MongoDB documents. If you were doing this with a relational database, you'd have to devise a schema in advance, probably consisting of multiple tables, and then declare those tables. Here, none of that is required, yet you'll still preserve the rich structure of the tweet documents, and you'll be able to query them effectively.

Let's call the app TweetArchiver. TweetArchiver will consist of two components: the archiver and the viewer. The archiver will call the Twitter search API and store the relevant tweets, and the viewer will display the results in a web browser.

3.3.1 *Setting up*

This application requires three Ruby libraries. You can install them like so:

```
gem install mongo
gem install twitter
gem install sinatra
```

It'll be useful to have a configuration file that you can share between the archiver and viewer scripts. Create a file called config.rb, and initialize the following constants:

```
DATABASE_NAME    = "twitter-archive"
COLLECTION_NAME = "tweets"
TAGS = ["mongodb", "ruby"]
```

First you specify the names of the database and collection you'll be using for your application. Then you define an array of search terms, which you'll send to the Twitter API.

The next step is to write the archiver script. You start with a `TweetArchiver` class. You'll instantiate the class with a search term. Then you'll call the `update` method on the `TweetArchiver` instance, which issues a Twitter API call, and save the results to a MongoDB collection.

Let's start with the class's constructor:

```
def initialize(tag)
  connection = Mongo::Connection.new
  db         = connection[DATABASE_NAME]
  @tweets    = db[COLLECTION_NAME]

  @tweets.create_index([['id', 1]], :unique => true)
  @tweets.create_index([['tags', 1], ['id', -1]])

  @tag = tag
  @tweets_found = 0
end
```

The `initialize` method instantiates a connection, a database object, and the collection object you'll use to store the tweets. This method also creates a couple of indexes.

Every tweet will have an id field (distinct from MongoDB's _id field) which references the tweet's internal Twitter ID. You're creating a *unique* index on this field to keep from inserting the same tweet twice.

You're also creating a compound index on tags ascending and id descending. Indexes can be specified in ascending or descending order. This matters mainly when creating compound indexes; you should always choose the directions based on your expected query patterns. Since you're going to want to query for a particular tag and show the results from newest to oldest, an index with tags ascending and ID descending will make that query use the index both for filtering results and for sorting them. As you can see here, you indicate index direction with 1 for *ascending* and -1 for *descending*.

3.3.2   *Gathering data*

MongoDB allows you to insert data regardless of its structure. Since you don't need to know which fields you'll be given in advance, Twitter is free to modify its API's return values with practically no consequences to your application. Normally, using an RDBMS, any change to Twitter's API (or more generally, to your data source) will require a database schema migration. With MongoDB, your application might need to change to accommodate new data schemas, but the database itself can handle any document-style schema automatically.

The Ruby Twitter library returns Ruby hashes, so you can pass these directly to your MongoDB collection object. Within your TweetArchiver, you add the following instance method:

```
def save_tweets_for(term)
  Twitter::Search.new.containing(term).each do |tweet|
    @tweets_found  += 1
    tweet_with_tag = tweet.to_hash.merge!({"tags" => [term]})
    @tweets.save(tweet_with_tag)
  end
end
```

Before saving each tweet document, you make one small modification. To simplify later queries, you add the search term to a tags attribute. Then you pass the modified document to the save method. Here, then, is the complete listing for the archiver class.

Listing 3.1   A class for fetching tweets and archiving them in MongoDB

```
require 'rubygems'
require 'mongo'
require 'twitter'

require 'config'

class TweetArchiver

  # Create a new instance of TweetArchiver
  def initialize(tag)
    connection = Mongo::Connection.new
    db         = connection[DATABASE_NAME]
    @tweets    = db[COLLECTION_NAME]
```

```
    @tweets.create_index([['id', 1]], :unique => true)
    @tweets.create_index([['tags', 1], ['id', -1]])

    @tag = tag
    @tweets_found = 0
  end

  def update
    puts "Starting Twitter search for '#{@tag}'..."
    save_tweets_for(@tag)
    print "#{@tweets_found} tweets saved.\n\n"
  end

  private

  def save_tweets_for(term)
    Twitter::Search.new(term).each do |tweet|
      @tweets_found += 1
      tweet_with_tag = tweet.to_hash.merge!({"tags" => [term]})
      @tweets.save(tweet_with_tag)
    end
  end

end
```

All that remains is to write a script to run the `TweetArchiver` code against each of the search terms. Create a file called update.rb containing the following:

```
require 'config'
require 'archiver'

TAGS.each do |tag|
  archive = TweetArchiver.new(tag)
  archive.update
end
```

Next, run the update script:

```
ruby update.rb
```

You'll see some status messages indicating that tweets have been found and saved. You can verify that the script works by opening up the MongoDB shell and querying the collection directly:

```
> use twitter-archive
switched to db twitter-archive
> db.tweets.count()
30
```

To keep the archive current, you can rerun the update script once every few minutes using a cron job. But that's an administrative detail. What's important here is that you've managed to store tweets from Twitter searches in only a few lines of code.[5] Now comes the task of displaying the results.

---

[5] It's possible to accomplish this in far fewer lines of code. Doing so is left as an exercise to the reader.

3.3.3   *Viewing the archive*

You'll use Ruby's Sinatra web framework to build a simple app to display the results. Create a file called viewer.rb and place it in the same directory as the other scripts. Next, make a subdirectory called `views`, and place a file there called tweets.erb. The project's file structure should looks like this:

```
- config.rb
- archiver.rb
- update.rb
- viewer.rb
- /views
    - tweets.erb
```

Now edit viewer.rb with the following code.

Listing 3.2   A simple Sinatra application for displaying and searching the Tweet archive

```
require 'rubygems'
require 'mongo'                                       ❶ Require
require 'sinatra'                                        libraries

require 'config'

configure do                                          ❷ Instantiate
  db = Mongo::Connection.new[DATABASE_NAME]              collection
  TWEETS = db[COLLECTION_NAME]                           for tweets
end

get '/' do
  if params['tag']                                    ❸ Dynamically build
    selector = {:tags => params['tag']}                  query selector
  else                            ❹ Or use
    selector = {}                    blank selector
  end

  @tweets = TWEETS.find(selector).sort(["id", -1])    ◁──❺ Issue query

  erb :tweets                     ◁──❻ Render view
end
```

The first lines require the necessary libraries along with your config file ❶. Next there's a configuration block that creates a connection to MongoDB and stores a reference to your `tweets` collection in the constant `TWEETS` ❷.

The real meat of the application is in the lines beginning with `get '/' do`. The code in this block handles requests to the application's root URL. First, you build your query selector. If a `tags` URL parameter has been provided then you create a query selector that restricts the result set to the given tags ❸. Otherwise, you create a blank selector, which returns all documents in the collection ❹. You then issue the query ❺. By now you should know that what gets assigned to the `@tweets` variable isn't a result set, but a cursor. You'll iterate over that cursor in your view.

The last line ❻ renders the view file tweets.erb, whose full code listing is shown next.

Listing 3.3   HTML with embedded Ruby for rendering the Tweets

```
<!DOCTYPE html PUBLIC "-//W3C//DTD XHTML 1.0 Transitional//EN"
  "http://www.w3.org/TR/xhtml1/DTD/xhtml1-transitional.dtd">
<html lang='en' xml:lang='en' xmlns='http://www.w3.org/1999/xhtml'>
<head>
  <meta http-equiv="Content-Type" content="text/html; charset=UTF-8"/>

  <style>
    body {
      background-color: #DBD4C2;
      width: 1000px;
      margin: 50px auto;
    }

    h2 {
      margin-top: 2em;
    }
  </style>

</head>

<body>

<h1>Tweet Archive</h1>

<% TAGS.each do |tag| %>
  <a href="/?tag=<%= tag %>"><%= tag %></a>
<% end %>

<% @tweets.each do |tweet| %>
  <h2><%= tweet['text'] %></h2>
  <p>
    <a href="http://twitter.com/<%= tweet['from_user'] %>">
      <%= tweet['from_user'] %>
    </a>
    on <%= tweet['created_at'] %>
  </p>

  <img src="<%= tweet['profile_image_url'] %>" width="48" />
<% end %>

</body>
</html>
```

Most of the code is just HTML with some ERB mixed in.[6] The important parts come near the end, with the two iterators. The first of these cycles through the list of tags to display links for restricting the result set to a given tag. The second iterator, beginning with the @tweets.each code, cycles through each tweet to display the tweet's text, creation date, and user profile image. You can see results by running the application:

```
$ ruby viewer.rb
```

---

[6]   *ERB* stands for *embedded Ruby*. The Sinatra app runs the tweets.erb file through an ERB processor and evaluates any Ruby code between <% and %> in the context of the application.

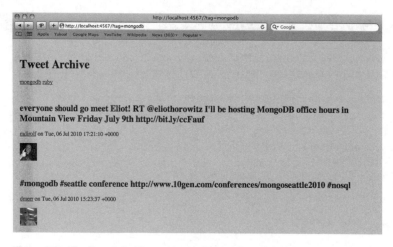

Figure 3.3   The Tweet Archiver output rendered in a web browser

If the application starts without error, you'll see the standard Sinatra startup message:

```
$ ruby viewer.rb
== Sinatra/1.0.0 has taken the stage on 4567 for development
with backup from Mongrel
```

You can then point your web browser to http://localhost:4567. The page should look something like the screenshot in figure 3.3. Try clicking on the links at the top of the screen to narrow the results to a particular tag.

That's the extent of the application. It's admittedly simple, but it demonstrates some of the ease of using MongoDB. You didn't have to define your schema in advance; you took advantage of secondary indexes to make your queries fast and prevent duplicate inserts; and you had a relatively simple integration with your programming language.

3.4   *Summary*

You've just learned the basics of talking to MongoDB through the Ruby programming language. You saw how easy it is to represent documents in Ruby, and how similar Ruby's CRUD API is to that of the MongoDB shell. We dove into some internals, learning how the drivers in general are built and looking in detail at object IDs, BSON, and the MongoDB network protocol. Finally, you built a simple application to show the use of MongoDB with real data. Though you certainly shouldn't feel you've reached MongoDB mastery, the prospect of writing applications with the database should be in reach.

Beginning with chapter 4, we're going to take everything you've learned so far and drill down. Specifically, we'll investigate how you might build an e-commerce application in MongoDB. That would be an enormous project, so we'll focus solely on a few sections on the back end. I'll present some data models for that domain, and you'll see how to insert and query that kind of data.

Part 2

Application development in MongoDB

The second part of this book is a deep exploration of MongoDB's document data model, query language, and CRUD (create, read, update, and delete) operations.

We'll make these topics concrete by progressively designing an e-commerce data model and the CRUD operations necessary for managing such data. Thus each chapter will present its subject matter in a top-down fashion, first by presenting examples within the sample e-commerce application's domain, and then by systematically filling in the details. On your first reading, you may want to read the e-commerce examples only and save the detailed material for later, or vice versa.

In chapter 4, you'll learn some schema design principles and then construct a basic e-commerce data model for products, categories, users, orders, and product reviews. Then you'll learn about how MongoDB organizes data on the database, collection, and document levels. This will include a summary of BSON's core data types.

Chapter 5 covers MongoDB's query language and aggregation functions. You'll learn how to issue common queries against the data model developed in the previous chapter, and you'll practice a few aggregations. Then, in the nuts and bolts sections, you'll see the semantics of query operators presented in detail. The chapter ends with an explanation of the map-reduce and grouping functions.

In presenting MongoDB's update and delete operations, chapter 6 brings us full circle by showing the rationale for the e-commerce data model. You'll learn how to maintain the category hierarchy and how to manage inventory transactionally. In addition, the update operators will be covered in detail along with the powerful `findAndModify` command.

Document-oriented data

This chapter takes a closer look at document-oriented data modeling and at how data is organized at the database, collection, and document levels in MongoDB. I'll start with a brief, general discussion of schema design. This is helpful because a large number of MongoDB users have never designed schemas for databases other than the traditional RDBMS. This exploration of principles sets the stage for the second part of the chapter, where we examine the design of an e-commerce schema in MongoDB. Along the way, you'll see how this schema differs from an equivalent RDBMS schema, and you'll learn how the typical relationships between entities, such as one-to-many and many-to-many, are represented in MongoDB. The e-commerce schema presented here will also serve as a basis for our discussions of queries, aggregation, and updates in subsequent chapters.

Since documents are the raw materials of MongoDB, I'll devote the final portion of this chapter to the small details and corner cases surrounding documents and their environs. This implies a more detailed discussion of databases, collections, and documents than you've seen up to this point. But if you read to the end, you'll be familiar with most of the obscure features and limitations of document data in MongoDB. You may also find yourself returning to this final section of the chapter later on, as it contains many of the gotchas you'll encounter when using MongoDB in the wild.

4.1 *Principles of schema design*

Database schema design is the process of choosing the best representation for a data set given the features of the database system, the nature of the data, and the application requirements. The principles of schema design for relational database systems are well established. With RDBMSs, you're encouraged to shoot for a *normalized* data model, which helps to ensure generic queryability and avoid updates to data that might result in inconsistencies. Moreover, the established patterns prevent developers from having to wonder how to model, say, one-to-many and many-to-many relationships. But schema design is never an exact science, even with relational databases. Performance-intensive applications, or applications that have to consume unstructured data, may require a more generic data model. Some applications are so demanding in their storage and scaling requirements that they're forced to break all the old schema design rules. FriendFeed is a great example of this, and the article describing the site's unorthodox data model is well worth your time (see http://mng.bz/ycG3).

If you're coming from the RDBMS world, you may be troubled by MongoDB's lack of hard schema design rules. Good practices have emerged, but there's still usually more than one good way to model a given data set. The premise of this section is that principles can drive schema design, but the reality is that those principles are pliable. To get you thinking, here are a few questions you can bring to the table when modeling data with *any* database system.

- *What's the basic unit of data?* In an RDBMS, you have tables with columns and rows. In a key-value store, you have keys pointing to amorphous values. In MongoDB, the basic unit of data is the BSON document.
- *How can you query and update that data?* Once you understand the basic data type, you need to know how to manipulate it. RDBMSs feature ad hoc queries and joins. MongoDB also allows ad hoc queries, but joins aren't supported. Simple key-value stores only permit fetching values by a single key.

  Databases also diverge in the kinds of updates they permit. With an RDBMS, you can update documents in sophisticated ways using SQL and wrap multiple updates in a transaction to get atomicity and rollback. MongoDB doesn't support transactions, but it does support a variety of atomic update operations that can work on the internal structures of a complex document. With simple key-value stores, you might be able to update a value, but every update will usually mean replacing the value completely.

  The essential point is that building the best data model means understanding the features of your database. If you want to model data well in MongoDB, you must start with the knowledge of exactly which sorts of queries and updates it's best at.

- *What are your application access patterns?* In addition to understanding the basic unit of data and the features of the database, you also need to pin down the needs of your application. If you read the FriendFeed article just mentioned, you'll see how the idiosyncrasies of an application can easily demand a schema that goes against firmly held data modeling principles. The upshot is that you must ask numerous questions about the application before you can determine the ideal data model. What's the read/write ratio? What sorts of queries do you need? How is the data updated? What concurrency issues can you expect? How well structured is the data?

The best schema designs are always the product of deep knowledge of the database you're using, good judgment about the requirements of the application at hand, and plain old experience. The examples in this chapter, and the schema design patterns in appendix B, have been designed to help you develop a good sense for schema design in MongoDB. Having studied these examples, you'll be well prepared to design the best schemas for your own applications.

4.2 Designing an e-commerce data model

Demonstrations of next-generation data stores typically revolve around social media: Twitter-like demo apps are the norm. Unfortunately, such apps tend to have rather simple data models. That's why, in this and in subsequent chapters, we'll look at the much richer domain of e-commerce. E-commerce has the advantage of including a large number of familiar data modeling patterns. Plus, it's not hard to imagine how products, categories, product reviews, and orders are typically modeled in an RDBMS. This should make the upcoming examples more instructive, since you'll be able to contrast them with some of your preconceived notions of schema design.

E-commerce has often been a domain exclusive to RDBMSs, and this is true for a couple of reasons. The first is that e-commerce sites generally require transactions, and transactions are an RDBMS staple. The second is that, until recently, domains that require rich data models and sophisticated queries have been assumed to fit best within the realm of the RDBMS. The following examples call into question this second assumption.

Before we proceed, a note on scope is in order. Building an entire e-commerce back end isn't practical within the space of this book. What we'll do instead is pick out a handful of e-commerce entities and show how they might be modeled in MongoDB. In particular, we'll look at products and categories, users and orders, and product reviews. For each entity, I'll show an example document. Then, we'll hint at some of the database features that complement the document's structure.

For many developers, *data model* goes hand in hand with *object mapping*, and for that purpose you've probably used an object-relational mapping library, such as Java's Hibernate framework or Ruby's ActiveRecord. Such libraries are all but necessary for building applications efficiently on an RDBMS. But they're less necessary with MongoDB. This is due in part to the fact that a document is already an object-like representation. It's also partly due to drivers, which provide a fairly high-level interface to MongoDB. You can frequently build entire applications on MongoDB using the driver interface alone.

That said, object mappers are convenient because they facilitate validation, type checking, and associations. A number of mature MongoDB object mappers provide an extra layer of abstraction above the basic language drivers, and you might consider using one on a larger project.[1] But regardless of the object mapper, you're always ultimately dealing with documents. That's why this chapter focuses on the documents themselves. Knowing the shape of documents in a well-designed MongoDB schema will prepare you to work with the database intelligently, with or without an object mapper.

4.2.1 Products and categories

Products and categories are the mainstays of any e-commerce site. Products, in a normalized RDBMS model, tend to require a large number of tables. There's always a table for basic product information, such as the name and SKU, but there'll be other tables to relate shipping information and pricing histories. If the system allows products with arbitrary attributes, then a complicated series of tables will be necessary to define and store those attributes, as you saw in chapter 1 in the Magento example. This multitable schema will be facilitated by the RDBMS's ability to join tables.

Modeling a product in MongoDB should be less complicated. Because collections don't enforce a schema, any product document will have room for whichever dynamic attributes the product needs. And by using arrays to contain inner document structures, you can typically condense a multitable RDBMS representation into a single MongoDB collection. More concretely, here's a sample product from a gardening store.

Listing 4.1 A sample product document

```
doc =
{ _id: new ObjectId("4c4b1476238d3b4dd5003981"),
  slug: "wheel-barrow-9092",
  sku: "9092",
  name: "Extra Large Wheel Barrow",
  description: "Heavy duty wheel barrow...",

  details: {
    weight: 47,
    weight_units: "lbs",
    model_num: 4039283402,
    manufacturer: "Acme",
    color: "Green"
  },

  total_reviews: 4,
  average_review: 4.5,
```

---

[1] To find out which object mappers are most current for your language of choice, consult the recommendations at http://mongodb.org.

```
        pricing:  {
          retail: 589700,
          sale: 489700,
        },

        price_history: [
            {retail: 529700,
             sale: 429700,
             start: new Date(2010, 4, 1),
             end: new Date(2010, 4, 8)
             },

            {retail:  529700,
             sale:  529700,
             start: new Date(2010, 4, 9),
             end: new Date(2010, 4, 16)
             },
        ],

        category_ids: [new ObjectId("6a5b1476238d3b4dd5000048"),
                        new ObjectId("6a5b1476238d3b4dd5000049")],

        main_cat_id: new ObjectId("6a5b1476238d3b4dd5000048"),

        tags: ["tools", "gardening", "soil"],

}
```

The document contains the basic name, sku, and description fields. There's also the standard MongoDB object ID stored in the _id field. In addition, you've defined a slug, wheel-barrow-9092, to provide a meaningful URL. MongoDB users sometimes complain about the ugliness of object IDs in URLs. Naturally, you don't want URLs that look like this:

http://mygardensite.org/products/4c4b1476238d3b4dd5003981

Meaningful IDs are so much better:

http://mygardensite.org/products/wheel-barrow-9092

I generally recommend building a slug field if a URL will be generated for the document. Such a field should have a unique index on it so that the value can be used as a primary key. Assuming you're storing this document in the products collection, you can create the unique index like so:

db.products.ensureIndex({slug: 1}, {unique: true})

If you have a unique index on slug, you'll need to insert your product document using safe mode so that you'll know if the insert fails. That way, you can retry with a different slug if necessary. To take an example, imagine your gardening store has multiple wheelbarrows for sale. When you start selling a new wheelbarrow, your code will need to generate a unique slug for the new product. Here's how you'd perform the insert from Ruby:

```
@products.insert({:name => "Extra Large Wheel Barrow",
        :sku  => "9092",
```

```
:slug => "wheel-barrow-9092"},
:safe => true)
```

What's important to note here is that you specify `:safe => true`. If the insert succeeds without raising an exception, you know you've chosen a unique slug. But if an exception is raised, your code will need to retry with a new value for the slug.

Continuing on, you have a key, `details`, that points to a sub-document containing various product details. You've specified the weight, weight units, and the manufacturer's model number. You might store other ad hoc attributes here as well. For instance, if you were selling seeds, you might include attributes for the expected yield and time to harvest, and if you were selling lawnmowers, you could include horsepower, fuel type, and mulching options. The `details` attribute provides a nice container for these kinds of dynamic attributes.

Note that you can also store the product's current and past prices in the same document. The `pricing` key points to an object containing retail and sale prices. `price_history`, by contrast, references a whole array of pricing options. Storing copies of documents like this is a common versioning technique.

Next, there's an array of tag names for the product. You saw a similar tagging example in chapter 1, but the technique bears repeating. Since you can index array keys, this is the simplest and best way of storing relevant tags on an item while at the same time assuring efficient queryability.

But what about relationships? You've been able to use rich document structures such as sub-documents and arrays to store product details, prices, and tags all in a single document. And yet, you eventually need to relate to documents in other collections. To start, you'll relate products to a category structure. This relationship between products and categories is usually conceived of as many-to-many, where each product can belong to more than one category, and each category can contain multiple products. In an RDMBS, you'd use a join table to represent a many-to-many relationship like this one. Join tables store all the relationship references between two tables in a single table. Using a SQL join, it's then possible to issue a single query to retrieve a product with all its categories, and vice versa.

MongoDB doesn't support joins, so you need a different many-to-many strategy. Looking at your wheelbarrow document, you'll see a field called `category_ids` containing an array of object IDs. Each object ID acts as a pointer to the `_id` field of some category document. For reference, here's a sample category document.

Listing 4.2 A category document

```
doc =
{  _id: new ObjectId("6a5b1476238d3b4dd5000048"),
   slug: "gardening-tools",
   ancestors: [{ name: "Home",
                 _id:  new ObjectId("8b87fb1476238d3b4dd500003"),
                 slug: "home"
               },

               { name: "Outdoors",
```

```
                    _id:  new ObjectId("9a9fb1476238d3b4dd5000001"),
                    slug: "outdoors"
                }
        ],

        parent_id: new ObjectId("9a9fb1476238d3b4dd5000001"),

        name: "Gardening Tools",
        description: "Gardening gadgets galore!",
    }
```

If you go back to the product document and look carefully at the object IDs in its category_ids field, you'll see that the product is related to the Gardening Tools category just shown. Having the category_ids array key in the product document enables all the kinds of queries you might issue on a many-to-many relationship. For instance, to query for all products in the Gardening Tools category, the code is simple:

```
db.products.find({category_ids => category['_id']})
```

To query for all categories from a given product, you use the $in operator. This is analogous to SQL's IN directive:

```
db.categories.find({_id: {$in: product['category_ids']}})
```

With the many-to-many relationship described, I'll say a few words about the category document itself. You'll notice the standard _id, slug, name, and description fields. These are straightforward, but the array of parent documents may not be. Why are you redundantly storing such a large percentage of each of the document's ancestor categories? The fact is that categories are always conceived of as a hierarchy, and the ways of representing such a hierarchy in a database are many.[2] The strategy you choose is always dependent on the needs of the application. In this case, because MongoDB doesn't support joins, we've elected to denormalize the parent category names in each child document. This way, when querying for the Gardening Products category, there's no need to perform additional queries to get the names and URLs of the parent categories, Outdoors and Home.

Some developers would consider this level of denormalization unacceptable. There are other options for representing a tree, and one of these is discussed in appendix B. But for the moment, try to be open to the possibility that what best determine the schema are the demands of the application, and not necessarily the dictates of theory. When you see more examples of querying and updating this structure in the next two chapters, the rationale will become clearer.

4.2.2 Users and orders

Looking at how you model users and orders illustrates another common relationship: one-to-many. That is, every user has many orders. In an RDBMS, you'd use a foreign key in your orders table; here, the convention is similar. Examine the following listing:

---

[2] Two such methods, the adjacency list and the nested set, are presented in this MySQL developer article: http://mng.bz/83w4.

Listing 4.3   An e-commerce order, with line items, pricing, and a shipping address

```
doc =
{ _id: ObjectId("6a5b1476238d3b4dd5000048")
  user_id: ObjectId("4c4b1476238d3b4dd5000001")

  state: "CART",

  line_items:  [
    { _id: ObjectId("4c4b1476238d3b4dd5003981"),
      sku:  "9092",
      name:  "Extra Large Wheel Barrow",
      quantity:  1,
      pricing:  {
        retail:  5897,
        sale:  4897,
      }
    },

    { _id:  ObjectId("4c4b1476238d3b4dd5003981"),
      sku:  "10027",
      name:  "Rubberized Work Glove, Black",
      quantity:  2,
      pricing: {
        retail:  1499,
        sale:  1299
      }
    }
  ],

  shipping_address:  {
    street: "588 5th Street",
    city: "Brooklyn",
    state: "NY",
    zip: 11215
  },

  sub_total:  6196
}
```

The second order attribute, user_id, stores a given user's _id. It's effectively a pointer to the sample user, shown in listing 4.4 (we'll discuss this listing presently). This arrangement makes it easy to query either side of the relationship. To find all orders for a given user is simple:

```
db.orders.find({user_id: user['_id']})
```

The query for getting the user for a particular order is equally simple:

```
user_id = order['user_id']
db.users.find({_id: user_id})
```

Using an object ID as a reference in this way, it's easy to build a one-to-many relationship between orders and users.

We'll now look at some other salient aspects of the order document. In general, you're using the rich representation afforded by the document data model. You'll see that the document includes both the line items and the shipping address. These attributes, in a normalized relational model, would be located in separate tables. Here, the line items consist of an array of sub-documents, each describing a product in the shopping cart. The shipping address attribute points to a single object containing address fields.

Let's take a moment to discuss the merits of this representation. First, there's a win for the human mind. Your entire concept of an order, including line items, shipping address, and eventual payment information, can be encapsulated in a single entity. When querying the database, you can return the entire order object with one simple query. What's more, the products, as they appeared when purchased, are effectively frozen within your order document. Finally, as you'll see in the next two chapters, and as you may sense, you can easily query and modify this order document.

The user document presents similar patterns, as it stores a list of address documents along with a list of payment method documents. In addition, at the top level of the document, you find the basic attributes common to any user model. And as with the slug field on your product, keep a unique index on the username field.

Listing 4.4   A user document, with addresses and payment methods

```
{ _id: new ObjectId("4c4b1476238d3b4dd5000001"),
  username: "kbanker",
  email: "kylebanker@gmail.com",
  first_name: "Kyle",
  last_name: "Banker",
  hashed_password: "bd1cfa194c3a603e7186780824b04419",

  addresses: [
    {name: "home",
     street: "588 5th Street",
     city: "Brooklyn",
     state: "NY",
     zip: 11215},

    {name: "work",
     street: "1 E. 23rd Street",
     city: "New York",
     state: "NY",
     zip: 10010}
  ],

  payment_methods: [
    {name: "VISA",
     last_four: 2127,
     crypted_number: "43f6ba1dfda6b8106dc7",
     expiration_date: new Date(2014, 4)
    }
  ]
}
```

4.2.3   *Reviews*

We'll close the sample data model with product reviews. Relationally speaking, each product has many reviews. Here, that relationship is encoded using an object ID reference, `review_id`, which you can see in this sample review document.

Listing 4.5   A document representing a product review

```
{ _id: new ObjectId("4c4b1476238d3b4dd5000041"),
  product_id: new ObjectId("4c4b1476238d3b4dd5003981"),
  date: new Date(2010, 5, 7),
  title: "Amazing",
  text: "Has a squeaky wheel, but still a darn good wheel barrow.",
  rating: 4,

  user_id: new ObjectId("4c4b1476238d3b4dd5000041"),
  username: "dgreenthumb",

  helpful_votes: 3,
  voter_ids: [ new ObjectId("4c4b1476238d3b4dd5000041"),
               new ObjectId("7a4f0376238d3b4dd5000003"),
               new ObjectId("92c21476238d3b4dd5000032")
  ]
}
```

Most of the remaining attributes are self-explanatory. You store the review's date, title, and text; the rating provided by the user; and the user's ID. But it may come as a surprise that you store the username as well. After all, if this were an RDBMS, you'd be able to pull in the username with a join on the *users* table. Since you don't have the join option with MongoDB, you can proceed in one of two ways: either query against the user collection for each review or accept some denormalization. Issuing a query for every review might be unnecessarily costly when the attribute being queried (the username) is extremely unlikely to change. To be sure, you could go the normalized route and display all reviews in just two MongoDB queries. But here you're designing a schema for the common case. This does mean that a username update is more expensive, since a username will need to change in every place that it appears, but again, that happens infrequently enough to justify this as a reasonable design choice.

Also noteworthy is the decision to store votes in the review document itself. It's common for users to be able to vote on reviews. Here, you store the object ID of each voting user in an array of voter IDs. This allows you to prevent users from voting on a review more than once, and it also gives you the ability to query for all the reviews a user has voted on. Note also that you cache the total number of helpful votes, which among other things allows you to sort reviews based on helpfulness.

With that, we've covered a basic e-commerce data model. If this is your first time looking at a MongoDB data model, then contemplating the utility of this model may require a leap of faith. Rest assured that the mechanics of all of this—from adding votes uniquely, to modifying orders, to querying products intelligently—will be explored and explained in the next two chapters, which discuss querying and updating, respectively.

4.3 Nuts and bolts: on databases, collections, and documents

We're going to take a break from the e-commerce example to look at some of the core details of using databases, collections, and documents. Much of this involves definitions, special features, and edge cases. If you've ever wondered how MongoDB allocates data files, which data types are strictly permitted within a document, or what the benefits of using capped collections are, read on.

4.3.1 Databases

A database is a logical and physical grouping of collections. In this section, we'll discuss the details of creating and deleting databases. We'll also jump down a level to see how MongoDB allocates space for individual databases on the file system.

MANAGING DATABASES

There's no explicit way to create a database in MongoDB. Instead, a database is created automatically once you write to a collection in that database. Have a look at this Ruby code:

```
@connection = Mongo::Connection.new
@db = @connection['garden']
```

Assuming that the database doesn't exist already, the database has yet to be created on disk even after executing this code. All you've done is instantiate an instance of the class Mongo::DB. Only when you write to a collection are the data files created. Continuing on:

```
@products = @db['products']
@products.save({:name => "Extra Large Wheel Barrow"})
```

When you call save on the products collection, the driver tells MongoDB to insert the product document into the garden.products namespace. If that namespace doesn't exist, then it's created; part of this involves allocating the garden database on disk.

To delete a database, which means dropping all its collections, you issue a special command. You can drop the garden database from Ruby like so:

```
@connection.drop_database('garden')
```

From the MongoDB shell, you run the dropDatabase() method:

```
use garden
db.dropDatabase();
```

Do be careful when dropping databases; there's no way to undo this operation.

DATA FILES AND ALLOCATION

When you create a database, MongoDB allocates a set of data files on disk. All collections, indexes, and other metadata for the database are stored in these files. The data files reside in whichever directory you've designated as the dbpath when starting nmongod. When left unspecified, mongod stores all its files in /data/db.[3] Let's see how this directory looks after creating the garden database:

```
$ cd /data/db
$ ls -al
drwxr-xr-x  6 kyle   admin          204 Jul 31 15:48 .
drwxrwxrwx  7 root   admin          238 Jul 31 15:46 ..
-rwxr-xr-x  1 kyle   admin     67108864 Jul 31 15:47 garden.0
-rwxr-xr-x  1 kyle   admin    134217728 Jul 31 15:46 garden.1
-rwxr-xr-x  1 kyle   admin     16777216 Jul 31 15:47 garden.ns
-rwxr-xr-x  1 kyle   admin            6 Jul 31 15:48 mongod.lock
```

First note the mongod.lock file, which stores the server's process ID.[4] The database files themselves are all named after the database they belong to. garden.ns is the first file to be generated. The file's extension, *ns*, stands for *namespaces*. Every collection and index in a database gets its own namespace, and the metadata for each namespace is stored in this file. By default, the .ns file is fixed to 16 MB, which lets it store approximately 24,000 namespaces. This means that the sum of the number of indexes and collections in your database can't exceed 24,000. You're not likely to need anywhere close to this number of collections or indexes. But on the off chance that you need even more, you can makes the file larger by using the --nssize server option.

In addition to creating the namespace file, MongoDB allocates space for the collections and indexes in files ending with incrementing integers starting with 0. Study the directory listing and you'll see two core data files, the 64 MB garden.0 and the 128 MB garden.1. The initial size of these files often comes as a shock to new users. But MongoDB favors this preallocation to ensure that as much data as possible will be stored contiguously. This way, when you query and update the data, those operations are more likely to occur in proximity, rather than being spread across the disk.

As you add data to your database, MongoDB continues to allocate more data files. Each new data file gets twice the space of the previously allocated file until the largest preallocated size of 2 GB is reached. Thus, garden.2 will be 256 MB, garden.3 will use 512 MB, and so forth. The assumption here is that, if the total data size is growing at a constant rate, the data files should be allocated increasingly, which is a pretty standard allocation strategy. Certainly one consequence is that the difference between allocated space and actual space used can be high.[5]

---

[3] On Windows, it's c:\data\db.

[4] Never delete or alter the lock file unless you're recovering from an unclean shutdown. If you start mongod and get an error message about the lock file, there's a good chance that you've shut down uncleanly, and you may have to initiate a recovery process. We discuss this further in chapter 10.

[5] This may present a problem in deployments where space is at a premium. For those situations, you may use some combination of the --noprealloc and --smallfiles server options.

You can always check the amount of space used versus allocated using the `stats` command:

```
> db.stats()
{
  "collections" : 3,
  "objects" : 10004,
  "avgObjSize" : 36.005,
  "dataSize" : 360192,
  "storageSize" : 791296,
  "numExtents" : 7,
  "indexes" : 1,
  "indexSize" : 425984,
  "fileSize" : 201326592,
  "ok" : 1
}
```

In this example, the `fileSize` field indicates the total size of files allocated for this database. This is simply the sum of the sizes of the garden database's two data files, garden.0 and garden.1. Trickier is the difference between `dataSize` and `storageSize`. The former is the actual size of the BSON objects in the database; the latter includes extra space reserved for collection growth and also unallocated deleted space.[6] Finally, the `indexSize` value shows the total size of indexes for this database. It's important to keep an eye on total index size, as database performance will be best when all utilized indexes can fit in RAM. I'll elaborate on this in chapters 7 and 10 when presenting techniques for troubleshooting performance issues.

4.3.2 Collections

Collections are containers for structurally or conceptually similar documents. Here, I'll describe creating and deleting collections in more detail. Then I'll present MongoDB's special capped collections, and we'll look at some examples of how the core server uses collections internally.

MANAGING COLLECTIONS

As you saw in the previous section, you create collections implicitly by inserting documents into a particular namespace. But because more than one collection type exists, MongoDB also provides a command for creating collections. From the shell:

```
db.createCollection("users")
```

When creating a standard collection, you have the option of preallocating a specific number of bytes. This usually isn't necessary but can be done like so:

```
db.createCollection("users", {size: 20000})
```

Collection names may contain numbers, letters, or . characters, but must begin with a letter or number. Internally, a collection name is identified by its namespace name,

---

[6] Technically, collections are allocated space inside each data file in chunks called *extents*. The `storageSize` is the total space allocated for collection extents.

which includes the name of the database it belongs to. Thus, the products collection is technically referred to as `garden.products` when referenced in a message to or from the core server. This fully qualified collection name can't be longer than 128 characters.

It's sometimes useful to include the `.` character in collection names to provide a kind of virtual namespacing. For instance, you can imagine a series of collections with titles like the following:

```
products.categories
products.images
products.reviews
```

Keep in mind that this is just an organizational principle; the database treats collections named with a `.` just like any other collection.

Because I've already spoken about removing documents from collections and dropping collections completely, you only need to note that collections can also be renamed. As an example, you can rename the products collection with the shell's `renameCollection` method:

```
db.products.renameCollection("store_products")
```

CAPPED COLLECTIONS

In addition to the standard collections you've created so far, it's also possible to create what's known as a *capped collection*. Capped collections were originally designed for high-performance logging scenarios. They're distinguished from standard collections by their fixed size. This means that once a capped collection reaches its maximum size, subsequent inserts will overwrite the least-recently-inserted documents in the collection. This design prevents users from having to prune the collection manually when only recent data may be of value.

To understand how you might use a capped collection, imagine you want to keep track of users' actions on your site. Such actions might include viewing a product, adding to the cart, checking out, and purchasing. You can write a script to simulate logging these user actions to a capped collection. In the process, you'll see some of these collections' interesting properties. Here's a simple demonstration.

> **Listing 4.6   Simulating the logging of user actions to a capped collection**

```
require 'rubygems'
require 'mongo'

VIEW_PRODUCT = 0
ADD_TO_CART  = 1
CHECKOUT     = 2
PURCHASE     = 3

@con = Mongo::Connection.new
@db  = @con['garden']

@db.drop_collection("user.actions")

@db.create_collection("user.actions", :capped => true, :size => 1024)
```

```
@actions = @db['user.actions']

40.times do |n|
  doc = {
    :username => "kbanker",
    :action_code => rand(4),
    :time => Time.now.utc,
    :n => n
  }

  @actions.insert(doc)
end
```

First, you create a 1 KB capped collection called users.actions using the DB#create_
collection method.[7] Next, you insert 20 sample log documents. Each document contains a username, an action code (stored as an integer from 0 through 3), and a timestamp. You've included an incrementing integer, *n*, so that you can identify which
documents have aged out. Now let's query the collection from the shell:

```
> use garden
> db.user.actions.count();
10
```

Even though you've inserted 20 documents, only 10 documents exist in the collection.
If you query the collection, you'll see why:

```
db.user.actions.find();
{ "_id" : ObjectId("4c55f6e0238d3b201000000b"), "username" : "kbanker",
  "action_code" : 0, "n" : 10, "time" : "Sun Aug 01 2010 18:36:16" }
{ "_id" : ObjectId("4c55f6e0238d3b201000000c"), "username" : "kbanker",
  "action_code" : 4, "n" : 11, "time" : "Sun Aug 01 2010 18:36:16" }
{ "_id" : ObjectId("4c55f6e0238d3b201000000d"), "username" : "kbanker",
  "action_code" : 2, "n" : 12, "time" : "Sun Aug 01 2010 18:36:16" }
...
```

The documents are returned in order of insertion. If you look at the n values, it's clear
that the oldest document in the collection is the tenth document inserted, which
means that documents 0 through 9 have already aged out. Since this capped collection has a maximum size of 1024 bytes, and contains just 10 documents, you can conclude that each document is roughly 100 bytes in length. You'll see how to confirm
this assumption in the next subsection.

Before doing so, I should point out a couple more differences between capped
and standard collections. First, the index on _id isn't created by default for a capped
collection. This is a performance optimization; without an index, inserts take less
time. If you do want an index on _id, you can build the index manually. With no
indexes defined, it's best to think of a capped collection as a data structure that you
process sequentially in lieu of querying randomly. For this purpose, MongoDB provides a special sort operator for returning a collection's documents in natural

---

[7] The equivalent creation command from the shell would be db.createCollection("users.actions",
{capped: true, size: 1024}).

insertion order.[8] Your previous query returned items from your collection in forward natural order. To return them in reverse natural order, you must use the $natural sort operator:

```
> db.user.actions.find().sort({"$natural": -1});
```

In addition to ordering documents naturally and eschewing indexes, capped collections limit certain CRUD operations. For one, you can't delete individual documents from a capped collection; nor can you perform any update that will increase the size of a document.[9]

SYSTEM COLLECTIONS

Part of MongoDB's design lies in its own internal use of collections. Two of these special system collections that are always present are system.namespaces and system.indexes. You can query the former to see all the namespaces defined for the current database:

```
> db.system.namespaces.find();
{ "name" : "garden.products" }
{ "name" : "garden.system.indexes" }
{ "name" : "garden.products.$_id_" }
{ "name" : "garden.user.actions", "options" :
    { "create": "user.actions", "capped": true, "size": 1024 } }
```

The latter collection, system.indexes, stores each index definition for the current database. To see a list of indexes you've defined for the garden database, just query the collection:

```
> db.system.indexes.find();
{ "name" : "_id_", "ns" : "garden.products", "key" : { "_id" : 1 } }
```

system.namespaces and system.indexes are both standard collections, but MongoDB uses capped collections for replication. Each member of a replica set logs all its writes to a special capped collection called oplog.rs. Secondary nodes then read from this collection sequentially and apply new operations to themselves. We'll discuss this systems collection in more detail in chapter 9.

4.3.3 *Documents and insertion*

We'll round out this chapter with some details on documents and their insertion.

DOCUMENT SERIALIZATION, TYPES, AND LIMITS

As stated in the previous chapter, all documents must be serialized to BSON before being sent to MongoDB; they're later deserialized from BSON by the driver into the language's native document representation. Most of the drivers provide a simple interface for serializing to and from BSON, and it's useful knowing how this works for

---

[8] The natural order is the order in which documents are stored on disk.

[9] Since capped collections were originally designed for logging, there was no need to implement the deletion or updating of documents, as this would've complicated the code responsible for aging out old documents. Without these features, capped collections preserve the simplicity and efficiency they were designed for.

your driver in case you ever need to examine what's being sent to the database. For instance, when demonstrating capped collections, it was reasonable to assume that the sample document size was roughly 100 bytes. You can check this assumption using the Ruby driver's BSON serializer:

```
doc = {
  :_id => BSON::ObjectId.new,
  :username => "kbanker",
  :action_code => rand(5),
  :time => Time.now.utc,
  :n => 1
}

bson = BSON::BSON_CODER.serialize(doc)

puts "Document #{doc.inspect} takes up #{bson.length} bytes as BSON"
```

The serialize method returns a byte array. If you run the preceding code, you'll get a BSON object 82 bytes long, which isn't far from the estimate. If you ever want to check the BSON size of an object using the shell, that's also straightforward:

```
> doc = {
  _id: new ObjectId(),
  username: "kbanker",
  action_code: Math.ceil(Math.random() * 5),
  time: new Date(),
  n: 1
}

> Object.bsonsize(doc);
82
```

Again, you get 82 bytes. The difference between the 82-byte document size and the 100-byte estimate is due to normal collection and document overhead.

Deserializing BSON is just as straightforward. Try running this code to verify that it works:

```
deserialized_doc = BSON::BSON_CODER.deserialize(bson)

puts "Here's our document deserialized from BSON:"
puts deserialized_doc.inspect
```

Do note that you can't serialize just any Ruby hash. To serialize without error, the key names must be valid, and each of the values must be convertible into a BSON type. A valid key name consists of a null-terminated string with a maximum length of 255 bytes. The string may consist of any combination of ASCII characters, with three exceptions: it can't begin with a $, it must not contain any . characters, and it must not contain the null byte except in the final position. When programming in Ruby, you may use symbols as hash keys, but they'll be converted into their string equivalents when serialized.

It's important to consider the length of the key names you choose, since key names are stored in the documents themselves. This contrasts with an RDBMS, where column names are always kept separate from the rows they refer to. So when using BSON, if you can live with dob in place of date_of_birth as a key name, you'll save 10 bytes per document. That may not sound like much, but once you have a billion such documents, you'll have saved nearly 10 GB of storage space just by using a shorter key name. This doesn't mean you should go to unreasonable lengths to ensure small key names; be sensible. But if you expect massive amounts of data, economizing on key names will save space.

In addition to valid key names, documents must contain values that can be serialized into BSON. A table of BSON types, with examples and notes, can be found at http://bsonspec.org. Here, I'll only point out some of the highlights and gotchas.

Strings

All string values must be encoded as UTF-8. Though UTF-8 is quickly becoming the standard for character encoding, there are plenty of situations when an older encoding is still used. Users typically encounter issues with this when importing data generated by legacy systems into MongoDB. The solution usually involves either converting to UTF-8 before inserting or, barring that, storing the text as the BSON binary type.[10]

Numbers

BSON specifies three numeric types: double, int, and long. This means that BSON can encode any IEEE floating-point value and any signed integer up to eight bytes in length. When serializing integers in dynamic languages, the driver will automatically determine whether to encode as an int or a long. In fact, there's only one common situation where a number's type must be made explicit, which is when inserting numeric data via the JavaScript shell. JavaScript, unhappily, natively supports just a single numeric type called Number, which is equivalent to an IEEE double. Consequently, if you want to save a numeric value from the shell as an integer, you need to be explicit, using either NumberLong() or NumberInt(). Try this example:

```
db.numbers.save({n: 5});
db.numbers.save({ n: NumberLong(5) });
```

You've just saved two documents to the numbers collection. And though their values are equal, the first is saved as a double and the second as a long integer. Querying for all documents where n is 5 will return both documents:

```
> db.numbers.find({n: 5});
{ "_id" : ObjectId("4c581c98d5bbeb2365a838f9"), "n" : 5 }
{ "_id" : ObjectId("4c581c9bd5bbeb2365a838fa"), "n" : NumberLong( 5 ) }
```

But you can see that the second value is marked as a long integer. Another way to see this is to query by BSON type using the special $type operator. Each BSON type is identified by an integer, beginning with 1. If you consult the BSON spec at http://bsonspec.org, you'll see that doubles are type 1 and that 64-bit integers are type 18. Thus, you can query the collection for values by type:

---

[10] Incidentally, if you're new to character encodings, you owe it to yourself to read Joel Spolsky's well-known introduction (http://mng.bz/LVO6). If you're a Rubyist, you may also want to read James Edward Gray's series on character encodings in Ruby 1.8 and 1.9 (http://mng.bz/wc4J).

```
> db.numbers.find({n: {$type: 1}});
{ "_id" : ObjectId("4c581c98d5bbeb2365a838f9"), "n" : 5 }

> db.numbers.find({n: {$type: 18}});
{ "_id" : ObjectId("4c581c9bd5bbeb2365a838fa"), "n" : NumberLong( 5 ) }
```

This verifies the difference in storage. You'll probably never use the $type operator in production, but as seen here, it's a great tool for debugging.

The only other issue that commonly arises with BSON numeric types is the lack of decimal support. This means that if you're planning on storing currency values in MongoDB, you need to use an integer type and keep the values in cents.

Datetimes

The BSON datetime type is used to store temporal values. Time values are represented using a signed 64-bit integer marking milliseconds since the Unix epoch, in UTC (Coordinated Universal Time). A negative value marks milliseconds prior to the epoch.[11]

A couple usage notes follow. First, if you're creating dates in JavaScript, keep in mind that months in JavaScript dates are 0-based. This means that new Date(2011, 5, 11) will create a date object representing *June* 11, 2011. Next, if you're using the Ruby driver to store temporal data, the BSON serializer expects a Ruby Time object in UTC. Consequently, you can't use date classes that maintain a time zone since a BSON datetime can't encode that data.

Custom types

But what if you must store your times with their time zones? Sometimes the basic BSON types don't suffice. Though there's no way to create a custom BSON type, you can compose the various primitive BSON values to create your own virtual type. For instance, if you wanted to store times with zone, you might use a document structure like this, in Ruby:

```
{:time_with_zone =>
  {:time => Time.utc.now,
   :zone => "EST"
  }
}
```

It's not difficult to write an application so that it transparently handles these composite representations. This is usually how it's done in the real world. For example, MongoMapper, an object mapper for MongoDB written in Ruby, allows you to define to_mongo and from_mongo methods for any object to accommodate these sorts of custom composite types.

---

[11] The Unix epoch is defined as midnight, January 1, 1970, coordinated universal time.

Limits on document size

BSON documents in MongoDB v2.0 are limited to 16 MB in size.[12] The limit exists for two related reasons. First, it's there to prevent developers from creating ungainly data models. Though poor data models are still possible with this limit, the 16 MB limit helps discourage documents with especially deep levels of nesting, which is a common data modeling error made by novice MongoDB users. Deeply nested documents are difficult to work with; it's often better to expand the nested documents into separate collections.

The second reason for the 16 MB limit is performance-related. On the server side, querying a large document requires that the document be copied into a buffer before being sent to the client. This copying can get expensive, especially (as is often the case) when the client doesn't need the entire document.[13] In addition, once sent, there's the work of transporting the document across the network and then deserializing it on the driver side. This can become especially costly if large batches of multi-megabyte documents are being requested at once.

The upshot is that if you have especially large objects, you're probably better off splitting them up, modifying your data model, and using an extra collection or two. If you're simply storing large binary objects, like images or videos, that's a slightly different case. See appendix C for techniques on handling large binary objects.

BULK INSERTS

As soon as you have valid documents, the process of inserting them is straightforward. Most of the relevant details about inserting documents, including object ID generation, how inserts work on the network layer, and safe mode, were covered in chapter 3. But one final feature, bulk inserts, is worth discussing here.

All of the drivers make it possible to insert multiple documents at once. This can be extremely handy if you're inserting lots of data, as in an initial bulk import or a migration from another database system. Recall the earlier example of inserting 40 documents into the user.actions collection. If you look at the code, you'll see that you're inserting just one document at a time. With the following code, you build an array of 40 documents in advance and then pass the entire array of documents to the insert method:

```
docs = (0..40).map do |n|
  { :username => "kbanker",
    :action_code => rand(5),
    :time => Time.now.utc,
    :n => n
  }
end
```

---

[12] The number has varied by server version and is continually increasing. To see the limit for your server version, run db.ismaster from the shell, and examine the maxBsonObjectSize field. If you can't find this field, then the limit is 4 MB (and you're using a very old version of MongoDB).

[13] As you'll see in the next chapter, you can always specify which fields of a document to return in a query to limit response size. If you're doing this frequently, it may be worth reevaluating your data model.

```
@col = @db['test.bulk.insert']
@ids = @col.insert(docs)

puts "Here are the ids from the bulk insert: #{@ids.inspect}"
```

Instead of returning a single object ID, a bulk insert returns an array with the object IDs of all documents inserted. Users commonly ask what the ideal bulk insert size is, but the answer to this is dependent on too many factors to respond concretely, and the ideal number can range from 10 to 200. Benchmarking will be the best counsel in this case. The only limitation imposed by the database here is a 16 MB cap on any one insert operation. Experience shows that the most efficient bulk inserts will fall well below this limit.

4.4   Summary

We've covered a lot of ground in this chapter; congratulations for making it this far!

We began with a theoretical discussion of schema design and then proceeded to outline the data model for an e-commerce application. This gave you a chance to see what documents might look like in a production system, and it should've gotten you thinking in a more concrete way about the differences between schemas in RDMBSs and MongoDB.

We ended the chapter with a harder look at databases, documents, and collections; you may return to this section later on for reference. I've explained the rudiments of MongoDB, but we haven't really started moving data around. That'll all change in the next chapter, where we explore the power of ad hoc queries.

Queries and aggregation

MongoDB doesn't use SQL. Rather, it features its own JSON-like query language. We've been exploring this language throughout the book, but here we turn to some meatier, real-world examples. In particular, we're going to revisit the e-commerce data model introduced in the last chapter and present a variety of queries against it. Among the queries you'll practice are _id lookups, ranges, ordering, and projections. We'll also survey the MongoDB query language as a whole, looking at each available query operator in detail.

In addition to queries, we'll cover the related topic of aggregation. Queries allow you to get at the data as it's stored; aggregation functions summarize and reframe that data. First you'll see how to aggregate over this book's sample e-commerce data set, focusing on MongoDB's group and map-reduce functions. Later I'll present a complete reference to these functions.

Keep in mind as you're reading this chapter that MongoDB's query language and aggregation functions are still works in progress, and refinements are being added with each release. As it stands, mastering queries and aggregations in

MongoDB isn't so much a matter of mapping out every nook as it is finding the best ways to accomplish everyday tasks. Through the examples in this chapter, I'll point out the clearest routes to take. By the end of the chapter, you should have a good intuitive understanding of queries and aggregation in MongoDB, and you'll be ready to apply these tools to the design of application schemas.

5.1 E-commerce queries

This section continues our exploration of the e-commerce data model sketched out in the previous chapter. We've defined a document structure for products, categories, users, orders, and product reviews. Now, with that structure in mind, we'll look at how you might query these entities in a typical e-commerce application. Some of these queries are simple. For instance, _id lookups shouldn't be a mystery at this point. But we'll also examine a few more sophisticated patterns, including querying for and displaying a category hierarchy, as well as providing filtered views of product listings. In addition, we'll keep efficiency in mind by looking at possible indexes for some of these queries.

5.1.1 Products, categories, and reviews

Most e-commerce applications provide at least two basic views of products and categories. First is the product home page, which highlights a given product, displays reviews, and gives some sense of the product's categories. Second is the product listing page, which allows users to browse the category hierarchy and view thumbnails of all the products within a selected category. Let's begin with the product home page, in many ways the simpler of the two.

Imagine that your product page URLs are keyed on a product slug. In that case, you can get all the data you need for your product page with the following three queries:

```
db.products.findOne({'slug': 'wheel-barrow-9092'})
db.categories.findOne({'_id': product['main_cat_id']})
db.reviews.find({'product_id': product['_id']})
```

The first query finds the product with the slug wheel-barrow-9092. Once you have your product, you query for its category information with a simple _id query on the categories collection. Finally, you issue another simple lookup that gets all the reviews associated with the product.

You'll notice that the first two queries use the find_one method but that the last uses find instead. All of the MongoDB drivers provide these two methods, and so it's worth recalling the difference between them. As discussed in chapter 3, find returns a cursor object, whereas findOne returns a document. The findOne just referenced is equivalent to the following:

```
db.products.find({'slug': 'wheel-barrow-9092'}).limit(1)
```

If you're expecting a single document, findOne will return that document if it exists. If you need to return multiple documents, remember that you'll be using find, and

that this method will return a cursor. You'll then need to iterate over that cursor somewhere in your application.

Now look again at the product page queries. See anything unsettling? If the query
for reviews seems a bit liberal, you're right. This query says to return all reviews for the
given product, but this wouldn't be prudent in cases where a product had hundreds of
reviews. Most applications paginate reviews, and for this MongoDB provides `skip` and
`limit` options. You can use these options to paginate the review document like so:

```
db.reviews.find({'product_id': product['_id']}).skip(0).limit(12)
```

You also want to display reviews in a consistent order, which means you have to sort
your query results. If you want to sort by the number of helpful votes received by each
review, you can specify that easily:

```
db.reviews.find({'product_id': product['id']}).sort(
               {helpful_votes: -1}).limit(12)
```

In short, this query tells MongoDB to return the first 12 reviews sorted by the total
number of helpful votes in descending order. Now, with the skip, limit, and sort in
place, you simply need to decide whether to paginate in the first place. For this, you
can issue a count query. You then use the results of the count in combination with the
page of reviews you want. Your queries for the product page are complete:

```
product  = db.products.findOne({'slug': 'wheel-barrow-9092'})
category = db.categories.findOne({'_id': product['main_cat_id']})
reviews_count = db.reviews.count({'product_id': product['_id']})
reviews = db.reviews.find({'product_id': product['_id']}).
                     skip((page_number - 1) * 12).
                     limit(12).
                     sort({'helpful_votes': -1})
```

These lookups should use indexes. You've already seen that slugs, because they serve
as alternate primary keys, should have a unique index on them, and you know that all
`_id` fields will automatically have a unique index for standard collections. But it's also
important that you have an index on any fields acting as references. In this case, that
would include the `user_id` and `product_id` fields on the reviews collection.

With the queries for the product home pages in place, you can now turn to the
product listing page. Such a page will display a given category with a browsable listing
of products contained therein. Links to parent and sibling categories will also appear
on the page.

A product listing page is defined by its category; thus, requests for the page will use
the category's slug:

```
category = db.categories.findOne({'slug': 'outdoors'})
siblings = db.categories.find({'parent_id': category['_id']})
products = db.products.find({'category_id': category['_id']}).
                     skip((page_number - 1) * 12).
                     limit(12).
                     sort({helpful_votes: -1})
```

Siblings are any other categories with the same parent ID, so the query for siblings is straightforward. Since products all contain an array of category IDs, the query to find all products in a given category is also trivial. You also apply the same pagination pattern that you used for reviews, except that you sort by average product rating. You can imagine providing alternative sort methods (by name, price, and so forth). For those cases, you simply change the sort field.[1]

The product listing page has a base case, where you're viewing just the root-level categories but no products. A query against the categories collection for a `nil` parent ID is all that's required to get these root-level categories:

```
categories = db.categories.find({'parent_id': nil})
```

5.1.2 Users and orders

The queries in the previous section were generally limited to _id lookups and sorts. In looking at users and orders, we'll dig deeper, since you'll want to generate basic reports on orders.

But let's start with something simpler: user authentication. Users log in to the application by providing a username and password. Thus, you'd expect to see the following query pretty frequently:

```
db.users.findOne({username: 'kbanker',
  hashed_password: 'bd1cfa194c3a603e7186780824b04419'})
```

If the user exists and the password is correct, you'll get back an entire user document; otherwise, the query will return nothing. This query is acceptable. But if you're concerned with performance, you'll optimize by selecting the _id fields only so that you can initiate a session. After all, the user document stores addresses, payment methods, and other personal information. Why send that data across the network and deserialize on the driver side if all you need is a single field? You limit the fields returned using a projection:

```
db.users.findOne({username: 'kbanker',
  hashed_password: 'bd1cfa194c3a603e7186780824b04419'},
  {_id: 1})
```

The response now consists exclusively of the document's _id field:

```
{ _id: ObjectId("4c4b1476238d3b4dd5000001") }
```

There are a few other ways you might want to query the users collection. For instance, imagine you have an administrative back end allowing you to find users by different criteria. Frequently, you'll want to perform a lookup on a single field, such as last_name:

```
db.users.find({last_name: 'Banker'})
```

---

[1] It's important to consider whether these sorts will be efficient. You may choose to rely on your index to handle sorting for you, but as you add more sort options, the number of indexes grows, and the cost of maintaining those indexes may not be reasonable. This will be especially true if the number of products per category is small. We'll discuss this further in chapter 8, but start thinking about these trade-offs now.

This works, but there are limits to searching for an exact match. For one, you might not know how to spell a given user's name. In this case, you'll want some way of querying for a partial match. Suppose you know that the user's last name starts with *Ba*. In SQL, you could use a LIKE condition to represent this query:

```
SELECT * from users WHERE last_name LIKE 'Ba%'
```

The semantic equivalent in MongoDB is a regular expression:

```
db.users.find({last_name: /^Ba/})
```

As with an RDBMS, a prefix search like this one can take advantage of an index.[2]

When it comes to marketing to your users, you'll most likely want to target ranges of users. For instance, if you wanted to get all users residing in Upper Manhattan, you could issue this range query on a user's ZIP code:

```
db.users.find({'addresses.zip': {$gte: 10019, $lt: 10040}})
```

Recall that each user document contains an array of one or more addresses. This query will match a user document if any ZIP code among those addresses falls within the range specified. To make this query efficient, you'll want an index defined on addresses.zip.

Targeting users by location probably isn't the most effective way to generate conversions. Users can be much more meaningfully grouped by what they've purchased, which in this case requires a two-step query: you first need to get a set of orders based on a particular product, and once you have the orders, you can query for the associated users.[3] Suppose you want to target all users who've purchased the large wheelbarrow. Again you use MongoDB's dot notation to reach into the line_items array and search for a given SKU:

```
db.orders.find({'line_items.sku': "9092")
```

You can also imagine wanting to limit this result set to orders made within a certain time frame. If so, you can easily add a query condition that sets a minimum order date:

```
db.orders.find({'line_items.sku': "9092",
    'purchase_date': {$gte: new Date(2009, 0, 1)}})
```

Assuming these queries are issued frequently, you'll want a compound index ordered first by SKU and second by date of purchase. You can create such an index like so:

```
db.orders.ensureIndex({'line_items.sku': 1, 'purchase_date': 1})
```

When you query the orders collection, all you're looking for is a list of user IDs. Thus, you have an opportunity to be more efficient by using a projection. In the following code snippet, you first specify that you want the user_id field only. You then

---

[2] If you're not familiar with regular expressions, take note: the regular expression /^Ba/ can be read as "the beginning of the line followed by a *B* followed by an *a*."

[3] If you're coming from a relational database, the inability here to issue a JOIN query across orders and users might bother you, but try not to let it. It's common to perform this sort of client-side join with MongoDB.

transform the query results into a simple array of IDs and then use that array to query the users collection with the $in operator:

```
user_ids = db.orders.find({'line_items.sku': "9092",
  purchase_date: {'$gt': new Date(2009, 0, 1)}},
  {user_id: 1, _id: 0}).toArray().map(function(doc) { return doc['_id'] })
users = db.users.find({_id: {$in: user_ids}})
```

This technique of querying a collection using an array of IDs and $in will be efficient for arrays of IDs having up to a few thousand elements. For larger data sets, where you might have a million users who've purchased the wheelbarrow, it'll be more prudent to write those user IDs to a temporary collection and then process the query sequentially.

You'll see more examples of querying this data in the next chapter, and later on, you'll learn how to get insight from the data using MongoDB's aggregation functions. But with this introduction under your belt, we're now going to look at MongoDB's query language in some depth, explaining the syntax in general and each operator in particular.

5.2 MongoDB's query language

It's time we explore MongoDB's query language in all its glory. I'll begin with a general description of queries, their semantics, and their types. I'll then discuss cursors, since every MongoDB query is, fundamentally, the instantiation of a cursor and the fetching of that cursor's result set. With these fundamentals out of the way, I'll present a taxonomy of all MongoDB query operators.[4]

5.2.1 Query selectors

We begin with an overview of query selectors, paying particular attention to all the kinds of queries you can express with them.

SELECTOR MATCHING

The simplest way to specify a query is with a selector whose key-value pairs literally match against the document you're looking for. A couple of examples:

```
db.users.find({last_name: "Banker"})
db.users.find({first_name: "Smith", age: 40})
```

The second query reads, "Find me all users such that the first_name is Smith *and* the age is 40." Note that whenever you pass more than one key-value pair, both must match; the query conditions function as a Boolean AND. If you want to express a Boolean OR, see the upcoming section on Boolean operators.

RANGES

You frequently need to query for documents whose values span a certain range. In SQL, you use <, <=, >, and >=; with MongoDB, you get the analogous set of operators $lt, $lte, $gt, and $gte. You've been using these operators throughout the book,

---

[4] Unless you're a glutton for details, this taxonomy may safely be skimmed on first reading.

and their behavior is as expected. But beginners sometimes struggle with combining these operators. A common mistake is to repeat the search key:

```
db.users.find({age: {$gte: 0}, age: {$lte: 30}})
```

Because keys can't be at the same level in the same document, this query selector is invalid, and will apply only one of the two range operators. You can properly express this query as follows:

```
db.users.find({age: {$gte: 0, $lte: 30})
```

The only other surprise regarding the range operators involves types. Range queries will match values only if they have the same type as the value to be compared against.[5] For example, suppose you have a collection with the following documents:

```
{ "_id" : ObjectId("4caf82011b0978483ea29ada"), "value" : 97 }
{ "_id" : ObjectId("4caf82031b0978483ea29adb"), "value" : 98 }
{ "_id" : ObjectId("4caf82051b0978483ea29adc"), "value" : 99 }
{ "_id" : ObjectId("4caf820d1b0978483ea29ade"), "value" : "a" }
{ "_id" : ObjectId("4caf820f1b0978483ea29adf"), "value" : "b" }
{ "_id" : ObjectId("4caf82101b0978483ea29ae0"), "value" : "c" }
```

You then issue the following query:

```
db.items.find({value: {$gte: 97})
```

You may think that this query should return all six documents, since the strings are numerically equivalent to the integers 97, 98, and 99. But this isn't the case. This query returns the integer results only. If you want the string results, you must query with a string instead:

```
db.items.find({value: {$gte: "a"})
```

You won't need to worry about this type restriction as long as you never store multiple types for the same key within the same collection. This is a good general practice, and you should abide by it.

SET OPERATORS

Three query operators—$in, $all, and $nin—take a list of one or more values as their predicate. $in returns a document if any of the given values matches the search key. You might use this operator to return all products belonging to some discrete set of categories. If the following list of category IDs

```
[ObjectId("6a5b1476238d3b4dd5000048"),
 ObjectId("6a5b1476238d3b4dd5000051"),
 ObjectId("6a5b1476238d3b4dd5000057")
]
```

corresponds to the lawnmowers, hand tools, and work clothing categories, then the query to find all products belonging to these categories looks like this:

---

[5] Note that the numeric types—integer, long integer, and double—have type equivalence for these queries.

```
db.products.find({main_cat_id: { $in:
              [ObjectId("6a5b1476238d3b4dd5000048"),
               ObjectId("6a5b1476238d3b4dd5000051"),
               ObjectId("6a5b1476238d3b4dd5000057") ] } } )
```

Another way of thinking about the $in operator is as a kind of Boolean inclusive OR against a single attribute. Expressed this way, the previous query might be read, "Find me all products whose category is lawnmowers or hand tools or work clothing." Note that if you need a Boolean OR over multiple attributes, you'll want to use the $or operator, described in the next section.

$in is frequently used with lists of IDs. See the example earlier in this chapter for an example of another query that uses $in to return all users who've bought a particular product.

$nin returns a document only when none of the given elements matches. You might use $nin to find all products that are neither black nor blue:

```
db.products.find('details.color': { $nin: ["black", "blue"] }
```

Finally, $all matches if every given element matches the search key. If you wanted to find all products tagged as *gift* and *garden*, $all would be a good choice:

```
db.products.find(tags: { $all: ["gift", "garden"] }
```

Naturally, this query make sense only if the tags attribute stores an array of terms, like this:

```
{ name: "Bird Feeder",
  tags: [ "gift", "birds", "garden" ]
}
```

When using the set operators, keep in mind that $in and $all can take advantage of indexes, but $nin can't and thus requires a collection scan. If you use $nin, try to use it in combination with another query term that *does* use an index. Better yet, find a different way to express the query. You may, for instance, be able to store an attribute whose presence indicates a condition equivalent to your $nin query. For example, if you commonly issue a query for {timeframe: {$nin: ['morning', 'afternoon']}}, you may be able to express this more directly as {timeframe: 'evening'}.

BOOLEAN OPERATORS

MongoDB's Boolean operators include $ne, $not, $or, $and, and $exists.

$ne, the *not equal to* operator, works as you'd expect. In practice, it's best used in combination with at least one other operator; otherwise, it's likely to be inefficient because it can't take advantage of indexes. For example, you might use $ne to find all products manufactured by ACME that aren't tagged with *gardening*:

```
db.products.find('details.manufacturer': 'ACME', tags: {$ne: "gardening"} }
```

$ne works on keys pointing to single values and to arrays, as shown in the example where you match against the tags array.

Whereas $ne matches the negation of a specified value, $not negates the result of another MongoDB operator or regular expression query. Before you use $not, keep in mind that most query operators already have a negated form ($in and $nin, $gt and $lte, etc.); $not shouldn't be used with any of these. Reserve $not for times when the operator or regex you're using lacks a negated form. For example, if you wanted to query for all users with last names not beginning with *B* you could use $not like so:

```
db.users.find(last_name: {$not: /^B/} }
```

$or expresses the logical disjunction of two values for two different keys. This is an important point: if the possible values are scoped to the same key, use $in instead. Trivially, finding all products that are either blue or green looks like this:

```
db.products.find('details.color': {$in: ['blue', 'green']} }
```

But finding all products that are either blue or made by ACME requires $or:

```
db.products.find({ $or: [{'details.color': 'blue'}, 'details.manufacturer':
    'ACME'}] })
```

$or takes an array of query selectors, where each selector can be arbitrarily complex and may itself contain other query operators.[6]

Like $or, the $and operator also takes an array of query selectors. Because MongoDB interprets all query selectors containing more than one key by ANDing the conditions, you should use $and only when you can't express an AND in a simpler way. For example, suppose you want to find all products that are tagged with *gift* or *holiday* and either *gardening* or *landscaping*. The only way to express this query is with the conjunction of two $in queries:

```
db.products.find({$and: [
{tags: {$in: ['gift', 'holiday']}},
{tags: {$in: ['gardening', 'landscaping']}}
                        ]
                        }
                        )
```

The final operator we'll discuss in this section is $exists. This operator is necessary because collections don't enforce a fixed schema, so you occasionally need a way to query for documents containing a particular key. Recall that we'd planned to use each product's details attribute to store custom fields. You might for instance store a color field inside the details attribute. But if only a subset of all products specify a set of colors, then you can query for the ones that don't like so:

```
db.products.find({'details.color': {$exists: false}})
```

The opposite query is also possible:

```
db.products.find({'details.color': {$exists: true}})
```

---

[6] Not including $or.

Here you're basically checking for existence. But there's another way to check for existence which is practically equivalent: to match an attribute against the null value. Using this technique, you can alter the preceding queries. The first could be expressed like this:

```
db.products.find({'details.color': null})
```

And the second like this:

```
db.products.find({'details.color': {$ne: null}})
```

MATCHING SUB-DOCUMENTS

Some of the entities in this book's e-commerce data model have keys that point to a single embedded object. The product's details attribute is one good example. Here's part of the relevant document, expressed as JSON:

```
{ _id:  ObjectId("4c4b1476238d3b4dd5003981"),
  slug: "wheel-barrow-9092",
  sku:  "9092",

  details: {
      model_num: 4039283402,
      manufacturer: "Acme",
      manufacturer_id: 432,
      color:  "Green"
  }
}
```

Yoiu can query such objects by separating the relevant keys with a . (dot). For instance, if you want to find all products manufactured by Acme, you can use this query:

```
db.products.find({'details.manufacturer_id': 432});
```

Such queries can be specified arbitrarily deep. Thus, supposing you had the following slightly modified representation:

```
{ _id:  ObjectId("4c4b1476238d3b4dd5003981"),
  slug: "wheel-barrow-9092",
  sku:  "9092",

  details: {
      model_num: 4039283402,
      manufacturer: { name: "Acme",
                      id:   432 },
      color:  "Green"
    }
}
```

The key in the query selector would contain two dots:

```
db.products.find({'details.manufacturer.id': 432});
```

But in addition to matching against an individual sub-document attribute, you can also match an object as a whole. For example, imagine you're using MongoDB to store market positions. To save space, you forgo the standard object ID and replace it with a compound key consisting of a stock symbol and a timestamp. Here's how a representative document might look:[7]

```
{ _id: {sym: 'GOOG', date: 20101005}
  open:   40.23,
  high:   45.50,
  low:    38.81,
  close:  41.22
}
```

You could then find the summary of GOOG for October 5, 2010 with the following _id query:

```
db.ticks.find({_id: {sym: 'GOOG', date: 20101005} });
```

It's important to realize that a query matching an entire object like this will perform a strict byte-by-byte comparison, which means that the order of the keys matters. The following query isn't equivalent and won't match the sample document:

```
db.ticks.find({_id: {date: 20101005, sym: 'GOOG'} });
```

Though the order of keys will be preserved in JSON documents entered via the shell, this isn't necessarily true for document representations in all the various language drivers. For example, hashes in Ruby 1.8 aren't order-preserving. To preserve key order in Ruby 1.8, you must use an object of class BSON::OrderedHash instead:

```
doc = BSON::OrderedHash.new
doc['sym']  = 'GOOG'
doc['date'] = 20101005
@ticks.find(doc)
```

Be sure to check whether the language you're using supports ordered dictionaries; if not, the language's MongoDB driver will always provide an ordered alternative.

ARRAYS

Arrays give the document model much of its power. As you've seen, arrays are used to store lists of strings, object IDs, and even other documents. Arrays afford rich yet comprehensible documents; it stands to reason that MongoDB would let query and index the array type with ease. And it's true: the simplest array queries look just like queries on any other document type. Take product tags again. These tags are represented as a simple list of strings:

```
{ _id:   ObjectId("4c4b1476238d3b4dd5003981"),
  slug:  "wheel-barrow-9092",
  sku:   "9092",

  tags:  ["tools", "equipment", "soil"] }
```

Querying for products with the tag *soil* is trivial and uses the same syntax as querying a single document value:

```
db.products.find({tags: "soil"})
```

---

[7] In a potential high-throughput scenario, you'd want to limit document size as much as possible. You could accomplish this in part by using short key names. Thus you might use the key name *o* in place of *open*.

Importantly, this query can take advantage of an index on the `tags` field. So if you build the required index and run your query with `explain()`, you'll see that a B-tree cursor is used:

```
db.products.ensureIndex({tags: 1})
db.products.find({tags: "soil"}).explain()
```

When you need more control over your array queries, you can use dot notation to query for a value at a particular position within the array. Here's how you'd restrict the previous query to the first of a product's tags:

```
db.products.find({'tags.0': "soil"})
```

It might not make much sense to query tags in this way, but imagine you're dealing with user addresses. These you might represent with an array of sub-documents:

```
{ _id:        ObjectId("4c4b1476238d3b4dd5000001")
  username: "kbanker",
  addresses: [
    {name:      "home",
     street:  "588 5th Street",
     city:    "Brooklyn",
     state:   "NY",
     zip:     11215},

    {name:     "work",
     street: "1 E. 23rd Street",
     city:    "New York",
     state    "NY",
     zip      10010},
  ]
}
```

You might stipulate that the zeroth element of the array always be the user's primary shipping address. Thus, to find all users whose primary shipping address is in New York, you could again specify the zeroth position and combine that with a dot to target the `state` field:

```
db.users.find({'addresses.0.state': "NY"})
```

You can just as easily omit the position and specify a field alone. The following query will return a user document if *any* of the addresses in the list is in New York:

```
db.users.find({'addresses.state': "NY"})
```

As before, you'll want to index this dotted field:

```
db.users.ensureIndex({'addresses.state': 1})
```

Note that you use the same dot notation regardless of whether a field points to a sub-document or to an array of sub-documents. This is powerful, and the consistency is reassuring. But ambiguity can arise when querying against more than one attribute within an array of sub-objects. For example, suppose you want to fetch a list of all users whose home address is in New York. Can you think of a way to express this query?

```
db.users.find({'addresses.name': 'home', 'addresses.state': 'NY'})
```

The problem with this query is that the field references aren't restricted to a single address. In other words, this query will match as long as one of the addresses is designated as "home" and one is in New York, but what you want is for both attributes to apply to the *same* address. Fortunately, there's a query operator for this. To restrict multiple conditions to the same sub-document, you use the $elemMatch operator. You can properly satisfy the query like so:

```
db.users.find({addresses: {$elemMatch: {name: 'home', state: 'NY'}}})
```

Logically, you use $elemMatch only when you need to match two or more attributes in a sub-document.

The only array operator left to discuss is the $size operator. This operator allows you to query for an array by its size. For example, if you want to find all users with exactly three addresses, you can use the $size operator like so:

```
db.users.find({addresses: {$size: 3}})
```

At the time of this writing, the $size operator doesn't use an index and is limited to exact matches (you can't specify a range of sizes).[8] Therefore, if you need to perform queries based on the size of an array, you should cache the size in its own attribute within the document and update it manually as the array changes. For instance, you might consider adding an address_length field to your user document. You could then build an index on this field and issue all the range and exact match queries you require.

JavaScript

If you can't express your query with the tools described thus far, then you may need to write some JavaScript. You can use the special $where operator to pass a JavaScript expression to any query. Within a JavaScript context, the keyword this refers to the current document. Let's take a contrived example:

```
db.reviews.find({$where: "function() { return this.helpful_votes > 3; }"}})
```

There's also an abbreviated form for simple expressions like this one:

```
db.reviews.find({$where: "this.helpful_votes > 3"}})
```

This query works, but you'd *never* want to use it because you can easily express it using the standard query language. The problem is that JavaScript expressions can't use an index, and they incur substantial overhead because they must be evaluated within a JavaScript interpreter context. For these reasons, you should issue JavaScript queries only when you can't express your query using the standard query language. If you do find yourself needing JavaScript, try to combine the JavaScript expression with at least one standard query operator. The standard query operator will pare down the result set, reducing the number of documents that must be loaded into a JS context. Let's take a quick example to see how this might make sense.

---

[8] See https://jira.mongodb.org/browse/SERVER-478 for updates on this issue.

Imagine that, for each user, you've calculated a rating reliability factor. This is essentially an integer that, when multiplied by the user's rating, results in a more normalized rating. Suppose further that you want to query a particular user's reviews and only return a normalized rating greater than 3. Here's how that query would look:

```
db.reviews.find({user_id: ObjectId("4c4b1476238d3b4dd5000001"),
            $where: "(this.rating * .92) > 3"})
```

This query meets both recommendations: it uses a standard query on a presumably-indexed `user_id` field, and it employs a JavaScript expression that's absolutely beyond the capabilities of the standard query language.

In addition to recognizing the attendant performance penalties, it's good to be aware of the possibility of JavaScript *injection attacks*. An injection attack becomes possible whenever a user is allowed to enter code directly into a JavaScript query. Though there's never any danger of users being able to write or delete in this way, they might be able to read sensitive data. An incredibly unsafe JavaScript query in Ruby might look something like this:

```
@users.find({$where => "this.#{attribute} == #{value}"})
```

Assuming that users could control the values of `attribute` and `value`, they might manipulate the query to search the collection on any attribute pair. Though this wouldn't be the worst imaginable intrusion, you'd be wise to prevent its possibility.

REGULAR EXPRESSIONS

We saw near the beginning the chapter that you can use a regular expression within a query. In that example, I showed a prefix expression, `/^Ba/`, to find last names beginning with *Ba*, and I pointed out that this query would use an index. In fact, much more is possible. MongoDB is compiled with PCRE (http://mng.bz/hxmh), which supports a huge gamut of regular expressions.

With the exception of the prefix-style query just described, regular expressions queries can't use an index. Thus I recommend using them as you would a JavaScript expression—in combination with at least one other query term. Here's how you might query a given user's reviews for text containing the words *best* or *worst*. Note that you use the `i` regex flag[9] to indicate case insensitivity:

```
db.reviews.find({user_id: ObjectId("4c4b1476238d3b4dd5000001"),
            text: /best|worst/i })
```

If the language you're using has a native regex type, you can use a native regex object to perform the query. You can express an identical query in Ruby like so:

```
@reviews.find({:user_id => BSON::ObjectId("4c4b1476238d3b4dd5000001"),
            :text => /best|worst/i })
```

---

[9] The case-insensitive option will always prevent an index from being used to serve the query, even in the case of a prefix match.

If you're querying from an environment that doesn't support a native regex type, you can use the special $regex and $options operators. Using these operators from the shell, you can express the query in yet another way:

```
db.reviews.find({user_id: ObjectId("4c4b1476238d3b4dd5000001"),
              text: {$regex: "best|worst", $options: "i" })
```

MISCELLANEOUS QUERY OPERATORS

Two more query operators aren't easily categorized and thus deserve their own section. The first is $mod, which allows you to query documents matching a given modulo operation. For instance, you can find all order subtotals that are evenly divisible by 3 using the following query:

```
db.orders.find({subtotal: {$mod: [3, 0]}})
```

You can see that the $mod operator takes an array having two values. The first is the divisor and the second is the expected remainder. Thus, this query technically reads, "Find all documents with subtotals that return a remainder of 0 when divided by 3." This is a contrived example, but it demonstrates the idea. If you end up using the $mod operator, keep in mind that it won't use an index.

The second miscellaneous operator is the $type operator, which matches values by their BSON type. I don't recommend storing multiple types for the same field within a collection, but if the situation ever arises, you have a query operator that essentially lets you test against type. This came in handy recently when I discovered a user whose _id queries weren't always matching when they should. The problem was that the user had been storing IDs as both strings and as proper object IDs. These are represented as BSON types 2 and 7, respectively, and to a new user, the distinction is easy to miss.

Correcting the issue first required finding all documents with ids stored as strings. The $type operator can help do just that:

```
db.users.find({_id: {$type: 2}})
```

5.2.2   *Query options*

All queries require a query selector. Even if empty, the query selector essentially defines the query. But when issuing a query, you have a variety of query options to choose from which allow you to further constrain the result set. I describe those options here.

PROJECTIONS

You can use a projection to select a subset of fields to return from each document in a query result set. Especially in cases where you have large documents, using a projection will minimize the costs of network latency and deserialization. Projections are most commonly defined as a set of fields to return:

```
db.users.find({}, {username: 1})
```

This query returns user documents excluding all but two fields: the username and the _id field, which is always included by default.

In some situations you may want to specify fields to exclude, instead. For instance, this book's user document contains shipping addresses and payment methods, but you don't usually need these. To exclude them, add those fields to the projection with a value of 0:

```
db.users.find({}, {addresses: 0, payment_methods: 0})
```

In addition to including and excluding fields, you can also return a range of values stored in an array. For example, you might want to store product reviews within the product document itself. In this case, you'd still want to be able to paginate those reviews, and for that you could use the $slice operator. To return the first 12 reviews, or the last 5, you'd use $slice like so:

```
db.products.find({}, {reviews: {$slice: 12}})
db.products.find({}, {reviews: {$slice: -5}})
```

$slice can also take a two-element array whose values represent numbers to skip and limit, respectively. Here's how to skip the first 24 reviews and limit the number of reviews to 12:

```
db.products.find({}, {reviews: {$slice: [24, 12]}})
```

Finally, note that using $slice won't prevent other fields from being returned. If you want to limit the other fields in the document, you must do so explicitly. For example, here's how you can modify the previous query to return the reviews and the review rating only:

```
db.products.find({}, {reviews: {$slice: [24, 12]}, 'reviews.rating': 1})
```

SORTING

You can sort any query result by one or more fields in ascending or descending order. A simple sort of reviews by rating, descending from highest to lowest, looks like this:

```
db.reviews.find({}).sort({rating: -1})
```

Naturally, it might be more useful to sort by helpfulness and then by rating:

```
db.reviews.find({}).sort({helpful_votes:-1, rating: -1})
```

In compound sorts like this, the order does matter. As noted elsewhere, JSON entered via the shell is ordered. Since Ruby hashes aren't ordered, you indicate sort order in Ruby with an array of arrays, which *is* ordered:

```
@reviews.find({}).sort([['helpful_votes', -1], [rating, -1]])
```

The way you specify sorts in MongoDB is straightforward, but two topics, discussed elsewhere, are essential to a good understand of sorting. The first is knowing how to sort according to insertion order using the $natural operator. This is discussed in chapter 4. The second, and more relevant, is knowing how to ensure that sorts can efficiently use indexes. We'll get to that in chapter 8, but feel free to skip ahead if you're heavily using sorts now.

SKIP AND LIMIT

There's nothing mysterious about the semantics of skip and limit. These query options should always work as you expect.

But you should beware of passing large values (say, values greater than 10,000) for skip because serving such queries requires scanning over a number of documents equal to the skip value. For example, imagine that you're paginating a million documents sorted by date, descending, with 10 results per page. This means that the query to display the 50,000th page will include a skip value of 500,000, which is incredibly inefficient. A better strategy is to omit the skip altogether and instead add a range condition to the query that indicates where the next result set begins. Thus, this query

```
db.docs.find({}).skip(500000).limit(10).sort({date: -1})
```

becomes this:

```
db.docs.find({date: {$gt: previous_page_date}}).limit(10).sort({date: -1})
```

This second query will scan far fewer items than the first. The only potential problem is that if date isn't unique for each document, the same document may be displayed more than once. There are many strategies for dealing with this, but the solutions are left as exercises for the reader.

5.3 Aggregating orders

You've already seen a basic example of MongoDB's aggregation in the count command, which you used for pagination. Most databases provide count plus a lot of other built-in aggregation functions for calculating sums, averages, variances, and the like. These features are on the MongoDB roadmap, but until they're implemented, you can use group and map-reduce to script any aggregate function, from simple sums to standard deviations.

5.3.1 Grouping reviews by user

It's common to want to know which users provide the most valuable reviews. Since the application allows users to votes on reviews, it's technically possible to calculate the total number of votes for all of a user's reviews along with the average number of votes a user receives per review. Though you could get these stats by querying all reviews and doing some basic client-side processing, you can also use MongoDB's group command to get the result from the server.

group takes a minimum of three arguments. The first, key, defines how your data will be grouped. In this case, you want your results to be grouped by user, so your grouping key is user_id. The second argument, known as the reduce function, is a JavaScript function that aggregates over a result set. The final argument to group is an initial document for the reduce function.

This sounds more complicated than it is. To see why, let's look more closely at the initial document you'll use and at its corresponding reduce function:

```
initial = {review: 0, votes: 0};

reduce  = function(doc, aggregator) {
```

```
        aggregator.reviews += 1.0;
        aggregator.votes   += doc.votes;
    }
```

You can see that the initial document defines the values that you want for each grouping key. In other words, once you've run `group`, you want a result set that, for each `user_id`, gives you the total number of reviews written and the sum of votes for all those reviews. The work of generating those sums is done by the `reduce` function. Suppose I've written five reviews. This means that five review documents will be tagged with my user ID. Each of those five documents will be passed to the `reduce` function as the `doc` argument. At first the value of `aggregator` is the `initial` document. Successive values are added to the aggregator for each document processed.

Here's how you'd execute this `group` command from the JavaScript shell.

Listing 5.1 Using MongoDB's `group` command

```
results = db.reviews.group({
  key:       {user_id: true},
  initial:   {reviews: 0, votes: 0.0},
  reduce:    function(doc, aggregator) {
                 aggregator.reviews += 1;
                 aggregator.votes   += doc.votes;
             }
  finalize:  function(doc) {
                 doc.average_votes = doc.votes / doc.reviews;
             }
})
```

You should note that you've passed an extra argument to `group`. You originally wanted the average number of votes per review. But this average can't be calculated until you have the total number of votes for all reviews and the total number of reviews. This is what the finalizer is for. It's a JavaScript function that's applied to each grouped result before the `group` command returns. In this case, you use the finalizer to calculate the average number of votes per review.

Here are the results of running this aggregation on a sample data set.

Listing 5.2 Results of the `group` command

```
[
  {user_id: ObjectId("4d00065860c53a481aeab608"),
   votes: 25.0,
   reviews: 7,
   average: 3.57
  },
  {user_id: ObjectId("4d00065860c53a481aeab608"),
   votes: 25.0,
   reviews: 7,
   average: 3.57
  }
]
```

We'll revisit the group command and all of its other options and idiosyncrasies at the end of the chapter.

5.3.2   *Map-reduce for orders by region*

You can think of MongoDB's map-reduce as a more flexible variation on group. With map-reduce, you have finer-grained control over the grouping key, and you have a variety of output options, including the ability to store the results in a new collection, allowing for flexible retrieval of that data later on. Let's use an example to see these differences in practice.

Chances are that you'll want to be able to generate some sales stats. How many items are you selling each month? What are the total dollars in sales for each month over the past year? You can easily answer these questions using map-reduce. The first step, as the name implies, is to write a map function. The map function is applied to each document in the collection and, in the process, fulfills two purposes: it defines which keys which you're grouping on, and it packages all the data you'll need for your calculation. To see this process in action, look closely at the following function:

```
map = function() {
    var shipping_month = this.purchase_date.getMonth() +
        '-' + this.purchase_data.getFullYear();

    var items = 0;
    this.line_items.forEach(function(item) {
        tmpItems += item.quantity;
    });

    emit(shipping_month, {order_total: this.sub_total, items_total: 0});
}
```

First, know that the variable this always refers to a document being iterated over. In the function's first line, you get an integer value denoting the month the order was created.[10] You then call emit(). This is a special method that every map function must invoke. The first argument to emit() is the key to group by, and the second is usually a document containing values to be reduced. In this case, you're grouping by month, and you're going to reduce over each order's subtotal and item count. The corresponding reduce function should make this more clear:

```
reduce = function(key, values) {
    var tmpTotal = 0;
    var tmpItems = 0;

    tmpTotal += doc.order_total;
    tmpItems += doc.items_total;

    return ( {total: tmpTotal, items: tmpItems} );
}
```

---

[10] Because JavaScript months are zero-based, the month value will range from 0–11. You'll need to add 1 to get a sensible numerical month representation. Added to this is a - followed by the year. So the keys look like 1-2011, 2-2011, and so on.

The `reduce` function will be passed a key and an array of one or more values. Your job in writing a reduce function is to make sure that those values are aggregated together in the desired way and then returned as a single value. Because of map-reduce's iterative nature, `reduce` may be invoked more than once, and your code must take this into account. All this means in practice is that the value returned by the `reduce` function must be identical in form to the value emitted by the map function. Look closely and you'll see that this is the case.

The shell's map-reduce method requires a map and a `reduce` function as arguments. But this example adds two more. The first is a query filter, which limits the documents involved in the aggregation to orders made since the beginning of 2010. The second argument is the name of the output collection:

```
filter = {purchase_date: {$gte: new Date(2010, 0, 1)}}
db.orders.mapReduce(map, reduce, {query: filter, out: 'totals'})
```

The results are stored in a collection called `totals`, and you can query this collection like you do any other. The following listing displays the results of querying one of these collections. The `_id` field holds your grouping key and the year and month, and the `value` field references the reduced totals.

> **Listing 5.3 Querying the `map-reduce` output collection**

```
> db.totals.find()
{ _id: "1-2011", value: { total: 32002300, items: 59 }}
{ _id: "2-2011", value: { total: 45439500, items: 71 }}
{ _id: "3-2011", value: { total: 54322300, items: 98 }}
{ _id: "4-2011", value: { total: 75534200, items: 115 }}
{ _id: "5-2011", value: { total: 81232100, items: 121 }}
```

The examples here should give you some sense of MongoDB's aggregation capabilities in practice. In the next section, we'll cover most of the hairy details.

5.4   Aggregation in detail

Here I'll provide some extra details on MongoDB's aggregation functions.

5.4.1   Maxima and minima

You'll commonly need to find min and max values for a given value in a collection. Databases using SQL provide special `min()` and `max()` functions, but MongoDB doesn't. Instead, you must specify these queries literally. To find a maximum value, you can sort descending by the desired value and limit the result set to just one document. You can get a corresponding minimum by reversing the sort. For example, if you wanted to find the review with the greatest number of helpful votes, your query would need to sort by that value and limit by one:

```
db.reviews.find({}).sort({helpful_votes: -1}).limit(1)
```

The `helpful_votes` field in the returned document will contain the maximum value for that field. To get the minimum value, just reverse the sort order:

```
db.reviews.find({}).sort({helpful_votes: 1}).limit(1)
```

If you're going to issue this query in a production situation, you'll ideally have an index on `helpful_votes`. If you want the review with the greatest number of helpful votes for a particular product, you'll want a compound index on `product_id` and `helpful_votes`. If the reason for this isn't clear, refer to chapter 7.

5.4.2 *Distinct*

MongoDB's `distinct` command is the simplest tool for getting a list of distinct values for a particular key. The command works for both single keys and array keys. `distinct` covers an entire collection by default but can be constrained with a query selector.

You can use `distinct` to get a list of all the unique tags on the products collection as follows:

```
db.products.distinct("tags")
```

It's that simple. If you want to operate on a subset of the `products` collection, you can pass a query selector as the second argument. Here, the query limits the distinct tag values to products in the Gardening Tools category:

```
db.products.distinct("tags",
        {category_id: ObjectId("6a5b1476238d3b4dd5000048")})
```

> **AGGREGATION COMMAND LIMITATIONS**   For all their practicality, `distinct` and `group` suffer from a significant limitation: they can't return a result set greater than 16 MB. The 16 MB limit isn't a threshold imposed on these commands *per se* but rather on all initial query result sets. `distinct` and `group` are implemented as commands, which means that they're implemented as queries on the special `$cmd` collection, and their being queries is what subjects them to this limitation. If `distinct` or `group` can't handle your aggregation result size, then you'll want to use `map-reduce` instead, where the results can be stored in a collection rather than being returned inline.

5.4.3 *Group*

`group`, like `distinct`, is a database command, and thus its result set is subject to the same 16 MB response limitation. Furthermore, to reduce memory consumption, `group` won't process more than 10,000 unique keys. If your aggregate operation fits within these bounds, then `group` can be a good choice because it's frequently faster than `map-reduce`.

You've already seen a semi-involved example of grouping reviews by user. Let's quickly review the options to be passed to `group`:

- key—A document describing the fields to group by. For instance, to group by `category_id`, you'd use {category_id: true} as your key. The key can also be compound. For instance, if you wanted to group a series of posts by `user_id` and `rating`, your key would look like this: {user_id: true, rating: true}. The key option is required unless you're using `keyf`.

- keyf—A JavaScript function that, when applied to a document, generates a key for that document. This is useful when the key for grouping needs to be calculated. For instance if you wanted to group a result set by the day of the week each document was created on but didn't actually store that value, then you could use a key function to generate the key:

```
function(doc) {
  return {day: doc.created_at.getDay();
}
```

This function will generate keys like this one: {day: 1}. Note that keyf is required if you don't specify a standard key.

- initial—A document that will be used as the starting basis for the results of the aggregation. When the reduce function is first run, this initial document will be used as the first value of the aggregator and will usually contain all the keys you aggregate over. So, for instance, if you're calculating sums of votes and total documents for each grouped item, then your initial document will look like this: {vote_sum: 0.0, doc_count: 0}.

   Note that this parameter is required.

- reduce—A JavaScript function to perform the aggregation. This function will receive two arguments: the current document being iterated and an aggregator document to store the results of the aggregation. The initial value of the aggregator will be the value of the initial document. Here's a sample reduce function aggregating votes and view sums:

```
function(doc, aggregator) {
  aggregator.doc_count += 1;
  aggregator.vote_sum  += doc.vote_count;
}
```

Note that the reduce function doesn't need to return anything; it merely needs to modify the aggregator object. Note also that the reduce function is required.

- cond—A query selector that filters the documents to be aggregated over. If you don't want your group operation to process the entire collection, then you must supply a query selector. For example, if you wanted to aggregate over only those documents having more than five votes, you could provide the following query selector: {vote_count: {$gt: 5}}

- finalize—A JavaScript function that will be applied to each result document before returning the result set. This function gives you a way to post-process the results of a group operation. A common use is averaging. You can use the existing values in a grouped result to add another value to store the average:

```
function(doc) {
  doc.average = doc.vote_count / doc.doc_count;
}
```

group is admittedly tricky at first, what with all the options just presented. But with a little practice, you'll quickly grow accustomed to its ways.

5.4.4   *Map-reduce*

You may be wondering why MongoDB would support both `group` and `map-reduce`, since they provide such similar functionality. In fact, `group` preceded `map-reduce` as MongoDB's sole aggregator. `map-reduce` was added later on for a couple of related reasons. First, operations in the map-reduce style were becoming more mainstream, and it seemed prudent to integrate this budding way of thinking into the product.[11] The second reason was much more practical: iterating over large data sets, especially in a sharded configuration, required a distributed aggregator. Map-reduce (the paradigm) provided just that.

map-reduce includes many options. Here they are in all their byzantine detail:

- map—A JavaScript function to be applied to each document. This function must call `emit()` to select the keys and values to be aggregated. Within the function context, the value of `this` is a reference to the current document. So, for example, if you wanted to group your results by user ID and produce totals on a vote count and document count, then your map function would look like this:

```
function() {
  emit(this.user_id, {vote_sum: this.vote_count, doc_count: 1});
}
```

- reduce—A JavaScript function that receives a key and a list of values. This function must always return a value having the same structure as each of the values provided in the values array. A `reduce` function typically iterates over the list of values and aggregates them in the process. Sticking to our example, here's how you'd reduce the mapped values:

```
function(key, values) {
  var vote_sum = 0;
  var doc_sum  = 0;

  values.forEach(function(value) {
    vote_sum += value.vote_sum;
    doc_sum  += value.doc_sum;

  });
  return {vote_sum: vote_sum, doc_sum: doc_sum};
}
```

  Note that the value of the key parameter frequently isn't used in the aggregation itself.

- query—A query selector that filters the collection to be mapped. This parameter serves the same function as `group`'s `cond` parameter.

---

[11] A lot of developers first saw map-reduce in a famous paper by Google on distributed computations (http://labs.google.com/papers/mapreduce.html). The ideas in this paper helped form the basis for Hadoop, an open source framework that uses distributed map-reduce to process large data sets. The map-reduce idea then spread. CouchDB, for instance, employed a map-reduce paradigm for declaring indexes.

- sort—A sort to be applied to the query. This is most useful when used in conjunction with the limit option. That way, you could run map-reduce on the 1,000 most-recently-created documents.
- limit—An integer specifying a limit to be applied to the query and sort.
- out—This parameter determines how the output is returned. To return all output as the result of the command itself, pass {inline: 1} as the value. Note that this works only when the result set fits within the 16 MB return limit.

  The other option is to place the results into an output collection. To do this, the value of out must be a string identifying the name of the collection where the results are to be stored.

  One problem with writing to an output collection is that you may overwrite existing data if you've recently run a similar map-reduce. Therefore, two other collection output options exist: one for merging the results with the old data and another for reducing against the data. In the merge case, notated as {merge: "collectionName"}, the new results will overwrite any existing items having the same key. In the reduce case, {reduce: "collectionName"}, existing keys' values will be reduced against new values using the reduce function. The reduce output method is especially helpful for performing iterative map-reduce, where you want to integrate new data into an existing aggregation. When you run the new map-reduce against the collection, you simply add a query selector to limit the data set over which the aggregation is run.
- finalize—A JavaScript function to be applied to each resulting document after the reduce phase is complete.
- scope—A document that specifies values for variables to be globally accessible by the map, reduce, and finalize functions.
- verbose—A Boolean that, when true, will include in the command's return document statistics on the execution time of the map-reduce job.

Alas, there's one important limitation to be aware of when thinking about MongoDB's map-reduce and group: speed. On large data sets, these aggregation functions often won't perform as quickly as some users may need. This can be blamed almost entirely on the MongoDB's JavaScript engine. It's hard to achieve high performance with a JavaScript engine that runs single-threaded and interpreted (not compiled).

But despair not. map-reduce and group are widely used and adequate in a lot of situations. For those cases when they're not, an alternative and a hope for the future exist. The alternative is to run aggregations elsewhere. Users with especially large data sets have experienced great success running the data through a Hadoop cluster. The hope for the future is a newer set of aggregation functions that use compiled, multi-threaded code. These are planned to be released some time after MongoDB v2.0; you can track progress at https://jira.mongodb.org/browse/SERVER-447.

5.5   *Summary*

Queries and aggregations make up a critical corner of the MongoDB interface. So once you've skimmed this chapter's reference, you're encouraged to put the query and aggregation mechanisms to the test. If you're ever unsure of how a particular combination of query operators will serve you, the shell is always a ready test bed.

We'll be using MongoDB queries pretty consistently from now on, and the next chapter is a good reminder of that. There, we tackle document updates. Since queries play a key role in most updates, you can look forward to yet more exploration of the query language elaborated here.

Updates, atomic operations, and deletes

6

In this chapter

- Updating documents
- Processing documents atomically
- Category hierarchies and inventory management

To update is to write to existing documents. But to do this effectively requires a thorough understanding of the kinds of document structures available and of the query expressions made possible by MongoDB. Having studied the e-commerce data model throughout the last two chapters, you should have a good sense for the ways in which schemas are designed and queried. We'll use all of this knowledge in our study of updates.

Specifically, we'll look more closely at why we model the category hierarchy in such a denormalized way, and how MongoDB's updates make that structure reasonable. We'll explore inventory management and solve a few tricky concurrency issues in the process. You'll get to know a host of new update operators, learn some tricks that take advantage of the atomicity of update operations, and experience the power of the findAndModify command. After numerous examples, there will be a section devoted to the nuts and bolts of each update operator. I'll also include some notes on concurrency and optimization, and then end with a brief but important summary of how to delete data in MongoDB.

By the end of the chapter, you'll have been exposed to the full range of MongoDB's CRUD operations, and you'll be well on your way to designing applications that best take advantage of MongoDB's interface and data model.

6.1   *A brief tour of document updates*

If you need to update a document in MongoDB, you have two ways of going about it. You can either replace the document altogether or you can use some combination of update operators to modify specific fields within the document. As a way of setting the stage for the more detailed examples to come, I'll begin this chapter with a simple demonstration of these two techniques. I'll then provide some reasons for preferring one over the other.

To start, recall the sample user document. The document includes a user's first and last names, email address, and shipping addresses. You'll undoubtedly need to update an email address from time to time, so let's begin with that. To replace the document altogether, we first query for the document, then modify it on the client side, and then issue the update with the modified document. Here's how that looks in Ruby:

```
user_id = BSON::ObjectId("4c4b1476238d3b4dd5000001")
doc     = @users.find_one({:_id => user_id})

doc['email'] = 'mongodb-user@10gen.com'
@users.update({:_id => user_id}, doc, :safe => true)
```

With the user's _id at hand, you first query for the document. Next you modify the document locally, in this case changing the email attribute. Then you pass the modified document to the update method. The final line says, "Find the document in the users collection with the given _id, and replace that document with the one I've provided."

That's how you modify by replacement; now let's look at modification by operator:

```
@users.update({:_id => user_id},
  {'$set' => {:email => 'mongodb-user@10gen.com'}},
  :safe => true)
```

The example uses $set, one of several special update operators, to modify the email address in a single request to the server. In this case, the update request is much more targeted: find the given user document and set its email field to mongodb-user@10gen.com.

How about another example? This time you want to add another shipping address to the user's list of addresses. Here's how you'd do that as a document replacement:

```
doc = @users.find_one({:_id => user_id})

new_address = {
        :name   => "work",
```

```
           :street  =>  "17 W. 18th St.",
           :city    =>  "New York",
           :state   =>  "NY",
           :zip     =>  10011
   }
doc['shipping_addresses'].append(new_address)
@users.update({:_id => user_id}, doc)
```

And here's the targeted approach:

```
@users.update({:_id => user_id},
   {'$push' => {:addresses =>
     {:name => "work",
    :street => "17 W. 18th St.",
    :city   => "New York",
    :state => "NY",
    :zip    => 10011
       }
     }
   })
```

The replacement approach, like before, fetches the user document from the server, modifies it, and then resends it. The update statement here is identical to the one you used to update the email address. By contrast, the targeted update uses a different update operator, $push, to push the new address onto the existing addresses array.

Now that you've seen a couple of updates in action, can you think of some reasons why you might use one method over the other? Which one do you find more intuitive? Which do you think is better for performance?

Modification by replacement is the more generic approach. Imagine that your application presents an HTML form for modifying user information. With document replacement, data from the form post, once validated, can be passed right to MongoDB; the code to perform the update is the same regardless of which user attributes are modified. So, for instance, if you were going to build a MongoDB object mapper that needed to generalize updates, then updates by replacement would probably make for a sensible default.[1]

But targeted modifications generally yield better performance. For one thing, there's no need for the initial round trip to the server to fetch the document to modify. And just as importantly, the document specifying the update is generally small. If you're updating via replacement, and your documents average 100 KB in size, then that's 100 KB sent to the server per update! Contrast that with the way updates are specified using $set and $push in the preceding examples; the documents specifying these updates can be less than 100 bytes each, regardless of the size of the document being modified. For this reason, the use of targeted updates frequently means less time spent serializing and transmitting data.

---

[1] This is the strategy employed by most MongoDB object mappers, and it's easy to understand why. If users are given the ability to model entities of arbitrary complexity, then issuing an update via replacement is much easier than calculating the ideal combination of special update operators to employ.

In addition, targeted operations allow you to update documents atomically. For instance, if you need to increment a counter, then updates via replacement are far from ideal; the only way to make them atomic is to employ some sort of optimistic locking. With targeted updates, you can use $inc to modify a counter atomically. This means that even with a large number of concurrent updates, each $inc will be applied in isolation, all or nothing.[2]

> **OPTIMISTIC LOCKING**   *Optimistic locking*, or *optimistic concurrency control*, is a technique for ensuring a clean update to a record without having to lock it. The easiest way to understand this technique is to think of a wiki. It's possible to have more than one user editing a wiki page at the same time. But the situation you never want is for a user to be editing and updating an out-of-date version of the page. Thus, an optimistic locking protocol is used. When a user tries to save their changes, a timestamp is included in the attempted update. If that timestamp is older than the latest saved version of the page, then the user's update can't go through. But if no one has saved any edits to the page, the update is allowed. This strategy allows multiple users to edit at the same time, which is much better than the alternative concurrency strategy of requiring each user to take out a lock to edit any one page.

Now that you understand the kinds of updates available, you'll be in a position to appreciate the strategies I'll introduce in the next section. There, we'll return to the e-commerce data model to answer some of the more difficult questions about operating on that data in production.

6.2   E-commerce updates

It's easy to provide stock examples for updating this or that attribute in a MongoDB document. But with a production data model and a real application, complications will arise, and the update for any given attribute might not be a simple one-liner. In the following sections, I'll use the e-commerce data model you saw in the last two chapters to provide a representative sample of the kinds of updates you'd expect to make in a production e-commerce site. You may find certain updates intuitive and other not so much. But overall, you'll develop a better appreciation for the schema developed in chapter 4 and an improved understanding of the features and limitations of MongoDB's update language.

6.2.1   Products and categories

Here you'll see a couple of examples of targeted updates in action, first looking at how you calculate average product ratings and then at the more complicated task of maintaining the category hierarchy.

---

[2] The MongoDB documentation uses the term *atomic updates* to signify what I'm calling *targeted updates*. This new terminology is an attempt to clarify the use of the word *atomic*. In fact, all updates issued to the core server occur atomically, isolated on a per-document basis. The update operators are called atomic because they make it possible to update a document without first having to query it.

AVERAGE PRODUCT RATINGS

Products are amenable to numerous update strategies. Assuming that administrators are provided with an interface for editing product information, the easiest update involves fetching the current product document, merging that data with the user's edits, and issuing a document replacement. At other times, you may need to update just a couple of values, where a targeted update is clearly the way to go. This is the case with average product ratings. Because users need to sort product listings based on average product rating, you store that rating in the product document itself and update the value whenever a review is added or removed.

Here's one way of issuing this update:

```
average = 0.0
count   = 0
total   = 0
cursor = @reviews.find({:product_id => product_id}, :fields => ["rating"])
while cursor.has_next? && review = cursor.next()
  total += review['rating']
  count += 1
end

average = total / count

@products.update({:_id => BSON::ObjectId("4c4b1476238d3b4dd5003981")},
    {'$set' => {:total_reviews => count, :average_review => average}})
```

This code aggregates and produces the rating field from each product review and then produces an average. You also use the fact that you're iterating over each rating to count the total ratings for the product. This saves an extra database call to the count function. With the total number of reviews and their average rating, the code issues a targeted update, using $set.

Performance-conscious users may balk at the idea of reaggregating all product reviews for each update. The method provided here, though conservative, will likely be acceptable for most situations. But other strategies are possible. For instance, you could store an extra field on the product document that caches the review ratings total. After inserting a new review, you'd first query for the product to get the current total number of reviews and the ratings total. Then you'd calculate the average and issue an update using a selector like the following:

```
{'$set' => {:average_review => average, :ratings_total => total},
  '$inc' => {:total_reviews => 1}})
```

Only by benchmarking against a system with representative data can you say whether this approach is worthwhile. But the example shows that MongoDB frequently provides more than one valid path. The requirements of the application will help you decide which is best.

THE CATEGORY HIERARCHY

With many databases, there's no easy way to represent a category hierarchy. This is true of MongoDB, although the document structure does help the situation somewhat. Documents permit a strategy that optimizes for reads, since each category can contain a list of its ancestors. The one tricky requirement is keeping all the ancestor lists up to date. Let's look at an example to see how this is done.

What you need first is a generic method for updating the ancestor list for any given category. Here's one possible solution:

```
def generate_ancestors(_id, parent_id)
  ancestor_list = []
  while parent = @categories.find_one(:_id => parent_id) do
    ancestor_list.unshift(parent)
    parent_id = parent['parent_id']
  end

  @categories.update({:_id => _id},
    {"$set" {:ancestors => ancestor_list}})
end
```

This method works by walking backward up the category hierarchy, making successive queries to each node's `parent_id` attribute until reaching the root node (where `parent_id` is `nil`). All the while, it builds an in-order list of ancestors, storing that result in the `ancestor_list` array. Finally, it updates the category's `ancestors` attribute using `$set`.

Now that you have that basic building block, let's look at the process of inserting a new category. Imagine you have a simple category hierarchy that looks like the one you see in figure 6.1.

Suppose you want to add a new category called Gardening and place it under the Home category. You insert the new category document and then run your method to generate its ancestors:

```
category = {
  :parent_id => parent_id,
  :slug => "gardening",
  :name => "Gardening",
  :description => "All gardening implements, tools, seeds, and soil."
}
gardening_id = @categories.insert(category)
generate_ancestors(gardening_id, parent_id)
```

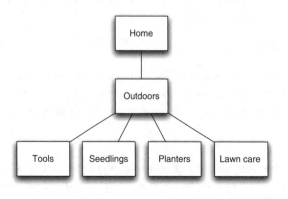

Figure 6.1 An initial category hierarchy

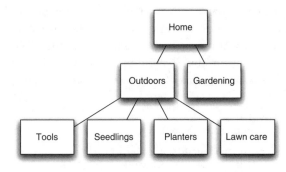

Figure 6.2   Adding a Gardening category

Figure 6.2 displays the updated tree.

That's easy enough. But what if you now want to place the Outdoors category underneath Gardening? This is potentially complicated because it alters the ancestor lists of a number of categories. You can start by changing the parent_id of Outdoors to the _id of Gardening. This turns out to be not too difficult:

```
@categories.update({:_id => outdoors_id},
                   {'$set' => {:parent_id => gardening_id}})
```

Since you've effectively moved the Outdoors category, all the descendants of Outdoors are going to have invalid ancestor lists. You can rectify this by querying for all categories with Outdoors in their ancestor lists and then regenerating those lists. MongoDB's power to query into arrays makes this trivial:

```
@categories.find({'ancestors.id' => outdoors_id}).each do |category|
  generate_ancestors(category['_id'], outdoors_id)
end
```

That's how you handle an update to a category's parent_id attribute, and you can see the resulting category arrangement in figure 6.3.

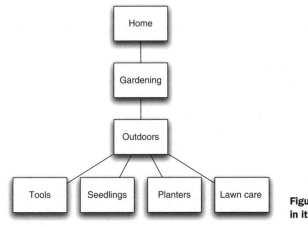

Figure 6.3   The category tree in its final state

But now what if you update a category name? If you change the name of Outdoors to The Great Outdoors, then you also have to change Outdoors wherever it appears in the ancestor lists of other categories. You may be justified in thinking, "See? This is where denormalization comes to bite you," but it should make you feel better to know that you can perform this update without recalculating any ancestor list. Here's how:

```
doc = @categories.find_one({:_id => outdoors_id})
doc['name'] = "The Great Outdoors"
@categories.update({:_id => outdoors_id}, doc)

@categories.update({'ancestors.id' => outdoors_id},
  {'$set' => {'ancestors.$'=> doc}}, :multi => true)
```

You first grab the Outdoors document, alter the `name` attribute locally, and then update via replacement. Now you use the updated Outdoors document to replace its occurrences in the various ancestor lists. You accomplish this using the positional operator and a multi-update. The multi-update is easy to understand; recall that you need to specify `:multi => true` if you want the update to affect all documents matching the selector. Here, you want to update each category that has the Outdoors category in its ancestor list.

The positional operator is more subtle. Consider that you have no way of knowing where in a given category's ancestor list the Outdoors category will appear. You thus need a way for the update operator to dynamically target the position of the Outdoors category in the array for any document. Enter the positional operator. This operator, here the `$` in `ancestors.$`, substitutes the array index matched by the query selector with itself, and thus enables the update.

Because of the need to update individual sub-documents within arrays, you'll always want to keep the positional operator at hand. In general, these techniques for updating the category hierarchy will be applicable whenever you're dealing with arrays of sub-documents.

6.2.2   Reviews

Not all reviews are created equal, which is why this application allows users to vote on them. These votes are elementary; they indicate that the given review is helpful. You've modeled reviews so that they cache the total number of helpful votes and keep a list of each voter's ID. The relevant section of each review document looks like this:

```
{helpful_votes: 3,
 voter_ids: [ ObjectId("4c4b1476238d3b4dd5000041"),
              ObjectId("7a4f0376238d3b4dd5000003"),
              ObjectId("92c21476238d3b4dd5000032")
           ]}
```

You can record user votes using targeted updates. The strategy is to use the $push operator to add the voter's ID to the list and the $inc operator to increment the total number of votes, both in the same update operation:

```
db.reviews.update({_id: ObjectId("4c4b1476238d3b4dd5000041")},
  {$push: {voter_ids: ObjectId("4c4b1476238d3b4dd5000001")},
```

```
  $inc: {helpful_votes: 1}
})
```

This is almost correct. But you need to ensure that the update happens only if the voting user hasn't yet voted on this review. So you modify the query selector to match only when the `voter_ids` array doesn't contain the ID you're about to add. You can easily accomplish this using the `$ne` query operator:

```
query_selector = {_id: ObjectId("4c4b1476238d3b4dd5000041"),
  voter_ids: {$ne: ObjectId("4c4b1476238d3b4dd5000001")}}
db.reviews.update(query_selector,
  {$push: {voter_ids: ObjectId("4c4b1476238d3b4dd5000001")},
  $inc : {helpful_votes: 1}
})
```

This is an especially powerful demonstration of MongoDB's update mechanism and how it can be used with a document-oriented schema. Voting, in this case, is both atomic and efficient. The atomicity ensures that, even in a high-concurrency environment, it'll be impossible for any one user to vote more than once. The efficiency lies in the fact that the test for voter membership and the updates to the counter and the voter list all occur in the same request to the server.

Now, if you do end up using this technique to record votes, it's especially important that any other updates to the review document also be targeted. This is because updating by replacement could conceivably result in an inconsistency. Imagine, for instance, that a user updates the content of their review and that this update occurs via replacement. When updating by replacement, you first query for the document you want to update. But between the time that you query for the review and replace it, it's possible that a different user might vote on the review. This sequence of events is illustrated in figure 6.4.

It should be clear that the document replacement at T3 will overwrite the votes update happening at T2. It's possible to avoid this using the optimistic locking

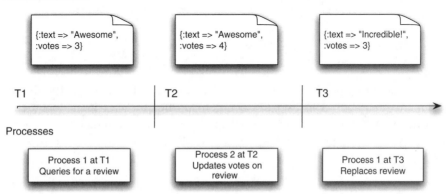

Figure 6.4 When a review is updated concurrently via targeted and replacement updates, data can be lost.

technique described earlier, but it's probably easier to ensure that all updates in this case are targeted.

6.2.3   *Orders*

The atomicity and efficiency of updates that you saw in reviews can also be applied to orders. Specifically, you're going to see how to implement an Add to Cart function using a targeted update. This is a two-step process. First, you construct the product document that you'll be storing in the order's line-item array. Then you issue a targeted update, indicating that this is to be an *upsert*—an update that will insert a new document if the document to be updated doesn't exist. (I'll describe upserts in detail in the next section.) The upsert will create a new order object if it doesn't yet exist, seamlessly handling both initial and subsequent additions to the shopping cart.[3]

Let's begin by constructing a sample document to add to the cart:

```
cart_item = {
  _id:  ObjectId("4c4b1476238d3b4dd5003981"),
  slug: "wheel-barrow-9092",
  sku:  "9092",

  name: "Extra Large Wheel Barrow",

  pricing: {
    retail: 589700,
    sale:   489700
  }
}
```

You'll most likely build this document by querying the products collection and then extracting whichever fields need to be preserved as a line item. The product's _id, sku, slug, name, and price fields should suffice.[4] With the cart item document, you can then upsert into the orders collection:

```
selector = {user_id: ObjectId("4c4b1476238d3b4dd5000001"),
            state:   'CART',
            'line_items.id':
              {'$ne': ObjectId("4c4b1476238d3b4dd5003981")}
           }

update = {'$push': {'line_items': cart_item}}

db.orders.update(selector, update, true, false)
```

To make the code more clear, I'm constructing the query selector and the update document separately. The update document pushes the cart item document onto the array of line items. As the query selector indicates, this update won't succeed unless this particular item doesn't yet exist in that array. Of course, the first time a user

---

[3] I'm using the terms *shopping cart* and *order* interchangeably because they're both represented using the same document. They're formally differentiated only by the document's state field (a document with a state of CART is a shopping cart).

[4] In a real e-commerce application, you'll want to verify that the price has not changed at checkout time.

executes the Add to Cart function, no shopping cart will exist at all. That's why you use an upsert here. The upsert will construct the document implied by the keys and values of the query selector and those of the update document. Therefore, the initial upsert will produce an order document looking like this one:

```
{
user_id: ObjectId("4c4b1476238d3b4dd5000001"),
state:  'CART',
line_items: [{
    _id:  ObjectId("4c4b1476238d3b4dd5003981"),
    slug: "wheel-barrow-9092",
    sku:  "9092",

    name: "Extra Large Wheel Barrow",

    pricing: {
      retail: 589700,
      sale:   489700
    }
  }]
}
```

You then need to issue another targeted update to ensure that the item quantities and order subtotal are correct:

```
selector = {user_id: ObjectId("4c4b1476238d3b4dd5000001"),
            state:   "CART",
            'line_items.id': ObjectId("4c4b1476238d3b4dd5003981")}

update = {$inc:
            {'line_items.$.qty': 1,
             sub_total: cart_item['pricing']['sale']
            }
        }

db.orders.update(selector, update)
```

Notice that you use the $inc operator to update the overall subtotal and quantity on the individual line item. This latter update is facilitated by the positional operator ($), introduced in the previous subsection. The main reason you need this second update is to handle the case where the user clicks Add to Cart on an item that's already in the cart. For this case, the first update won't succeed, but you'll still need to adjust the quantity and subtotal. Thus, after clicking Add to Cart twice on the wheelbarrow product, the cart should look like this:

```
{
'user_id': ObjectId("4c4b1476238d3b4dd5000001"),
'state'  : 'CART',
'line_items': [{
    _id:  ObjectId("4c4b1476238d3b4dd5003981"),
    qty:  2,
    slug: "wheel-barrow-9092",
    sku:  "9092",

    name: "Extra Large Wheel Barrow",
```

```
    pricing: {
      retail: 589700,
      sale:    489700
    }
  }],

  subtotal: 979400
}
```

There are now two wheelbarrows in the cart, and the subtotal reflects that.

There are still more operations you'll need to fully implement a shopping cart. Most of these, such as removing an item from the cart or clearing a cart altogether, can be implemented with one or more targeted updates. If that's not obvious, the upcoming subsection describing each query operator should make it clear. As for the actual order processing, that can be handled by advancing the order document through a series of states and applying each state's processing logic. We'll demonstrate this in the next section, where I explain atomic document processing and the find-AndModify command.

6.3   *Atomic document processing*

One tool you won't want to do without is MongoDB's findAndModify command.[5] This command allows you to atomically update a document and return it in the same round trip. This is a big deal because of what it enables. For instance, you can use findAndModify to build job queues and state machines. You can then use these primitive constructs to implement basic transactional semantics, which greatly expand the range of applications you can build using MongoDB. With these transaction-like features, you can construct an entire e-commerce site on MongoDB—not just the product content, but the checkout mechanism and the inventory management as well.

To demonstrate, we'll look at two examples of the findAndModify command in action. First, I'll show how to handle basic state transitions on the shopping cart. Then we'll look at a slightly more involved example of managing a limited inventory.

6.3.1   *Order state transitions*

All state transitions have two parts: a query ensuring a valid initial state and an update that effects the change of state. Let's skip forward a few steps in the order process and assume that the user is about to click the Pay Now button to authorize the purchase. If you're going to authorize the user's credit card synchronously on the application side, then you need to ensure these things:

1 You authorize for the amount that the user sees on the checkout screen.
2 The cart's contents never change while in the process of authorization.

---

[5] The way this command is identified can vary by environment. The shell helper is invoked camel case as db.orders.findAndModify, whereas Ruby uses underscores: find_and_modify. To confuse the issue even more, the core server knows the command as findandmodify. You'll use this final form if you ever need to issue the command manually.

3 Errors in the authorization process return the cart to its previous state.

4 If the credit card is successfully authorized, the payment information is posted to the order, and that order's state is transitioned to SHIPMENT PENDING.

The first step is to get the order into the new PRE-AUTHORIZE state. You use `find-AndModify` to find the user's current order object and ensure that the object is in a CART state:

```
db.orders.findAndModify({
  query: {user_id: ObjectId("4c4b1476238d3b4dd5000001"),
          state: "CART" },

  update: {"$set": {"state": "PRE-AUTHORIZE"},
  new: true}
})
```

If successful, `findAndModify` will return the transitioned order object.[6] Once the order is in the PRE-AUTHORIZE state, the user won't be able to edit the cart's contents. This is because all updates to the cart always ensure a state of CART. Now, in the pre-authorization state, you take the returned order object and recalculate the various totals. Once you have those totals, you issue a new `findAndModify` which transitions the document's state to AUTHORIZING only if the new totals match the old totals. Here's what that `findAndModify` looks like:

```
db.orders.findAndModify({
  query: {user_id:  ObjectId("4c4b1476238d3b4dd5000001"),
          total: 99000,
          state: "PRE-AUTHORIZE" },

  update: {"$set": {"state": "AUTHORIZING"}}
})
```

If this second `findAndModify` fails, then you must return the order's state to CART and report the updated totals to the user. But if it succeeds, then you know that the total to be authorized is the same total that was presented to the user. This means that you can move on to the actual authorization API call. Thus, the application now issues a credit card authorization request on the user's credit card. If the credit card fails to authorize, you record the failure and, like before, return the order to its CART state.

But if the authorization is successful, you write the authorization info to the order and transition it to the next state. The following strategy does both in the same `find-AndModify` call. Here, the example uses a sample document representing the authorization receipt, which is attached to the original order:

```
auth_doc = {ts: new Date(),
            cc: 3432003948293040,
            id: 29238382910293844483949348,
            gateway: "Authorize.net"}
```

---

[6] By default, the `findAndModify` command returns the document as it appears prior to the update. To return the modified document, you must specify {`new: true`} as as in this example.

```
db.orders.findAndModify({
  query: {user_id: ObjectId("4c4b1476238d3b4dd5000001"),
          state: "AUTHORIZING" },

  update: {"$set":
                {"state": "PRE-SHIPPING"},
                "authorization": auth}
})
```

It's important to be aware of the MongoDB features that facilitate this transactional process. There's the ability to modify any one document atomically. There's the guarantee of consistent reads along a single connection. And finally, there's the document structure itself, which allows these operations to fit within the single-document atomicity that MongoDB provides. In this case, that structure allows you to fit line items, products, pricing, and user ownership into the same document, ensuring that you only ever need to operate on that one document to advance the sale.

This ought to strike you as impressive. But it may lead you to wonder, as it did me, whether any *multi-object* transaction-like behavior can be implemented with MongoDB. The answer is a cautious affirmative and can be demonstrated by looking into another e-commerce centerpiece: inventory management.

6.3.2   *Inventory management*

Not every e-commerce site needs strict inventory management. Most commodity items can be replenished in a reasonable enough time to allow any order to go through regardless of the actual number of items on hand. In cases like these, managing inventory is easily handled by managing expectations; as soon as only a few items remain in stock, adjust the shipping estimates.

One-of-a-kind items present a different challenge. Imagine you're selling concert tickets with assigned seats or handmade works of art. These products can't be hedged; users will always need a guarantee that they can purchase the products they've selected. Here I'll present a possible solution to this problem using MongoDB. This will further illustrate the creative possibilities in the findAndModify command and the judicious use of the document model. It'll also show how to implement transactional semantics across multiple documents.

The way you model inventory can be best understood by thinking about a real store. If you're in a gardening store, you can see and feel the physical inventory; dozens of shovels, rakes, and clippers may line the aisles. If you take a shovel and place it in your cart, that's one less shovel available for the other customers. As a corollary, no two customers can have the same shovel in their shopping carts at the same time. You can use this simple principle to model inventory. For every physical piece of inventory in your warehouse, you store a corresponding document in an inventory collection. If there are 10 shovels in the warehouse, there are 10 shovel documents in the database. Each inventory item is linked to a product by sku, and each of these items can be in one of four states: AVAILABLE (0), IN_CART (1), PRE_ORDER (2), or PURCHASED (3).

Here's a method that inserts three shovels, three rakes, and three sets of clippers as available inventory:

```
3.times do
  @inventory.insert({:sku => 'shovel',   :state => AVAILABLE})
  @inventory.insert({:sku => 'rake',     :state => AVAILABLE})
  @inventory.insert({:sku => 'clippers', :state => AVAILABLE})
end
```

We'll handle inventory management with a special inventory fetching class. We'll first look at how this fetcher works and then we'll peel back the covers to reveal its implementation.

The inventory fetcher can add arbitrary sets of products to a shopping cart. Here you create a new order object and a new inventory fetcher. You then ask the fetcher to add three shovels and one set of clippers to a given order by passing an order ID and two documents specifying the products and quantities you want to the add_to_cart method:

```
@order_id = @orders.insert({:username => 'kbanker', :item_ids => []})
@fetcher  = InventoryFetcher.new(:orders    => @orders,
                                 :inventory => @inventory)

@fetcher.add_to_cart(@order_id,
                     {:sku => "shovel", :qty => 3},
                     {:sku => "clippers", :qty => 1})

order = @orders.find_one({"_id" => @order_id})
puts "\nHere's the order:"
p order
```

The add_to_cart method will raise an exception if it fails to add every item to a cart. If it succeeds, the order should look like this:

```
{"_id" => BSON::ObjectId('4cdf3668238d3b6e3200000a'),
 "username"=>"kbanker",
 "item_ids" => [BSON::ObjectId('4cdf3668238d3b6e32000001'),
                BSON::ObjectId('4cdf3668238d3b6e32000004'),
                BSON::ObjectId('4cdf3668238d3b6e32000007'),
                BSON::ObjectId('4cdf3668238d3b6e32000009')],
}
```

The _id of each physical inventory item will be stored in the order document. You can query for each of these items like so:

```
puts "\nHere's each item:"
order['item_ids'].each do |item_id|
  item = @inventory.find_one({"_id" => item_id})
  p item
end
```

Looking at each of these items individually, you can see that each has a state of 1, corresponding to the IN_CART state. You should also notice that each item records the time of the last state change with a timestamp. You can later use this timestamp to expire items that have been in a cart for too long. For instance, you might give users 15 minutes to check out from the time they add products to their cart:

```
{"_id" => BSON::ObjectId('4cdf3668238d3b6e32000001'),
  "sku"=>"shovel", "state"=>1, "ts"=>"Sun Nov 14 01:07:52 UTC 2010"}

{"_id"=>BSÓN::ObjectId('4cdf3668238d3b6e32000004'),
  "sku"=>"shovel", "state"=>1, "ts"=>"Sun Nov 14 01:07:52 UTC 2010"}

{"_id"=>BSON::ObjectId('4cdf3668238d3b6e32000007'),
  "sku"=>"shovel", "state"=>1, "ts"=>"Sun Nov 14 01:07:52 UTC 2010"}

{"_id"=>BSON::ObjectId('4cdf3668238d3b6e32000009'),
  "sku"=>"clippers", "state"=>1, "ts"=>"Sun Nov 14 01:07:52 UTC 2010"}
```

If this InventoryFetcher's API makes any sense, you should have a least a few hunches about how you'd implement inventory management. Unsurprisingly, the findAnd-Modify command resides at its core. The full source code for the InventoryFetcher, including a test suite, is included with the source code of this book. We're not going to look at every line of code, but we'll highlight the three key methods that make it work.

First, when you pass a list of items to be added to your cart, the fetcher attempts to transition each item from the state of AVAILABLE to IN_CART. If at any point this operation fails (if any one item can't be added to the cart), then the entire operation is rolled back. Have a look at the add_to_cart method that you invoked earlier:

```
def add_to_cart(order_id, *items)
  item_selectors = []
  items.each do |item|
    item[:qty].times do
      item_selectors << {:sku => item[:sku]}
    end
  end

  transition_state(order_id, item_selectors, :from => AVAILABLE,
      :to => IN_CART)
end
```

This method doesn't do much. It basically takes the specification for items to add to the cart and expands the quantities so that one item selector exists for each physical item that will be added to the cart. For instance, this document, which says that you want to add two shovels

```
{:sku => "shovel", :qty => 2}
```

becomes this:

```
[{:sku => "shovel"}, {:sku => "shovel"}]
```

You need a separate query selector for each item you want to add to your cart. Thus, the method passes the array of item selectors to another method called transition_state. For example, the code above specifies that the state should be transitioned from AVAILABLE to IN_CART:

```
def transition_state(order_id, selectors, opts={})
  items_transitioned = []

  begin
    for selector in selectors do
```

```
        query = selector.merge(:state => opts[:from])

        physical_item = @inventory.find_and_modify(:query => query,
          :update => {'$set' => {:state => opts[:to], :ts => Time.now.utc}})

        if physical_item.nil?
          raise InventoryFetchFailure
        end

        items_transitioned << physical_item['_id']

        @orders.update({:_id => order_id},
                       {"$push" => {:item_ids => physical_item['_id']}})
      end

    rescue Mongo::OperationFailure, InventoryFetchFailure
      rollback(order_id, items_transitioned, opts[:from], opts[:to])
      raise InventoryFetchFailure, "Failed to add #{selector[:sku]}"
    end

    items_transitioned.size
  end
```

To transition state, each selector gets an extra condition, {:state => AVAILABLE}, and
then the selector is passed to findAndModify which, if matched, sets a timestamp and
the item's new state. The method then saves the list of items transitioned and updates
the order with the ID of the item just added.

If the findAndModify command fails and returns nil, then you raise an Inventory-
FetchFailure exception. If the command fails because of networking errors, you rescue the inevitable Mongo::OperationFailure exception. In both cases, you rescue by
rolling back all the items transitioned thus far and then raise an InventoryFetch-
Failure, which includes the SKU of the item that couldn't be added. You can then rescue this exception on the application layer to fail gracefully for the user.

All that now remains is to examine the rollback code:

```
def rollback(order_id, item_ids, old_state, new_state)
  @orders.update({"_id" => order_id},
                 {"$pullAll" => {:item_ids => item_ids}})

  item_ids.each do |id|
    @inventory.find_and_modify(
      :query  => {"_id" => id, :state => new_state},
      :update => {"$set" => {:state => old_state, :ts => Time.now.utc}}
    )
  end
end
```

You use the $pullAll operator to remove all of the IDs just added to the order's
item_ids array. You then iterate over the list of item IDs and transition each one back
to its old state.

The transition_state method can be used as the basis for other methods that
move items through their successive states. It wouldn't be difficult to integrate this
into the order transition system that you built in the previous subsection. But that
must be left as an exercise for the reader.

You may justifiably ask whether this system is robust enough for production. This question can't be answered easily without knowing more particulars, but what can be stated assuredly is that MongoDB provides enough features to permit a usable solution when you need transaction-like behavior. Granted, no one should be building a banking system on MongoDB. But if some sort of transactional behavior is required, it's reasonable to consider MongoDB for the task, especially when you want to run the application entirely on one database.

6.4   *Nuts and bolts: MongoDB updates and deletes*

To really understand updates in MongoDB, you need a holistic understanding of MongoDB's document model and query language, and the examples in the preceding sections are great for helping with that. But here, as in all of this book's nuts-and-bolts sections, we get down to brass tacks. This mostly involves brief summaries of each feature of the MongoDB update interface, but I also include several notes on performance. For brevity's sake, all of the upcoming examples will be in JavaScript.

6.4.1   *Update types and options*

MongoDB supports both targeted updates and updates via replacement. The former are defined by the use of one or more update operators; the latter by a document that will be used to replace the document matched by the update's query selector.

> **Syntax note: updates versus queries**
>
> Users new to MongoDB sometimes have difficulty distinguishing between the update and query syntaxes. Targeted updates, at least, always begin with the update operator, and this operator is almost always a verb-like construct. Take the `$addToSet` operator, for example:
>
> ```
> db.products.update({}, {$addToSet: {tags: 'green'}})
> ```
>
> If you add a query selector to this update, note that the query operator is semantically adjectival and comes after the field name to query on:
>
> ```
> db.products.update({'price' => {$lte => 10}},
>    {$addToSet: {tags: 'cheap'}})
> ```
>
> Basically, update operators are prefix whereas query operators are usually infix.

Note that an update will fail if the update document is ambiguous. Here, we've combined an update operator, `$addToSet`, with replacement-style semantics, `{name: "Pitchfork"}`:

```
db.products.update({}, {name: "Pitchfork", $addToSet: {tags: 'cheap'}})
```

If your intention is to change the document's name, you must use the `$set` operator:

```
db.products.update({},
   {$set: {name: "Pitchfork"}, $addToSet: {tags: 'cheap'}})
```

MULTIDOCUMENT UPDATES

An update will, by default, only update the first document matched by its query selector. To update all matching documents, you need to explicitly specify a multi-document update. In the shell, you can express this by passing true as the fourth argument of the update method. Here's how you'd add the cheap tags to all documents in the products collection:

```
db.products.update({}, {$addToSet: {tags: 'cheap'}}, false, true)
```

With the Ruby driver (and most other drivers), you can express multidocument updates more clearly:

```
@products.update({}, {'$addToSet' => {'tags' => 'cheap'}}, :multi => true)
```

UPSERTS

It's common to need to insert if an item doesn't exist but update it if it does. You can handle this normally tricky-to-implement pattern using MongoDB upserts. If the query selector matches, the update takes place normally. But if no document matches the query selector, a new document will be inserted. The new document's attributes will be a logical merging of the query selector and the targeted update document.[7]

Here's a simple example of an upsert using the shell:

```
db.products.update({slug: 'hammer'}, {$addToSet: {tags: 'cheap'}}, true)
```

And here's an equivalent upsert in Ruby:

```
@products.update({'slug' => 'hammer'},
  {'$addToSet' => {'tags' => 'cheap'}}, :upsert => true)
```

As you should expect, upserts can can insert or update only one document at a time. You'll find upserts incredibly valuable when you need to update atomically and when there's uncertainly about a document's prior existence. For a practical example, see section 6.2.3, which describes adding products to a cart.

6.4.2 Update operators

MongoDB supports a host of update operators. Here I provide brief examples of each of them.

STANDARD UPDATE OPERATORS

This first set of operators is the most generic, and each works with almost any data type.

$inc

You use the $inc operator to increment or decrement a numeric value:

```
db.products.update({slug: "shovel"}, {$inc: {review_count: 1}})
db.users.update({username: "moe"}, {$inc: {password_retires: -1}})
```

But you can also use $inc to add or subtract from numbers arbitrarily:

```
db.readings.update({_id: 324}, {$inc: {temp: 2.7435}})
```

---

[7] Note that upserts don't work with replacement-style update documents.

$inc is as efficient as it is convenient. Because it rarely changes the size of a document, an $inc usually occurs in-place on disk, thus affecting only the value pair specified.[8]

As demonstrated in the code for adding products to a shopping cart, $inc works with upserts. For example, you can change the preceding update to an upsert like so:

```
db.readings.update({_id: 324}, {$inc: {temp: 2.7435}}, true)
```

If no reading with an _id of 324 exists, a new document will be created with said _id and a temp with the value of the $inc, 2.7435.

$set and $unset

If you need to set the value of a particular key in a document, you'll want to use $set. You can set a key to a value having any valid BSON type. This means that all of the following updates are possible:

```
db.readings.update({_id: 324}, {$set: {temp: 97.6}}})
db.readings.update({_id: 325}, {$set: {temp: {f: 212, c: 100} }})
db.readings.update({_id: 326}, {$set: {temps: [97.6, 98.4, 99.1]}}})
```

If the key being set already exists, then its value will be overwritten; otherwise, a new key will be created.

$unset removes the provided key from a document. Here's how to remove the temp key from the reading document:

```
db.readings.update({_id: 324}, {$unset: {temp: 1}})
```

You can also use $unset on embedded documents and on arrays. In both cases, you specify the inner object using dot notation. If you have these two documents in your collection

```
{_id: 325, 'temp': {f: 212, c: 100}}
{_id: 326, temps: [97.6, 98.4, 99.1]}
```

then you can remove the Fahrenheit reading in the first document and the zeroth element in the second document like so:

```
db.readings.update({_id: 325},
  {$unset: {'temp.f': 1}})

db.readings.update({_id: 236},
  {$pop: {temps: -1}})
```

This dot notation for accessing sub-documents and array elements can also be used with $set.

$rename

If you need to change the name of a key, use $rename:

```
db.readings.update({_id: 324}, {$rename: {'temp': 'temperature'}})
```

You can also rename a sub-document:

```
db.readings.update({_id: 325}, {$rename: {'temp.f': 'temp.farenheit'}})
```

---

[8] Exceptions to this rule arise when the numeric type changes. If the $inc results in a 32-bit integer being converted to a 64-bit integer, then the entire BSON document will have to be rewritten in-place.

> **Using $unset with arrays**
>
> Note that using $unset on individual array elements may not work exactly like you want it to. Instead of removing the element altogether, it merely sets that element's value to null. To completely remove an array element, see the $pull and $pop operators.
>
> ```
> db.readings.update({_id: 325}, {$unset: {'temp.f': 1})
> db.readings.update({_id: 326}, {$unset: {'temp.0': 1})
> ```

ARRAY UPDATE OPERATORS

The centrality of arrays in MongoDB's document model should be apparent. Naturally, MongoDB provides a handful of update operators that apply exclusively to arrays.

$push and $pushAll

If you need to append values to an array, $push and $pushAll are your friends. The first of these, $push, will add a single value to an array, whereas $pushAll supports adding a list of values. For example, adding a new tag to the shovel product is easy enough:

```
db.products.update({slug: 'shovel'}, {$push: {'tags': 'tools'}})
```

If you need to add a few tags in the same update, that's not a problem either:

```
db.products.update({slug: 'shovel'},
  {$pushAll: {'tags': ['tools', 'dirt', 'garden']}})
```

Note you can push values of any type onto an array, not just scalars. For an example of this, see the code in the previous section that pushed a product onto the shopping cart's line items array.

$addToSet and $each

$addToSet also appends a value to an array but does so in a more discerning way: the value is added only if it doesn't already exist in the array. Thus, if your shovel has already been tagged as a tool then the following update won't modify the document at all:

```
db.products.update({slug: 'shovel'}, {$addToSet: {'tags': 'tools'}})
```

If you need to add more than one value to an array uniquely in the same operation, then you must use $addToSet with the $each operator. Here's how that looks:

```
db.products.update({slug: 'shovel'},
{$addToSet: {'tags': {$each: ['tools', 'dirt', 'steel']}}})
```

Only those values in the $each that don't already exist in tags will be appended.

$pop

The most elementary way to remove an item from an array is with the $pop operator. If $push appends an item to an array, a subsequent $pop will remove that last item pushed. Though it's frequently used with $push, you can use $pop on its own. If your tags array contains the values ['tools', 'dirt', 'garden', 'steel'], then the following $pop will remove the steel tag:

```
db.products.update({slug: 'shovel'}, {$pop: {'tags': 1}})
```

Like $unset, $pop's syntax is {$pop: {'elementToRemove': 1}}. But unlike $unset, $pop takes a second possible value of -1 to remove the first element of the array. Here's how to remove the tools tag from the array:

```
db.products.update({slug: 'shovel'}, {$pop: {'tags': -1}})
```

One possible point of frustration is that you can't actually return the value that $pop removes from the array. Thus, despite its name, $pop doesn't work exactly like the stack operation you probably have in mind. Be aware of this.

$pull and $pullAll

$pull is $pop's more sophisticated cousin. With $pull, you specify exactly which array element to remove by value, not by position. Returning to the tags example, if you need to remove the tag dirt, you don't need to know where in the array it's located; you simply tell the $pull operator to remove it:

```
db.products.update({slug: 'shovel'}, {$pull {'tags': 'dirt'}})
```

$pullAll works analogously to $pushAll, allowing you to provide a list of values to remove. To remove both the tags dirt and garden, you can use $pullAll like so:

```
db.products.update({slug: 'shovel'}, {$pullAll {'tags': ['dirt', 'garden']}})
```

POSITIONAL UPDATES

It's common to model data in MongoDB using an array of sub-documents, but it wasn't so easy to manipulate those sub-documents until the positional operator came along. The positional operator allows you to update a sub-document in an array. You identify which sub-document you want to update by using dot notation in your query selector. This is hard to understand without an example, so suppose you have an order document, part of which looks like this:

```
{ _id: new ObjectId("6a5b1476238d3b4dd5000048"),
  line_items:  [
    { _id:  ObjectId("4c4b1476238d3b4dd5003981"),
      sku:  "9092",
      name: "Extra Large Wheel Barrow",
      quantity:  1,
      pricing:  {
        retail:  5897,
        sale:  4897,
      }
    },
    { _id:  ObjectId("4c4b1476238d3b4dd5003981"),
      sku:  "10027",
      name: "Rubberized Work Glove, Black",
      quantity:  2,
      pricing: {
        retail:  1499,
```

```
        sale:  1299,
      }
    }
  ]
}
```

You want to be able to set the quantity of the second line item, with the SKU of 10027, to 5. The problem is that you don't know where in the line_items array this particular sub-document resides. You don't even know whether it exists. But a simple query selector, and an update document using the positional operator, solve both of these problems:

```
query  = {_id: ObjectId("4c4b1476238d3b4dd5003981"),
         'line_items.sku': "10027"}
update = {$set: {'line_items.$.quantity': 5}}
```

```
db.orders.update(query, update)
```

The positional operator is the $ that you see in the 'line_items.$.quantity' string. If the query selector matches, then the index of the document having a SKU of 10027 will replace the positional operator internally, thereby updating the correct document.

If your data model includes sub-documents, then you'll find the positional operator very useful for performing nuanced document updates.

6.4.3   *The findAndModify command*

With so many fleshed-out examples of using the findAndModify command earlier in this chapter, it only remains to enumerate its options. Of the following, the only options required are query and either update or remove:

- query—A document query selector. Defaults to {}.
- update—A document specifying an update. Defaults to {}.
- remove—A Boolean value that, when true, removes the object and then returns it. Defaults to false.
- new—A Boolean that, if true, returns the modified document as it appears after the update has been applied. Defaults to false.
- sort—A document specifying a sort direction. Because findAndModify will modify only one document at a time, the sort option can be used to help control which matching document is processed. For example, you might sort by {created_at: -1} to process to most recently created matching document.
- fields—If you only need to return a subset of fields, use this option to specify them. This is especially helpful with larger documents. The fields are specified just as they would be in any query. See the section on fields in chapter 5 for examples.
- upsert—A Boolean that, when true, treats findAndModify as an upsert. If the document sought doesn't exist, it'll be created. Note that if you want to return the newly created document, you also need to specify {new: true}.

6.4.4 Deletes

You'll be relieved to learn that removing documents poses few challenges. You can remove an entire collection or you can pass a query selector to the `remove` method to delete only a subset of a collection. Deleting all reviews is simple:

```
db.reviews.remove({})
```

But it's much more common to delete only the reviews of a particular user:

```
db.reviews.remove({user_id: ObjectId('4c4b1476238d3b4dd5000001')})
```

Thus, all calls to `remove` take an optional query specifier for selecting exactly which documents to delete. As far as the API goes, that's all there is to say. But you'll have a few questions surrounding the concurrency and atomicity of these operations. I'll explain that in the next section.

6.4.5 Concurrency, atomicity, and isolation

It's important to understand how concurrency works in MongoDB. As of MongoDB v2.0, the locking strategy is rather coarse; a single global reader-writer lock reigns over the entire `mongod` instance. What this means is that at any moment in time, the database permits either one writer or multiple readers (but not both). This sounds a lot worse than it is in practice because there exist quite a few concurrency optimizations around this lock. One is that the database keeps an internal map of which document are in RAM. For requests to read or write documents not residing in RAM, the database yields to other operations until the document can be paged into memory.

A second optimization is the yielding of write locks. The issue is that if any one write takes a long time to complete, all other read and write operations will be blocked for the duration of the original write. All inserts, updates, and removes take a write lock. Inserts rarely take a long time to complete. But updates that affect, say, an entire collection, as well as deletes that affect a lot of documents, can run long. The current solution to this is to allow these long-running ops to yield periodically for other readers and writers. When an operation yields, it pauses itself, releases its lock, and resumes later.[9]

But when updating and removing documents, this yielding behavior can be a mixed blessing. It's easy to imagine situations where you'd want all documents updated or removed before any other operation takes place. For these cases, you can use a special option called `$atomic` to keep the operation from yielding. You simply add the `$atomic` operator to the query selector like so:

```
db.reviews.remove({user_id: ObjectId('4c4b1476238d3b4dd5000001'),
{$atomic: true}})
```

---

[9] Granted, the yielding and resuming generally happen within the space of a few of milliseconds. So we're not necessarily talking about an egregious interruption here.

The same can be applied to any multi-update. This forces the entire multi-update to complete in isolation:

```
db.reviews.update({$atomic: true}, {$set: {rating: 0}}, false, true)
```

This update sets each review's rating to 0. Because the operation happens in isolation, the operation will never yield, ensuring a consistent view of the system at all times.[10]

6.4.6 *Update performance notes*

Experience shows that having a basic mental model of how updates affect a document on disk helps users design systems with better performance. The first thing you should understand is the degree to which an update can be said to happen "in-place." Ideally, an update will affect the smallest portion of a BSON document on disk, as this leads to the greatest efficiency. But this isn't always what happens. Here, I'll explain how this can be so.

There are essentially three kinds of updates to a document on disk. The first, and most efficient, takes place when only a single value is updated and the size of the overall BSON document doesn't change. This most commonly happens with the $inc operator. Because $inc is only incrementing an integer, the size of that value on disk won't change. If the integer represents an int it'll always take up four bytes on disk; long integers and doubles will require eight bytes. But altering the values of these numbers doesn't require any more space and, therefore, only that one value within the document must be rewritten on disk.

The second kind of update changes the size or structure of a document. A BSON document is literally represented as a byte array, and the first four bytes of the document always store the document's size. Thus, if you use the $push operator on a document, you're both increasing the overall document's size and changing its structure. This requires that the entire document be rewritten on disk. This isn't going to be horribly inefficient, but it's worth keeping in mind. If multiple update operators are applied in the same update, then the document must be rewritten once for each operator. Again, this usually isn't a problem, especially if writes are taking place in RAM. But if you have extremely large documents, say around 4 MB, and you're $pushing values onto arrays in those documents, then that's potentially lot of work on the server side.[11]

The final kind of update is a consequence of rewriting a document. If a document is enlarged and can no longer fit in its allocated space on disk, then not only does it need to be rewritten, but it must also be moved to a new space. This moving operation can be potentially expensive if it occurs often. MongoDB attempts to mitigate this by dynamically adjusting a padding factor on a per-collection basis. This means that if, within a given collection, lots of updates are taking place that require documents to be relocated, then the internal padding factor will be increased. The padding factor is

---

[10] Note that if an operation using $atomic fails halfway through, there's no implicit rollback. Half the documents will have been updated while the other half will still have their original value.

[11] It should go without saying that if you intend to do a lot of updates, it's best to keep your documents small.

multiplied by the size of each inserted document to get the amount of extra space to create beyond the document itself. This may reduce the number of future document relocations.

To see a given collection's padding factor, run the collection stats command:

```
db.tweets.stats()
{
  "ns" : "twitter.tweets",
  "count" : 53641,
  "size" : 85794884,
  "avgObjSize" : 1599.4273783113663,
  "storageSize" : 100375552,
  "numExtents" : 12,
  "nindexes" : 3,
  "lastExtentSize" : 21368832,
  "paddingFactor" : 1.2,
  "flags" : 0,
  "totalIndexSize" : 7946240,
  "indexSizes" : {
  "_id_" : 2236416,
  "user.friends_count_1" : 1564672,
  "user.screen_name_1_user.created_at_-1" : 4145152
},
"ok" : 1 }
```

This collection of tweets has a padding factor of 1.2, which indicates that when a 100-byte document is inserted, MongoDB will allocate 120 bytes on disk. The default padding value is 1, which indicates that no extra space will be allocated.

Now, a brief word of warning. The considerations mentioned here apply especially to deployments where the data size exceeds RAM or where an extreme write load is expected. So, if you're building an analytics system for a high-traffic site, take the information here with more than a grain of salt.

6.5   Summary

We've covered a lot in this chapter. The variety of updates may at first feel like a lot to take in, but the power that these updates represent should be reassuring. The fact is that MongoDB's update language is as sophisticated as its query language. You can update a simple document as easily as you can a complex, nested structure. When needed, you can atomically update individual documents and, in combination with findAndModify, build transactional workflows.

If you've finished this chapter and feel like you can apply the examples here on your own, then you're well on your way to becoming a MongoDB guru.

Part 3

MongoDB mastery

Having read the first two parts of the book, you should understand MongoDB quite well from a developer's perspective. Now it's time to switch roles. In this final part of the book, we'll look at MongoDB from the database administrator's perspective. This means we'll cover all the things you need to know about performance, deployments, fault tolerance, and scalability.

To get the best performance from MongoDB, you have to design efficient queries and then ensure that they're properly indexed. This is what you'll learn in chapter 7. You'll see why indexes are important, and you'll learn how they're chosen and then traversed by the query optimizer. You'll also learn how to use helpful tools like the query explainer and the profiler.

Chapter 8 is devoted to replication. You'll spend most of this chapter learning how replica sets work and how to deploy them intelligently for high availability and automatic failover. In addition, you'll learn how to use replication to scale application reads and to customize the durability of writes.

Horizontal scalability is the holy grail for modern database systems; MongoDB scales horizontally by partitioning data in a processes known as *sharding*. Chapter 9 presents sharding theory and practice, showing when to use it, how to design schemas around it, and how to deploy it.

The last chapter describes the niceties of deployment and administration. In chapter 10 we'll look at specific hardware and operating system recommendations. You'll then learn how to back up, monitor, and troubleshoot live MongoDB clusters.

Indexing and query optimization

7

Indexes are enormously important. With the right indexes in place, MongoDB can use its hardware efficiently and serve your application's queries quickly. But having the wrong indexes produces the opposite result: slow queries and poorly utilized hardware. It stands to reason that anyone wanting to use MongoDB effectively must understand indexing.

But for many developers, indexes are a topic shrouded in mystery. This need not be the case. Once you've finished this chapter, you should have a good mental model for thinking clearly about indexes. To introduce the concepts of indexing, we'll begin with a modest thought experiment. We'll then explore some core indexing concepts and provide an overview of the B-tree data structure underlying each MongoDB index.

Then it's on to indexing in practice. We'll discuss unique, sparse, and multikey indexes, and provide a number of pointers on index administration. Next, we'll delve into query optimization, describing how to use `explain()` and work harmoniously with the query optimizer.

7.1   Indexing theory

We'll proceed gradually, beginning with an extended analogy and ending with an exposition of some of MongoDB's key implementation details. Along the way, I'll define and provide examples of a number of important terms. If you're not too familiar with compound-key indexes, virtual memory, and index data structures, then you should find this section eminently edifying.

7.1.1   A thought experiment

To understand indexing, you need a picture in your head. So imagine a cookbook. And not just any cookbook: a massive cookbook, 5,000 pages long with the most delicious recipes for every occasion, cuisine, and season, with all the good ingredients you might find at home. This is the cookbook to end them all. Let's call it The Cookbook Omega.

Although this might be the best of all possible cookbooks, there are two tiny problems with The Cookbook Omega. The first is that the recipes are in random order. On page 3,475 you have Australian Braised Duck, and on page 2 you'll find Zacatecan Tacos.

That would be manageable were it not for the second problem: The Cookbook Omega has no index.

So here's the first question to ask yourself: with no index, how do you find the recipe for Rosemary Potatoes in The Cookbook Omega? Your only choice is to scan through every page of the book until you find the recipe. If the recipe is on page 3,973, that's how many pages you have to look through. In the worst case, where the recipe is on the last page, you have to look at every single page.

That would be madness. The solution is to build an index.

There are several ways you can imagine searching for a recipe, but the recipe's name is probably a good place to start. If you create an alphabetical listing of each recipe name followed by its page number, then you'll have indexed the book by recipe name. A few entries might look like this:

- Tibetan Yak Soufflé: 45
- Toasted Sesame Dumplings: 4,011
- Turkey à la King: 943

As long as you know the name of the recipe (or even the first few letters of that name), you can use this index to quickly find any recipe in the book. If that's the only way you expect to search for recipes, then your work is done.

But this is unrealistic because you can also imagine wanting to find recipes based on, say, the ingredients you have in your pantry. Or perhaps you want to search by cuisine. For those cases, you need more indexes.

So here's a second question. With just one index on the recipe name, how do you find all the chicken recipes? Again, lacking the proper indexes, you'd have to scan the entire book, all 5,000 pages. This is true for any search on ingredients or cuisine.

So you need to build another index, this time on ingredients. In this index, you have an alphabetical listing of ingredients each pointing to all the page numbers of recipes containing that ingredient. The most basic index on ingredients would thus look like this:

- Cashews: 3, 20, 42, 88, 103, 1,215...
- Cauliflower: 2, 47, 88, 89, 90, 275...
- Chicken: 7, 9, 80, 81, 82, 83, 84...
- Currants: 1,001, 1,050, 2,000, 2,133...

Is this the index you thought you were going to get? Is it even helpful?

This index is good if all you need is a list of recipes for a given ingredient. But if you want to include *any* other information about the recipe in your search, you still have some scanning to do—once you know the page numbers where Cauliflower is referenced, you then need to go to each of those pages to get the name of the recipe and what type of cuisine it is. This is better than paging through the whole book, but you can do better.

For example, imagine that you randomly discovered a great chicken recipe in The Cookbook Omega several months ago, but you've forgotten its name. As of now, you have two indexes, one on recipe name and the other on ingredients. Can you think of a way to use these two indexes in combination to find your long-lost chicken recipe?

In fact, this is impossible. If you start with the index on recipe name, but don't remember the name of the recipe, then searching this index is little better than paging through the entire book. If you start with the index on ingredients, then you'll have a list of page numbers to check, but those page numbers can in no way be plugged into the index on recipe name. Therefore, you can only use one index in this case, and it happens that the one on ingredients is more helpful.

ONE INDEX PER QUERY   Users commonly believe that a query on two fields can be resolved using two separate indexes on those fields. An algorithm exists for this: look up the page numbers in each index matching each term, and then scan the union of those pages for the individual recipes matching both terms. A number of pages won't match, but you'll still narrow down the total number of scanned items. Some databases implement this algorithm, but MongoDB doesn't. Even if it did, searching two fields that comprise a compound index will always be more efficient than what I just described. Keep in mind that the database will use a single index per query and that if you're going to be querying on more than one field, ensure that a compound index for those fields exists.

So what to do? Happily, there's a solution to the long-lost chicken recipe, and its answer lies in the use of compound indexes.

The two indexes you've created so far are single-key indexes: they both order just one key from each recipe. You're going to build yet another index for The Cookbook Omega, but this time, instead of using one key per index, you'll use two. Indexes that use more than one key like this are called *compound indexes*.

This compound index uses both ingredients and recipe name, *in that order*. You'll notate the index like this: `ingredient-name`. Part of this index would look like what you see in figure 7.1

The value of this index for a human is obvious. You can now search by ingredient and probably find the recipe you want, even if you only remember the initial part of the name. For a machine, it's still valuable for this use case and will keep the database from having to scan every recipe name listed for that ingredient. This compound index would be especially useful if, as with The Cookbook Omega, there were several hundred (or thousand) chicken recipes. Can you see why?

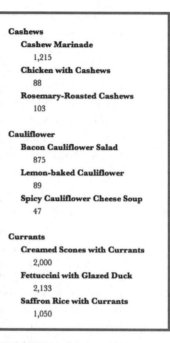

Cashews
    Cashew Marinade
      1,215
    Chicken with Cashews
      88
    Rosemary-Roasted Cashews
      103

Cauliflower
    Bacon Cauliflower Salad
      875
    Lemon-baked Cauliflower
      89
    Spicy Cauliflower Cheese Soup
      47

Currants
    Creamed Scones with Currants
      2,000
    Fettuccini with Glazed Duck
      2,133
    Saffron Rice with Currants
      1,050

Figure 7.1 A compound index inside a cookbook

One thing to notice: with compound indexes, order matters. Imagine the reverse compound index on `name-ingredient`. Would this index be interchangeable with the compound index we just explored?

Definitely not. With the new index, once you have the recipe name, your search is already limited to a single recipe, a single page in your cookbook. So if this index were used on a search for the recipe Cashew Marinade and the ingredient Bananas, then the index could confirm that no such recipe exists. But this use case is the opposite one: you know the ingredient, but not the recipe name.

The cookbook now has three indexes: one on `recipe` name, one on `ingredient`, and one on `ingredient-name`. This means that you can safely eliminate the single-key index on `ingredient`. Why? Because a search on a single ingredient can use the index on `ingredient-name`. That is, if you know the ingredient, you can traverse this compound index to get a list of all page numbers containing said ingredient. Look again at the sample entries for this index to see why this is so.

The goal of this section was to present an extended metaphor for readers who need a better mental model of indexes. From this metaphor, you can derive a few simple rules of thumb:

1 Indexes significantly reduce the amount of work required to fetch documents. Without the proper indexes, the only way to satisfy a query is to scan all documents linearly until the query conditions are met. This frequently means scanning entire collections.

2 Only one single-key index will be used to resolve a query.[1] For queries containing multiple keys (say, ingredient and recipe name), a compound index containing those keys will best resolve the query.

3 An index on `ingredients` can and should be eliminated if you have a second index on `ingredient-cuisine`. More generally, if you have a compound index on `a-b`, then a second index on `a` alone will be redundant.[2]

4 The order of keys in a compound index matters.

Bear in mind that this cookbook analogy can be taken only so far. It's a model for understanding indexes, but it doesn't fully correspond to the way MongoDB's indexes work. In the next section, we'll elaborate on the rules of thumb just presented, and we'll explore indexing in MongoDB in detail.

7.1.2 Core indexing concepts

The preceding thought experiment hinted at a number of core indexing concepts. Here and throughout the rest of the chapter, we'll unpack those ideas.

SINGLE-KEY INDEXES

With a single-key index, each entry in the index corresponds to a single value from each of the documents indexed. The default index on _id is a good example of a single-key index. Because this field is indexed, each document's _id also lives in an index for fast retrieval by that field.

COMPOUND-KEY INDEXES

For the moment, MongoDB uses one index per query.[3] But you often need to query on more than one attribute, and you want such a query to be as efficient as possible. For example, imagine that you've built two indexes on the *products* collection from this book's e-commerce example: one index on `manufacturer` and another on `price`. In this case, you've created two entirely distinct data structures that, when traversed, are ordered like the lists you see in figure 7.2.

Now, imagine your query looks like this:

```
db.products.find({'details.manufacturer': 'Acme',
                  'pricing.sale': {$lt: 7500}})
```

This query says to find all Acme products costing less than $75.00. If you issue this query with single-key indexes on manufacturer and price, only one of these will be

---

[1] The one exception is queries using the $or operator. But as a general rule, this isn't possible, or even desirable, in MongoDB.

[2] There are exceptions. If b is a multikey index, it may make sense to have indexes on both a-b and a.

[3] There are rare exceptions to this rule. For instance, queries with $or may use a different index for each clause of the $or query. But each individual clause by itself still uses just one index.

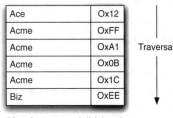

Ace	Ox12
Acme	OxFF
Acme	OxA1
Acme	Ox0B
Acme	Ox1C
Biz	OxEE

Traversal

7999	OxFF
7500	Ox12
7500	OxEE
7500	OxA1
7499	Ox0B
7499	Ox1C

Manufacturers and disk locations   Sale prices and disk locations

Figure 7.2 Single-key index traversal

used. The query optimizer will pick the more efficient of the two, but neither will give you an ideal result. To satisfy the query using these indexes, you'd have to traverse each structure separately and then grab the list of disk locations that match and calculate their union. MongoDB doesn't support this right now, in part because using a compound index for this case is so much more efficient.

A compound index is a single index where each entry is composed of more than one key. If you were to build a *compound-key* index on manufacturer and price, the ordered representation would look like what you see in figure 7.3.

In order to fulfill your query, the query optimizer only need find the first entry in the index where manufacturer is Acme and price is $75.00. From there, the results can be retrieved with a simple scan of the successive index entries, stopping when the value of *manufacturer* no longer equals *Acme*.

There are two things you should notice about the way this index and query work together. The first is that the order of the index's keys matters. If you had declared a compound index where price was the first key and manufacturer the second, then your query would've been far less efficient. Hard to see why? Take a look at the structure of the entries in such an index in figure 7.4.

Keys must be compared in the order in which they appear. Unfortunately, this index doesn't provide an easy way to jump to all the Acme products. So the only way to fulfill your query would be to look at *every* product whose price is less than $75.00 and then select only those products made by Acme. To put this in perspective, imagine that your collection had a million products, all priced under $100.00 and evenly distributed by price. Under these circumstances, fulfilling your query would require that you scan 750,000 index entries. By contrast, using the original compound index,

Ace - 8000	Ox12
Acme - 7999	OxFF
Acme - 7500	OxA1
Acme - 7499	Ox0B
Acme - 7499	Ox1C
Biz - 8999	OxEE

Traversal

7999 - Acme	OxFF
7500 - Ace	OxEE
7500 - Acme	Ox12
7500 - Biz	OxA1
7499 - Acme	Ox0B
7499 - Acme	Ox1C

Traversal

Manufacturers and prices, with disk locations   Prices and manufacturers, with disk locations

Figure 7.3 Compound-key index traversal   **Figure 7.4 A compound-key index with the keys reversed**

where manufacturer precedes price, the number of entries scanned would be the same as the number of entries returned. This is because once you've arrived at the entry for (Acme - 7500), it's a simple, in-order scan to serve the query.

So the order of keys in a compound index matters. If that seems clear, then the second thing you should understand is why we've chosen the first ordering over the second. This may be obvious from the diagrams, but there's another way to look at the problem. Look again at the query: the two query terms specify different kinds of matches. On manufacturer, you want to match the term exactly. But on price, you want to match a range of values, beginning with 7500. As a general rule, a query where one term demands an exact match and another specifies a range requires a compound index where the range key comes second. We'll revisit this idea in the section on query optimization.

INDEX EFFICIENCY

Although indexes are essential for good query performance, each new index imposes a small maintenance cost. It should be easy to see why. Whenever you add a document to a collection, each index on that collection must be modified to include the new document. So if a particular collection has 10 indexes, then that makes 10 separate structures to modify on each insert. This holds for any write operation, whether you're removing a document or updating a given document's indexed keys.

For read-intensive applications, the cost of indexes is almost always justified. Just realize that indexes do impose a cost and that they therefore must be chosen with care. This means ensuring that all of your indexes are used and that none of them are redundant. You can do this in part by profiling your application's queries, and I'll describe this process later in the chapter.

But there's a second consideration here. Even with all the right indexes in place, it's still possible that those indexes won't result in faster queries. This occurs when indexes and a working data set don't fit in RAM.

You may recall from chapter 1 that MongoDB tells the operating system to map all data files to memory using the mmap() system call. From this point on, the data files, which include all documents, collections, and their indexes, are swapped in and out of RAM by the operating system in 4 KB chunks called *pages*.[4] Whenever data from a given page is requested, the operating system must ensure that the page is available in RAM. If it's not, then a kind of exception known as a *page fault* is raised, and this tells the memory manager to load the page from disk into RAM.

With sufficient RAM, all of the data files in use will eventually be loaded into memory. Whenever that memory is altered, as in the case of a write, those changes will be flushed to disk asynchronously by the OS, but the write will be fast, occurring directly in RAM. When data fits into RAM, you have the ideal situation because the number of disk accesses is reduced to a minimum. But if the working data set can't fit into RAM, then page faults will start to creep up. This means that the operating system will be

---

[4] The 4 KB page size is standard but not universal.

going to disk frequently, greatly slowing read and write operations. In the worst case, as data size becomes much larger than available RAM, a situation can occur where, for any read or write, data must be paged *to and from* disk. This is known as *thrashing*, and it causes performance to take a severe dive.

Fortunately, this situation is relatively easy to avoid. At minimum, you need to make sure that your indexes will fit in RAM. This is one reason why it's important to avoid creating any unneeded indexes. With extra indexes in place, more RAM will be required to maintain those indexes. Along the same lines, each index should have only the keys it needs: a triple-key compound index might be necessary at times, but be aware that it'll use more space than a simple single-key index.

Ideally, indexes *and* a working data set fit in RAM. But estimating how much RAM this requires for any given deployment isn't always easy. You can always discover total index size by looking at the results of the `stats` command. But finding out working set size is less clear-cut because it's different for every application. The *working set* is the subset of total data commonly queried and updated. For instance, suppose you have a million users. If only half of them are active, then your working set for the user collection is half the total data size. If all users are active, then the working set is equal to the entire data set.

In chapter 10, we'll revisit the concept of the working set, and we'll look at specific ways to diagnose hardware-related performance issues. For now, be aware of the potential costs of adding new indexes, and keep an eye on the ratio of index and working set size to RAM. Doing so will help you to maintain good performance as your data grows.

7.1.3   *B-trees*

As mentioned, MongoDB represents indexes internally as *B-trees*. B-trees are ubiquitous (see http://mng.bz/wQfG), having remained in popular use for database records and indexes since at least the late 1970s.[5] If you've used other database systems, then you may already be familiar with the various consequences of using B-trees. This is good because it means you can effectively transfer most of your knowledge of indexing. If you *don't* know much about B-trees, that's okay, too; this section will present the concepts most relevant to your work with MongoDB.

B-trees have two overarching traits that make them ideal for database indexes. First, they facilitate a variety of queries, including exact matches, range conditions, sorting, prefix matching, and index-only queries. Second, they're able to remain balanced in spite of the addition and removal of keys.

We'll look at a simple representation of a B-tree and then discuss some principles that you'll want to keep in mind. So imagine that you have a collection of users and that you've created a compound index on last name and age.[6] An abstract representation of the resulting B-tree might look something like figure 7.5.

---

[5]   MongoDB uses B-trees for its indexes only; collections are stored as doubly-linked lists.

[6]   Indexing on last name and age is a bit contrived, but it nicely illustrates the concepts.

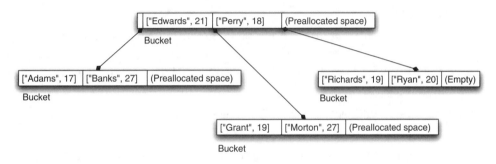

Figure 7.5 Sample B-tree structure

A B-tree, as you might guess, is a tree-like data structure. Each node in the tree can contain multiple keys. You can see in the example that the root node contains two keys, each of which is in the form of a BSON object representing an indexed value from the users collection. So in reading the contents of the root node, you can see the keys for two documents, indicating last names Edwards and Perry, with ages of 21 and 18, respectively. Each of these keys includes two pointers: one to the data file it belongs to and another to the child node. Additionally, the node itself points to another node with values less than the node's smallest value.

One thing to notice is that each node has some empty space (not to scale). In MongoDB's B-tree implementation, a new node is allocated 8,192 bytes, which means that in practice, each node may contain hundreds of keys. This depends on the average index key size; in this case, that average key size might be around 30 bytes. The maximum key size in MongoDB v2.0 is 1024 bytes. Add to this a per-key overhead of 18 bytes and a per-node overhead of 40 bytes, and this results in about 170 keys per node.[7]

This is relevant because users frequently want to know why index sizes are what they are. So you now know that each node is 8 KB, and you can estimate how many keys will fit into each node. To calculate this, keep in mind that B-tree nodes are usually intentionally kept around 60% full by default.

If the preceding made sense, then in addition to gaining a superficial mental model of B-trees, you should walk away with some ideas about how they use space and how they're maintained: a couple more reminders that indexes aren't free. Choose them carefully.

7.2 *Indexing in practice*

With most of the theory behind us, we'll now look at some refinements on our concept of indexing in MongoDB. We'll then proceed to some of the niceties of index administration.

---

[7] (8192 - 40) / (30 + 18) = 169.8

7.2.1   *Index types*

All indexes in MongoDB use the same underlying data structure, but indexes with a variety of properties are nevertheless permitted. In particular, unique, sparse, and multikey indexes are frequently used, and here I describe them in some detail.[8]

UNIQUE INDEXES

To create a unique index, specify the `unique` option:

```
db.users.ensureIndex({username: 1}, {unique: true})
```

Unique indexes enforce uniqueness across all their entries. Thus if you try to insert a document into this book's sample application's `users` collection with an already-indexed username value, then the insert will fail with the following exception:

```
E11000 duplicate key error index:
  gardening.users.$username_1  dup key: { : "kbanker" }
```

If using a driver, this exception will be caught only if you perform the insert using your driver's safe mode. See chapter 3 for a discussion of this.

If you need a unique index on a collection, it's usually best to create the index before inserting any data. If you create the index in advance, you guarantee the uniqueness constraint from the start. When creating a unique index on a collection that already contains data, you run the risk of failure since it's possible that duplicate keys may already exist in the collection. When duplicate keys exist, the index creation fails.

If you do find yourself needing to create a unique index on an established collection, you have a couple of options. The first is to repeatedly attempt to create the unique index and use the failure messages to manually remove the documents with duplicate keys. But if the data isn't so important, you can also instruct the database to drop documents with duplicate keys automatically using the `dropDups` option. To take an example, if your `users` collection already contains data, and if you don't care that documents with duplicate keys are removed, then you can issue the index creation command like this:

```
db.users.ensureIndex({username: 1}, {unique: true, dropDups: true})
```

Note that the choice of duplicate key documents to be preserved is arbitrary, so use this feature with extreme care.

SPARSE INDEXES

Indexes are dense by default. This means that for every document in an indexed collection, there will be a corresponding entry in the index even if the document lacks the indexed key. For example, recall the products collection from your e-commerce data model, and imagine that you've built an index on the product attribute `category_ids`. Now suppose that a few products haven't been assigned to any categories. For each of these categoryless products, there will still exist a null entry in the `category_ids` index. You can query for those null values like so:

---

[8]   Note that MongoDB also supports spatial indexes, but because they're so specialized, I explain them separately in appendix E.

```
db.products.find({category_ids: null})
```

Here, when searching for all products lacking a category, the query optimizer will still be able to use the index on `category_ids` to locate the corresponding products.

But there are two cases where a dense index is undesirable. The first is when you want a unique index on a field that doesn't appear in every document in the collection. For instance, you definitely want a unique index on every product's `sku` field. But suppose that, for some reason, products are entered into the system before a `sku` is assigned. If you have a unique index on `sku` and attempt to insert more than one product without a `sku`, then the first insert will succeed, but all subsequent inserts will fail because there will already be an entry in the index where `sku` is null. This is a case where a dense index doesn't serve your purpose. What you want instead is a *sparse index*.

In a sparse index, only those documents having some value for the indexed key will appear. If you want to create a sparse index, all you have to do is specify `{sparse: true}`. So for example, you can create a unique, sparse index on `sku` like so:

```
db.products.ensureIndex({sku: 1}, {unique: true, sparse: true})
```

There's another case where a sparse index is desirable: when a large number of documents in a collection don't contain the indexed key. For example, suppose you allowed anonymous reviews on your e-commerce site. In this case, half the reviews might lack a `user_id` field, and if that field were indexed, then half the entries in that index would be null. This would be inefficient for two reasons. First, it would increase the size of the index. Second, it would require updates to the index when adding and removing documents with null `user_id` fields.

If you rarely (or never) expect queries on anonymous reviews, you might elect to build a sparse index on `user_id`. Here again, setting the `sparse` option is simple:

```
db.reviews.ensureIndex({user_id: 1}, {sparse: true})
```

Now, only those reviews linked to a user via the `user_id` field will be indexed.

MULTIKEY INDEXES

You've seen in earlier chapters several examples of indexing fields whose values are arrays.[9] This is made possible by what's known as a *multikey index*, which allows multiple entries in the index to reference the same document. This makes sense if we take a simple example. Suppose you have a product document with a few tags like this:

```
{ name: "Wheelbarrow",
  tags: ["tools", "gardening", "soil"]
}
```

If you create an index on `tags`, then each value in this document's tags array will appear in the index. This means that a query on any one of these array values can use the index to locate the document. This is the idea behind a multikey index: multiple index entries, or keys, end up referencing the same document.

---

[9] Think of category IDs, for instance.

Multikey indexes are always enabled in MongoDB. Anytime an indexed field contains an array, each array value will be given its own entry in the index.

The intelligent use of multikey indexes is essential to proper MongoDB schema design. This should be evident from the examples presented in chapters 4 through 6; several more examples are provided in the design patterns section of appendix B.

7.2.2 Index administration

When it comes to administering indexes in MongoDB, there may be some gaps in your operational knowledge. Here we'll see index creation and deletion in detail and address questions surrounding compaction and backups.

CREATING AND DELETING INDEXES

By now you've created quite a few indexes, so there should be no mysteries surrounding the index creation syntax. Simply call one of the index creation helper methods, either in the shell or with your language of choice, and a document defining the new index will be placed into the special `system.indexes` collection.

Though it's usually easier to use a helper method to create an index, you can also insert an index specification manually (this is what the helper methods do). You just need to be sure you've specified the minimum set of keys: ns, key, and name. ns is the namespace, key is the field or combination of fields to index, and name is a name used to refer to the index. Any additional options, like sparse, can also be specified here. So for example, let's create a sparse index on the users collection:

```
spec = {ns: "green.users", key: {'addresses.zip': 1}, name: 'zip'}
db.system.indexes.insert(spec, true)
```

If no errors are returned on insert, then the index now exists, and you can query the `system.indexes` collection to prove it

```
db.system.indexes.find()
{ "_id" : ObjectId("4d2205c4051f853d46447e95"), "ns" : "green.users",
  "key" : { "addresses.zip" : 1 }, "name" : "zip", "v" : 1 }
```

If you're running MongoDB v2.0 or later, you'll see that an extra key, v, has been added. This version field allows for future changes in the internal index format but should be of little concern to application developers.

To delete an index, you might think that all you need to do is remove the index document from `system.indexes`, but this operation is prohibited. Instead, you must delete indexes using the database command `deleteIndexes`. As with index creation, there are helpers for deleting indexes, but if you want to run the command itself, you can do that too. The command takes as its argument a document containing the collection name and either the name of the index to drop or * to drop all indexes. To manually drop the index you just created, issue the command like so:

```
use green
db.runCommand({deleteIndexes: "users", index: "zip"})
```

In most cases, you'll simply use the shell's helpers to create and drop indexes:

```
use green
db.users.ensureIndex({zip: 1})
```

You can then check the index specifications with the getIndexSpecs() method:

```
> db.users.getIndexSpecs()
[
    {
        "v" : 1,
        "key" : {
            "_id" : 1
        },
        "ns" : "green.users",
        "name" : "_id_"
    },
    {
        "v" : 1,
        "key" : {
            "zip" : 1
        },
        "ns" : "green.users",
        "name" : "zip_1"
    }
]
```

Finally, you can drop the index using the dropIndex() method. Note that you must supply the index's name as specified in the spec:

```
use green
db.users.dropIndex("zip_1")
```

Those are the basics of creating and deleting indexes. For what to expect when an index is created, read on.

BUILDING INDEXES

Most of the time, you'll want to declare your indexes before putting your application into production. This allows indexes to be built incrementally, as the data is inserted. But there are two cases where you might choose to build an index after the fact. The first case occurs when you need to import a lot of data before switching into production. For instance, you might be migrating an application to MongoDB and need to seed the database with user information from a data warehouse. You could create the indexes on your user data in advance, but doing so after you've imported the data will ensure an ideally balanced and compacted index from the start. This will also minimize the net time to build the index.

The second (and more obvious) case for creating indexes on existing data sets is when you have to optimize for new queries.

Regardless of why you're creating new indexes, the process isn't always pleasing. For large data sets, building an index can take hours, even days. But you can monitor the progress of an index build from the MongoDB logs. Let's take an example from a data set that we'll use in the next section. First, you declare an index to be built:

```
db.values.ensureIndex({open: 1, close: 1})
```

BE CAREFUL DECLARING INDEXES   Because it's so easy to declare indexes, it's also easy to inadvertently trigger an index build. If the data set is large enough, then the build will take a long time. And in a production situation, this can be a nightmare since there's no easy way to kill an index build. If this ever happens to you, you'll have to fail over to a secondary node—if you have one. But the most prudent advice is to treat an index build as a kind of database migration, and ensure that your application code never declares indexes automatically.

The index builds in two steps. In the first step, the values to be indexed are sorted. A sorted data set makes for a much more efficient insertion into the B-tree. Note that the progress of the sort is indicated by the ratio of the number of documents sorted to the total number of documents:

```
[conn1] building new index on { open: 1.0, close: 1.0 } for stocks.values
     1000000/4308303   23%
     2000000/4308303   46%
     3000000/4308303   69%
     4000000/4308303   92%
     Tue Jan  4 09:59:13 [conn1]    external sort used : 5 files  in 55 secs
```

For step two, the sorted values are inserted into the index. Progress is indicated in the same way, and when complete, the time it took to complete the index build is indicated as the insert time into `system.indexes`:

```
1200300/4308303   27%
    2227900/4308303   51%
    2837100/4308303   65%
    3278100/4308303   76%
    3783300/4308303   87%
    4075500/4308303   94%
Tue Jan  4 10:00:16 [conn1] done building bottom layer, going to commit
Tue Jan  4 10:00:16 [conn1] done for 4308303 records 118.942secs
Tue Jan  4 10:00:16 [conn1] insert stocks.system.indexes 118942ms
```

In addition to examining the MongoDB log, you can check the index build progress by running the shell's `currentOp()` method:[10]

```
> db.currentOp()
{
  "inprog" : [
    {
      "opid" : 58,
      "active" : true,
      "lockType" : "write",
      "waitingForLock" : false,
      "secs_running" : 55,
      "op" : "insert",
      "ns" : "stocks.system.indexes",
```

---

[10] Note that if you've started the index build from the MongoDB shell, you'll have to open a new instance of the shell to run `currentOp` concurrently. For more about `db.currentOp()`, see chapter 10.

```
    "query" : {
    },
    "client" : "127.0.0.1:53421",
    "desc" : "conn",
    "msg" : "index: (1/3) external sort 3999999/4308303 92%"
  }
 ]
}
```

The last field, msg, describes the build's progress. Note also the lockType, which indicates that the index build takes a write lock. This means that no other client can read or write from the database at this time. If you're running in production, this is obviously a bad thing, and it's the reason why long index builds can be so vexing. We're going to look right now at two possible solutions to this problem.

Background indexing

If you're running in production and can't afford to halt access to the database, you can specify that an index be built in the background. Although the index build will still take a write lock, the job will yield to allow other readers and writers to access the database. If your application typically exerts a heavy load on MongoDB, then a background index build will degrade performance, but this may be acceptable under certain circumstances. For example, if you know that the index can be built within a time window where application traffic is at a minimum, then background indexing in this case might be a good choice.

To build an index in the background, specify {background: true} when you declare the index. The previous index can be built in the background like so:

```
db.values.ensureIndex({open: 1, close: 1}, {background: true})
```

Offline indexing

If your production data set is too large to be indexed within a few hours, then you'll need to make alternate plans. This will usually involve taking a replica node offline, building the index on that node by itself, and then allowing the node to catch up with the master replica. Once it's caught up, you can promote the node to primary and then take another secondary offline and build *its* version of the index. This tactic presumes that your replication oplog is large enough to prevent the offline node from becoming stale during the index build. The next chapter covers replication in detail and should help you plan for a migration such as this.

BACKUPS

Because indexes are hard to build, you may want to back them up. Unfortunately, not all backup methods include indexes. For instance, you might be tempted to use mongodump and mongorestore, but these utilities preserve collections and index declarations only. This means that when you run mongorestore, all the indexes declared for any collections you've backed up will be re-created. As always, if your data set is large, the time it takes to build these indexes may be unacceptable.

Consequently, if you want your backups to include indexes, then you'll want to opt for backing up the MongoDB data files themselves. More details about this, and general instructions for backups, can be found in chapter 10.

COMPACTION

If your application heavily updates existing data, or performs a lot of large deletions, then you may end up with a highly fragmented index. B-trees will coalesce on their own somewhat, but this isn't always sufficient to offset a high delete volume. The primary symptom of a fragmented index is an index size much larger than you'd expect for the given data size. This fragmented state can result in indexes using more RAM than necessary. In these cases, you may want to consider rebuilding one or more indexes. You can do this by dropping and recreating individual indexes or by running the reIndex command, which will rebuild all indexes for a given collection:

```
db.values.reIndex();
```

Be careful about reindexing: the command will take out a write lock for the duration of the rebuild, temporarily rendering your MongoDB instance unusable. Reindexing is best done offline, as described earlier for building indexes on a secondary. Note that the compact command, discussed in chapter 10, will also rebuild indexes for the collection on which it's run.

7.3   Query optimization

Query optimization is the process of identifying slow queries, discovering why they're slow, and then taking steps to speed them up. In this section, we'll look at each step of the query optimization process in turn so that by the time you finish reading, you'll have a framework for addressing problematic queries on any MongoDB installation.

Before diving in, I must warn that the techniques presented here can't be used to solve *every* query performance problem. The causes of slow queries vary too much. Poor application design, inappropriate data models, and insufficient physical hardware are all common culprits, and their remedies require a significant time investment. Here we'll look at ways to optimize queries by restructuring the queries themselves and by building the most useful indexes. I'll also describe other avenues for investigation when these techniques fail to deliver.

7.3.1   Identifying slow queries

If your MongoDB-based application feels sluggish, then it's past time to start profiling your queries. Any disciplined approach to application design should include a query audit; given how easy MongoDB makes this there's no excuse. Though the requirements will vary per application, it's safe to assume that for most apps, queries shouldn't take much longer than 100 milliseconds. The MongoDB logger has this assumption ingrained, since it prints a warning whenever any operation, including a query, takes more than 100 ms. The logs, therefore, are the first place you should look for slow queries.

It's unlikely that any of the data sets we've worked with up until now have been large enough to generate queries lasting longer than 100 ms. So for the following examples, we'll use a data set consisting of daily NASDAQ summaries. If you want to follow along, you'll want to have this data locally. To import it, first download the archive from http://mng.bz/ii49. Then unzip the file to a temporary folder. You'll see the following output:

```
$ unzip stocks.zip
Archive:  stocks.zip
   creating: dump/stocks/
  inflating: dump/stocks/system.indexes.bson
  inflating: dump/stocks/values.bson
```

Finally, restore the dump like so:

```
$ mongorestore -d stocks -c values dump/stocks
```

The stocks data set is large and easy to work with. For a certain subset of the NASDAQ stock exchange's symbols, there exists a document for each day's high, low, close, and volume for a 25-year period beginning in 1983. Given the number and size of the documents in this collection, it's easy to generate one of the log warnings. Try querying for the first occurrence of Google's stock price:

```
db.values.find({"stock_symbol": "GOOG"}).sort({date: -1}).limit(1)
```

You'll notice that this takes some time to run. And if you check the MongoDB log, you'll see the expected slow query warning. Here's a sample of the output to expect:

```
Thu Nov 16 09:40:26 [conn1] query stocks.values
          ntoreturn:1 scanAndOrder reslen:210 nscanned:4308303
          { query: { stock_symbol: "GOOG" }, orderby: { date: -1.0 } }
          nreturned:1 4011ms
```

There's a lot of information here, and we'll go over the meaning of all of it when we discuss explain(). For now, if you read the message carefully, you should be able to extract the most important parts: that it's a query on stocks.values; that the query selector consists of a match on stock_symbol and that a sort is being performed; maybe most significantly, that the query takes a whopping 4 seconds (4011ms).

Warnings like this must be addressed. They're so critical that it's worth your while to occasionally cull them from your MongoDB logs. This can be accomplished easily with grep:

```
grep -E '([0-9])+ms' mongod.log
```

If 100 ms is too high a threshold, you can lower it with the --slowms server option. If you define slow as taking longer than 50 ms, then start mongod with --slowms 50.

Of course, grepping logs isn't very systematic. You can use the MongoDB logs to check for slow queries, but the procedure is rather coarse, and should be reserved as a kind of sanity check in a staging or production environment. To identity slow queries before they become a problem, you want a precision tool. MongoDB's built-in query profiler is exactly that.

USING THE PROFILER

For identifying slow queries, you can't beat the built-in profiler. Profiling is disabled by default, so let's get started by enabling it. From the MongoDB shell, enter the following:

```
use stocks
db.setProfilingLevel(2)
```

First you select the database you want to profile; profiling is always scoped to a particular database. Then you set the profiling level to 2. This is the most verbose level; it directs the profiler to log every read and write. A couple other options are available. To log only slow (100 ms) operations, set the profiling level to 1. To disable the query profiler altogether, set it to 0. And to log only operations taking longer than a certain threshold in milliseconds, pass the number of milliseconds as the second argument like this:

```
use stocks
db.setProfilingLevel(1, 50)
```

Once you've enabled the profiler, it's time to issue some queries. Let's run another query on the stocks database. Try finding the highest closing price in the data set:

```
db.values.find({}).sort({close: -1}).limit(1)
```

The profiling results are stored in a special capped collection called system.profile. Recall that capped collections are fixed in size and that data is written to them in a circular way so that once the collection reaches its max size, new documents overwrite the oldest documents. The system.profile collection is allocated 128 KB, thus ensuring that the profile data never consumes much in the way of resources.

You can query system.profile as you would any capped collection. For instance, you can find all queries that took longer than 150 ms like so:

```
db.system.profile.find({millis: {$gt: 150}})
```

And because capped collections maintain natural insertion order, you can use the $natural operator to sort so that the most recent results are displayed first:

```
db.system.profile.find().sort({$natural: -1}).limit(5)
```

Returning to the query you just issued, you should see an entry in the result set that looks something like this:

```
{ "ts" : ISODate("2011-09-22T22:42:38.332Z"),
"op" : "query", "ns" : "stocks.values",
"query" : { "query" : { }, "orderby" : { "close" : -1 } },
"ntoreturn" : 1, "nscanned" : 4308303, "scanAndOrder" : true,
"nreturned" : 1, "responseLength" : 194, "millis" : 14576,
"client" : "127.0.0.1", "user" : "" }
```

Another expensive query: this one took nearly 15 seconds! In addition to the time it took to complete, you get all same information about the query that you saw in the MongoDB log's slow query warning, which is enough to start the deeper investigation that we'll cover in the next section.

But before moving on, a few more words about profiling strategy are in order. A good way to use the profiler is to start it with a coarse setting and work downward. First ensure that no queries take longer than 100 ms, then move down to 75 ms, and so on. While the profiler is enabled, you'll want to put your application through its paces. At a minimum, this means ensuring that every read and write is performed. But to be thorough, those reads and writes must be executed under real conditions, where the data sizes, query load, and hardware are representative of the application's production environment.

The query profiler is useful, but to get the most out of it, you need to be methodical. Better to be surprised with a few slow queries in development than in production, where the remedies are much more costly.

7.3.2 Examining slow queries

With MongoDB's profiler, finding slow queries is easy. Discovering *why* these queries are slow is trickier because the process may require some detective work. As mentioned, the causes of slow queries are manifold. If you're lucky, then resolving a slow query may be as easy as adding an index. In more difficult cases, you might have to rearrange indexes, restructure the data model, or upgrade hardware. But you should always look at the simplest case first, and that's what you're going to do here.

In the simplest case, a lack of indexes, inappropriate indexes, or less-than-ideal queries will be the root of the problem. You can find out for sure by running an *explain* on the offending queries. Let's explore how to do that now.

USING AND UNDERSTANDING EXPLAIN()

MongoDB's explain command provides detailed information about a given query's path.[11] Let's dive right in and see what information can be gleaned from running an explain on the last query you ran in the previous section. To run explain from the shell, you need only attach the explain() method call:

```
db.values.find({}).sort({close: -1}).limit(1).explain()
{
  "cursor" : "BasicCursor",
  "nscanned" : 4308303,
  "nscannedObjects" : 4308303,
  "n" : 1,
  "scanAndOrder" : true,
  "millis" : 14576,
  "nYields" : 0,
  "nChunkSkips" : 0,
  "indexBounds" : { }
}
```

The millis field indicates that this query takes more than 14 seconds, and there's an obvious reason for this. Look at the nscanned value: this shows that the query

---

[11] You may recall that I introduced explain in chapter 2, but only briefly. Here I'll provide a complete treatment of the command and its output.

engine had to scan 4,308,303 documents to fulfill the query. Now, quickly run a count on the *values* collection:

```
db.values.count()
4308303
```

The number of documents scanned is the same as the total number of documents in the collection. So you've performed a complete collection scan. If your query were expected to return every document in the collection, then this wouldn't be a bad thing. But since you're returning one document, as indicated by the explain value n, this *is* problematic. Generally speaking, you want the values of n and nscanned to be as close together as possible. When doing a collection scan, this is almost never the case. The cursor field tells you that you've been using a BasicCursor, which only confirms that you're scanning the collection itself and not an index.

A second datum here further explains the slowness of the query: the scanAndOrder field. This indicator appears when the query optimizer can't use an index to return a sorted result set. Therefore, in this case, not only does the query engine have to scan the collection, it also has to sort the result set manually.

The poor performance is unacceptable, but fortunately the fix is simple. All you need to do is build an index on the close field. Go ahead and do that now and then reissue the query:[12]

```
db.values.ensureIndex({close: 1})
db.values.find({}).sort({close: -1}).limit(1).explain()
{
  "cursor" : "BtreeCursor close_1 reverse",
  "nscanned" : 1,
  "nscannedObjects" : 1,
  "n" : 1,
  "millis" : 0,
  "nYields" : 0,
  "nChunkSkips" : 0,
  "indexBounds" : {
    "close" : [
      [
        {
          "$maxElement" : 1
        },
        {
          "$minElement" : 1
        }
      ]
    ]
  }
}
```

What a difference! The query now takes less than a millisecond to process. You can see from the cursor field that you're using a BtreeCursor on the index named *close_1*

---

[12] Note that building the index may take a few minutes.

and that you're iterating over the index in reverse order. In the indexBounds field, you see the special values $maxElement and $minElement. These indicate that the query spans the entire index. So in this case, the query optimizer walks the rightmost edge of the B-tree until it reaches the maximum key and then works its way backward. Since you've specified a limit of 1, the query is complete once the max element is found. And of course, since the index keeps the entries in order, there's no longer a need for the manual sort indicated by scanAndOrder.

You'll see slightly different output if you use the indexed key in your query selector. Take a look at the explain plan for a query selecting closing values greater than 500:

```
> db.values.find({close: {$gt: 500}}).explain()
{
  "cursor" : "BtreeCursor close_1",
  "nscanned" : 309,
  "nscannedObjects" : 309,
  "n" : 309,
  "millis" : 5,
  "nYields" : 0,
  "nChunkSkips" : 0,
  "indexBounds" : {
    "close" : [
      [
        500,
        1.7976931348623157e+308
      ]
    ]
  }
}
```

You're still scanning the same number of documents that you're returning (n and nscanned are the same), which is ideal. But note the difference in the way the index boundaries are specified. Instead of the $maxElement and $minElement keys, the boundaries are actual values. The lower bound is 500 and the upper bound is effectively infinite. These values must share the same class of data type that you're querying on; since you're querying on a number, the index bounds are numeric. If you were to query on a string range instead, then the boundaries would be strings. [13]

Before continuing on, try running explain() on a few queries of your own, and pay attention to the difference between n and nscanned.

MONGODB'S QUERY OPTIMIZER AND HINT()

The query optimizer is the piece of software that determines which index, if any, will most efficiently serve a given query. To select an ideal index for your queries, the query optimizer uses a fairly simple set of rules:

1 Avoid scanAndOrder. If the query includes a sort, attempt to sort using an index.

---

[13] If this isn't making any sense, recall that a given index can contain keys of multiple data types. Thus, query results will always be limited by the data type used in the query.

2 Satisfy all fields with useful indexing constraints—attempt to use indexes for the fields in the query selector.

3 If the query implies a range or includes a sort, then choose an index where that last key used can help satisfy the range or sort.

If all of these conditions can be met for any one index, then that index will be considered optimal and will be used. If more than one index qualifies as optimal, then one of the optimal indexes will be chosen arbitrarily. There's a lesson here: if you can build optimal indexes for your queries, you make the query optimizer's job a lot easier. Strive for that if you can.

Let's look at a query that satisfies an index (and the query optimizer) perfectly. Go back to the stock symbol data set. Now imagine you want to issue the following query, which fetches all of Google's closing values greater than 200:

```
db.values.find({stock_symbol: "GOOG", close: {$gt: 200}})
```

The optimal index for this query includes both keys but places the `close` key last to allow for the range query:

```
db.values.ensureIndex({stock_symbol: 1, close: 1})
```

You'll see that if you run the query, both keys are used, and the index bounds are as expected:

```
db.values.find({stock_symbol: "GOOG", close: {$gt: 200}}).explain()
{
  "cursor" : "BtreeCursor stock_symbol_1_close_1",
  "nscanned" : 730,
  "nscannedObjects" : 730,
  "n" : 730,
  "millis" : 1,
  "nYields" : 0,
  "nChunkSkips" : 0,
  "isMultiKey" : false,
  "indexOnly" : false,
  "indexBounds" : {
    "stock_symbol" : [
      [
        "GOOG",
        "GOOG"
      ]
    ],
    "close" : [
      [
        200,
        1.7976931348623157e+308
      ]
    ]
  }
}
>
```

This is the optimal `explain` output for this query: the values of n and nscanned are the same. But now consider the case where no one index perfectly serves the query. For example, imagine that you don't have an index on {stock_symbol: 1, close: 1} but that, instead, you have a separate index on each of those fields. Using the shorthand `getIndexKeys()` to list indexes, you'd see this:

```
db.values.getIndexKeys()
[ { "_id" : 1 }, { "close" : 1 }, { "stock_symbol" : 1 } ]
```

Because your query includes both the `stock_symbol` and `close` keys, there's no obvious index to use. This is where the query optimizer comes in, and the heuristic is more straightforward than you might imagine. It's based purely on the value of nscanned. In other words, the optimizer chooses the index that requires scanning the least number of index entries. When the query is first run, the optimizer creates a query plan for each index that might efficiently satisfy the query. The optimizer then runs each plan in parallel.[14] The plan that finishes with the lowest value for nscanned is declared the winner. The optimizer then halts any long-running plans and saves the winner for future use.

You can see this process in action by issuing your query and running `explain()`. First, drop the compound index on {stock_symbol: 1, close: 1} and build separate indexes on each of these keys:

```
db.values.dropIndex("stock_symbol_1_close_1")
db.values.ensureIndex({stock_symbol: 1})
db.values.ensureIndex({close: 1})
```

Then pass `true` to the explain method, which will include the list of plans the query optimizer attempts. You can see the output in listing 7.1.

Listing 7.1 Viewing query plans with `explain(true)`

```
db.values.find({stock_symbol: "GOOG", close: {$gt: 200}}).explain(true)
{
  "cursor" : "BtreeCursor stock_symbol_1",
  "nscanned" : 894,
  "nscannedObjects" : 894,
  "n" : 730,
  "millis" : 8,
  "nYields" : 0,
  "nChunkSkips" : 0,
  "isMultiKey" : false,
  "indexOnly" : false,
  "indexBounds" : {
    "stock_symbol" : [
      [
        "GOOG",
        "GOOG"
      ]
    ]
```

---

[14] Technically, the plans are interleaved.

```
    },
    "allPlans" : [
      {
        "cursor" : "BtreeCursor close_1",
        "indexBounds" : {
          "close" : [
            [
              100,
              1.7976931348623157e+308
            ]
          ]
        }
      },
      {
        "cursor" : "BtreeCursor stock_symbol_1",
        "indexBounds" : {
          "stock_symbol" : [
            [
              "GOOG",
              "GOOG"
            ]
          ]
        }
      },
      {
        "cursor" : "BasicCursor",
        "indexBounds" : {
        }
      }
    ]
}
```

You'll see right away that the query plan chooses the index on {stock_symbol: 1} to fulfill the query. Lower down, the allPlans key points to a list that includes two additional query plans: one for the index on {close: 1}, and the other a collection scan with a BasicCursor.

It's understandable why the optimizer rejects the collection scan, but it might be less clear why the index on {close :1} doesn't satisfy. You can use hint() to find out. hint() forces the query optimizer to use a particular index:

```
query = {stock_symbol: "GOOG", close: {$gt: 100}}
db.values.find(query).hint({close: 1}).explain()
{
  "cursor" : "BtreeCursor close_1",
  "nscanned" : 5299,
  "n" : 730,
  "millis" : 36,
  "indexBounds" : {
    "close" : [
      [
        200,
        1.7976931348623157e+308
      ]
    ]
  }
}
```

Look at the value for nscanned: 5,299. This is much greater than the 894 entries scanned previously, and the time it takes to complete the query bears this out.

All that's left to understand is how the query optimizer caches and expires its choice of query plan. After all, you wouldn't want the optimizer running all those plans in parallel on each query.

When a successful plan is discovered, the query pattern, the value for nscanned, and the index spec are recorded. For the query we've been working with, the recorded structure looks something like this:

```
{ pattern: {stock_symbol: 'equality', close: 'bound',
  index: {stock_symbol: 1},
  nscanned: 894 }
```

The query pattern records the kind of match for each key. Here, you're requesting an exact match on stock_symbol (equality), and a range match on close (bound).[15] Whenever a new query matches this pattern, the index will be used.

But this shouldn't hold forever, and it doesn't. The optimizer automatically expires a plan after any of the following events:

- 100 writes are made to the collection.
- Indexes are added or removed from the collection.
- A query using a cached query plan does a lot more work than expected. Here, what qualifies as "a lot more work" is a value for nscanned exceeding the cached nscanned value by at least a factor of 10.

In the last of these cases, the optimizer will immediately begin interleaving other query plans in case a different index proves more efficient.

7.3.3 Query patterns

Here I present several common query patterns and the indexes to use with them.

SINGLE-KEY INDEXES
To review single-key indexes, recall the index you created for the stock values collection on closing numbers, {close: 1}. This index can be used in the following scenarios.

Exact matches
An exact match. For instance, all entries with a closing value of 100:

```
db.values.find({close: 100})
```

Sorting
A sort on the indexed field. For example:

```
db.values.find({}).sort({close: 1})
```

In the case of a sort with no query selector, you'll probably want to tack on a limit unless you actually plan to iterate over the entire collection.

---

[15] In case you're interested, three kinds of range matches are stored: upper, lower, and upper-and-lower. The query pattern also includes any sort specification.

Range queries

A range query with or without a sort on the same field. For example, all closing values greater than or equal to 100:

```
db.values.find({close: {$gte: 100})
```

If you add a sort clause on the same key, the optimizer will still be able to use the same index:

```
db.values.find({close: {$gte: 100}).sort({close: 1})
```

COMPOUND-KEY INDEXES

Compound-key indexes are a little more complicated, but their uses are analogous to those of single-key indexes. The main thing to remember is that a compound-key index can efficiently serve just a single range or sort per query. Let's imagine a triple-compound key index, again for stock values, on {close: 1, open: 1, date: 1}. Following are some possible scenarios.

Exact matches

An exact match on the first key, the first and second keys, or the first, second, and third keys, in that order:

```
db.values.find({close: 1})
db.values.find({close: 1, open: 1})
db.values.find({close: 1, open: 1, date: "1985-01-08"})
```

Range matches

An exact match on any set of leftmost keys (including none), followed by either a range or a sort using the next key to the right. Thus, all the following queries are ideal for the triple-key index:

```
db.values.find({}).sort({close: 1})
db.values.find({close: {$gt: 1}})

db.values.find({close: 100}).sort({open: 1})
db.values.find({close: 100, open: {$gt: 1}})

db.values.find({close: 1, open: 1.01, date: {$gt: "2005-01-01"}})
db.values.find({close: 1, open: 1.01}).sort({date: 1})
```

COVERING INDEXES

If you've never heard of *covering indexes*, then realize from the start that the term is something of a misnomer. A covering index isn't, as the name would suggest, a *kind* of index but rather a *special use* of an index. In particular, an index can be said to cover a query if all the data required by the query resides in the index itself. Covered index queries are also known as *index-only queries*, since these queries are served without having to reference the indexed documents themselves. This can result in increased query performance.

Using a covering index in MongoDB is easy. Simply select a set of fields that reside in a single index, and exclude the _id field (since this field likely isn't part of the index you're using). Here's an example that uses the triple-compound index you created in the previous section:

```
db.values.find({open: 1}, {open: 1, close: 1, date: 1, _id: 0})
```

If you run `explain()` on this query, you'll see a field labeled `indexOnly` that's set to `true`. This indicates that the index, and no actual collection data, was used to serve the query.

Query optimization is always application-specific, but the hope is that the ideas and techniques provided here will help you tune your queries for the better. Empirical approaches are always useful. Make a habit of profiling and explaining your queries. In the process, you'll continue learning about the hidden corners of the query optimizer, and you'll ensure efficient queries for your application.

7.4 *Summary*

This chapter is hefty, no doubt, as indexing is an admittedly rich subject. If not all the ideas are clear, that's okay. You should at least come away with a few techniques for examining indexes and avoiding slow queries, and you should know enough to keep learning. With the complexity involved in indexing and query optimization, plain old experimentation may be your best teacher from here on out.

Replication

Replication is central to most database management systems because of one inevitable fact: failures happen. If you want your live production data to be available even after a failure, you need to be sure that your production databases are available on more than one machine. Replication ensures against failure, providing high availability and disaster recovery.

I begin this chapter by introducing replication in general and discussing its main use cases. I'll then cover MongoDB's replication through a detailed study of replica sets. Finally, I'll describe how to connect to replicated MongoDB clusters using the drivers, how to use write concern, and how to load balance reads across replicas.

8.1   *Replication overview*

Replication is the distribution and maintenance of a live database server across multiple machines. MongoDB provides two flavors of replication: *master-slave replication* and *replica sets*. For both, a single primary node receives all writes, and then all secondary nodes read and apply those writes to themselves asynchronously.

Master-slave replication and replica sets use the same replication mechanism, but replica sets additionally ensure automated failover: if the primary node goes offline for any reason, then one of the secondary nodes will automatically be promoted to primary, if possible. Replica sets provide other enhancements too, such as easier recovery and more sophistical deployment topologies. For these reasons, there are now few compelling reasons to use simple master-slave replication.[1] Replica sets are thus the recommend replication strategy for production deployments; consequently, I'll devote the bulk of this chapter to explanations and examples of replica sets, with only a brief overview of master-slave replication.

8.1.1   *Why replication matters*

All databases are vulnerable to failures of the environments in which they run. Replication provides a kind of insurance against these failures. What sort of failure am I talking about? Here are some of the more common scenarios:

- The network connection between the application and the database is lost.
- Planned downtime prevents the server from coming back online as expected. Any institution housing servers will be forced to schedule occasional downtime, and the results of this downtime aren't always easy to predict. A simple reboot will keep a database server offline for at least a few minutes. But then there's the question of what happens when the reboot is complete. There are times when newly installed software or hardware will prevent the operating system from starting up properly.
- There's a loss of power. Although most modern data centers feature redundant power supplies, nothing prevents user error within the data center itself or an extended brownout or blackout from shutting down your database server.
- A hard drive fails on the database server. Frequently having a mean time to failure of just a few years, hard drives fail more often than you might think.[2]

In addition to protecting against external failures, replication has been important for MongoDB in particular for durability. When running without journaling enabled, MongoDB's data files aren't guaranteed to be free of corruption in the event of an unclean shutdown. Without journaling, replication must always be run to guarantee a clean copy of the data files if a single node shuts down hard.

---

[1]   The only time you should opt for MongoDB's master-slave replication is when you'd require more than 11 slave nodes, since a replica set can have no more than 12 members.

[2]   You can read a detailed analysis of consumer hard drive failure rates in Google's "Failure Trends in a Large Disk Drive Population" (http://research.google.com/archive/disk_failures.pdf).

Of course, replication is desirable even when running *with* journaling. After all, you still want high availability and fast failover. In this case, journaling expedites recovery because it allows you to bring failed nodes back online simply by replaying the journal. This is much faster than resyncing from an existing replica or copying a replica's data files manually.

Journaled or not, MongoDB's replication greatly increases the reliability of the overall database deployments and is highly recommended.

8.1.2   *Replication use cases*

You may be surprised at how versatile a replicated database can be. In particular, replication facilitates redundancy, failover, maintenance, and load balancing. Here we take a brief look at each of these use cases.

Replication is designed primarily for redundancy. It essentially ensures that replicated nodes stay in sync with the primary node. These replicas can live in the same data center as the primary, or they can be distributed geographically as an additional failsafe. Because replication is asynchronous, any sort of network latency or partition between nodes will have no affect on the performance of the primary. As another form of redundancy, replicated nodes can also be delayed by a constant number of seconds behind the primary. This provides insurance against the case where a user inadvertently drops a collection or an application somehow corrupts the database. Normally, these operations will be replicated immediately; a delayed replica gives administrators time to react and possibly save their data.

It's important to note that although they're redundant, replicas aren't a replacement for backups. A backup represents a snapshot of the database at a particular time in the past, whereas a replica is always up to date. There are cases where a data set is large enough to render backups impractical, but as a general rule, backups are prudent and recommended even when running with replication.

Another use case for replication is failover. You want your systems to be highly available, but this is possible only with redundant nodes and the ability to switch over to those nodes in an emergency. Conveniently, MongoDB's replica sets can frequently make this switch automatically.

In addition to providing redundancy and failover, replication simplifies maintenance, usually by allowing you to run expensive operations on a node other than the primary. For example, it's common practice to run backups against a secondary node to keep unnecessary load off the primary and to avoid downtime. Another example involves building large indexes. Because index builds are expensive, you may opt to build on a secondary node first, swap the secondary with the existing primary, and then build again on the new secondary.

Finally, replication allows you to balance reads across replicas. For applications whose workloads are overwhelmingly read-heavy, this is the easiest way to scale MongoDB. But for all its promise, scaling reads with secondaries isn't practical if any of the following apply:

- The allotted hardware can't process the given workload. As an example, I mentioned working sets in the previous chapter. If your working data set is much larger than the available RAM, then sending random reads to the secondaries is still likely to result in excessive disk access, and thus slow queries.
- The ratio of writes to reads exceeds 50%. This is an admittedly arbitrary ratio, but it's a reasonable place to start. The issue here is that every write to the primary must eventually be written to all the secondaries as well. Therefore directing reads to secondaries that are already processing a lot of writes can sometimes slow the replication process and may not result in increased read throughput.
- The application requires consistent reads. Secondary nodes replicate asynchronously and therefore aren't guaranteed to reflect the latest writes to the primary node. In pathological cases, secondaries can run hours behind.

So you can balance read load with replication, but only in special cases. If you need to scale and any of the preceding conditions apply, then you'll need a different strategy, involving sharding, augmented hardware, or some combination of the two.

8.2 Replica sets

Replica sets are a refinement on master-slave replication, and they're the recommended MongoDB replication strategy. We'll start by configuring a sample replica set. I'll then describe how replication actually works, as this knowledge is incredibly important for diagnosing production issues. We'll end by discussing advanced configuration details, failover and recovery, and best deployment practices.

8.2.1 Setup

The minimum recommended replica set configuration consists of three nodes. Two of these nodes serve as first-class, persistent mongod instances. Either can act as the replica set primary, and both have a full copy of the data. The third node in the set is an *arbiter*, which doesn't replicate data, but merely acts as a kind of neutral observer. As the name suggests, the arbiter arbitrates: when failover is required, the arbiter helps to elect a new primary node. You can see an illustration of the replica set you're about to set up in figure 8.1.

Start by creating a data directory for each replica set member:

```
mkdir /data/node1
mkdir /data/node2
mkdir /data/arbiter
```

Next, start each member as a separate mongod. Since you'll be running each process on the same machine, it's probably easiest to start each mongod in a separate terminal window:

```
mongod --replSet myapp --dbpath /data/node1 --port 40000
mongod --replSet myapp --dbpath /data/node2 --port 40001
mongod --replSet myapp --dbpath /data/arbiter --port 40002
```

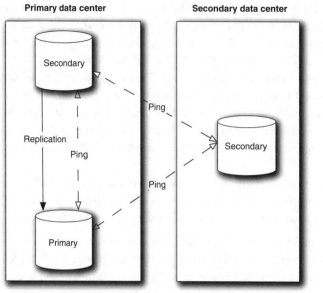

Figure 8.1   A basic replica set consisting of a primary, a secondary, and an arbiter

If you examine the mongod log output, the first thing you'll notice are error messages saying that the configuration can't be found. The is completely normal:

```
[startReplSets] replSet can't get local.system.replset
   config from self or any seed (EMPTYCONFIG)
[startReplSets] replSet info you may need to run replSetInitiate
```

To proceed, you need to configure the replica set. Do so by first connecting to one of the non-arbiter mongods just started. These examples were produced running these mongod processes locally, so you'll connect via the local hostname, in this case, arete.

Connect, and then run the rs.initiate() command:

```
> rs.initiate()
{
    "info2" : "no configuration explicitly specified -- making one",
    "me" : "arete:40000",
    "info" : "Config now saved locally.  Should come online in about a minute
    .",
    "ok" : 1
}
```

Within a minute or so, you'll have a one-member replica set. You can now add the other two members using rs.add():

```
> rs.add("localhost:40001")
{ "ok" : 1 }
> rs.add("arete.local:40002", {arbiterOnly: true})
{ "ok" : 1 }
```

Note that for the second node, you specify the arbiterOnly option to create an arbiter. Within a minute, all members should be online. To get a brief summary of the replica set status, run the db.isMaster() command:

```
> db.isMaster()
{
  "setName" : "myapp",
  "ismaster" : false,
  "secondary" : true,
  "hosts" : [
    "arete:40001",
    "arete:40000"
  ],
  "arbiters" : [
    "arete:40002"
  ],
  "primary" : "arete:40000",
  "maxBsonObjectSize" : 16777216,
  "ok" : 1
}
```

A more detailed view of the system is provided by the rs.status() method. You'll see state information for each node. Here's the complete status listing:

```
> rs.status()
{
    "set" : "myall",
    "date" : ISODate("2011-09-27T22:09:04Z"),
    "myState" : 1,
    "members" : [
        {
            "_id" : 0,
            "name" : "arete:40000",
            "health" : 1,
            "state" : 1,
            "stateStr" : "PRIMARY",
            "optime" : {
                "t" : 1317161329000,
                "i" : 1
            },
            "optimeDate" : ISODate("2011-09-27T22:08:49Z"),
            "self" : true
        },
        {
            "_id" : 1,
            "name" : "arete:40001",
            "health" : 1,
            "state" : 2,
            "stateStr" : "SECONDARY",
            "uptime" : 59,
            "optime" : {
                "t" : 1317161329000,
                "i" : 1
            },
            "optimeDate" : ISODate("2011-09-27T22:08:49Z"),
            "lastHeartbeat" : ISODate("2011-09-27T22:09:03Z"),
            "pingMs" : 0
        },
        {
            "_id" : 2,
```

```
            "name" : "arete:40002",
            "health" : 1,
            "state" : 7,
            "stateStr" : "ARBITER",
            "uptime" : 5,
            "optime" : {
                "t" : 0,
                "i" : 0
            },
            "optimeDate" : ISODate("1970-01-01T00:00:00Z"),
            "lastHeartbeat" : ISODate("2011-09-27T22:09:03Z"),
            "pingMs" : 0
        }
    ],
    "ok" : 1
}
```

Unless your MongoDB database contains a lot of data, the replica set should come online within 30 seconds. During this time, the stateStr field of each node should transition from RECOVERING to PRIMARY, SECONDARY, or ARBITER.

Now even if the replica set status claims that replication is working, you may want to see some empirical evidence of this. So go ahead and connect to the primary node with the shell and insert a document:

```
$ mongo arete:40000
> use bookstore
switched to db bookstore
> db.books.insert({title: "Oliver Twist"})
> show dbs
admin (empty)
bookstore 0.203125GB
local 0.203125GB
```

Initial replication should occur almost immediately. In another terminal window, open a new shell instance, but this time point it to the secondary node. Query for the document just inserted; it should have arrived:

```
$ mongo arete:40001
> show dbs
admin (empty)
bookstore 0.203125GB
local 0.203125GB
> use bookstore switched to db bookstore
> db.books.find()
{ "_id" : ObjectId("4d42ebf28e3c0c32c06bdf20"), "title" : "Oliver Twist" }
```

If replication is indeed working as displayed here, then you've successfully configured your replica set.

It should be satisfying to see replication in action, but perhaps more interesting is automated failover. Let's test that now. It's always tricky to simulate a network partition, so we'll go the easy route and just kill a node. You could kill the secondary, but that merely stops replication, with the remaining nodes maintaining their current status. If you want to see a change of system state, you need to kill the primary. A standard CTRL-C or kill -2 will do the trick. You can also connect to the primary using the shell and run db.shutdownServer().

Once you've killed the primary, note that the secondary detects the lapse in the primary's heartbeat. The secondary then elects itself primary. This election is possible because a majority of the original nodes (the arbiter and the original secondary) are still able to ping each other. Here's an excerpt from the secondary node's log:

```
[ReplSetHealthPollTask] replSet info arete:40000 is down (or slow to respond)
Mon Jan 31 22:56:22 [rs Manager] replSet info electSelf 1
Mon Jan 31 22:56:22 [rs Manager] replSet PRIMARY
```

If you connect to the new primary node and check the replica set status, you'll see that the old primary is unreachable:

```
> rs.status()
{
        "_id" : 0,
        "name" : "arete:40000",
        "health" : 1,
        "state" : 6,
        "stateStr" : "(not reachable/healthy)",
        "uptime" : 0,
        "optime" : {
          "t" : 1296510078000,
          "i" : 1
        },
        "optimeDate" : ISODate("2011-01-31T21:43:18Z"),
        "lastHeartbeat" : ISODate("2011-02-01T03:29:30Z"),
        "errmsg": "socket exception"
}
```

Post-failover, the replica set consists of just two nodes. Because the arbiter has no data, your application will continue to function as long as it communicates with the primary node only.[3] Even so, replication isn't happening, and there's now no possibility of failover. The old primary must be restored. Assuming that the old primary was shut down cleanly, you can bring it back online, and it'll automatically rejoin the replica set as a secondary. Go ahead and try that now by restarting the old primary node.

That's a clean overview of replica sets. Some of the details are, unsurprisingly, messier. In the next two sections, you'll see how replica sets actually work, and look at deployment, advanced configuration, and how to handle tricky scenarios that may arise in production.

8.2.2 How replication works

Replica sets rely on two basic mechanisms: an *oplog* and a *heartbeat*. The oplog enables the replication of data, and the heartbeat monitors health and triggers failover. You'll

---

[3] Applications sometimes query secondary nodes for read scaling. If that's happening, then this kind of failure will cause read failures. Thus it's important to design your application with failover in mind. More on this at the end of the chapter.

now see how both of these mechanisms work in turn. You should in the process begin to understand and predict replica set behavior, particularly in failure scenarios.

ALL ABOUT THE OPLOG

At the heart of MongoDB's replication stands the oplog. The oplog is a capped collection that lives in a database called `local` on every replicating node and records all changes to the data. Every time a client writes to the primary, an entry with enough information to reproduce the write is automatically added to the primary's oplog. Once the write is replicated to a given secondary, that secondary's oplog also stores a record of the write. Each oplog entry is identified with a BSON timestamp, and all secondaries use the timestamp to keep track of the latest entry they've applied.[4]

To better see how this works, let's look more closely at a real oplog and at the operations recorded therein. First connect with the shell to the primary node started in the previous section, and switch to the `local` database:

```
> use local
switched to db local
```

The `local` database stores all the replica set metadata and the oplog. Naturally, this database isn't replicated itself. Thus it lives up to its name; data in the `local` database is supposed to be unique to the local node and therefore shouldn't be replicated.

If you examine the `local` database, you'll see a collection called `oplog.rs`, which is where every replica set stores its oplog. You'll also see a few system collections. Here's the complete output:

```
> show collections
me
oplog.rs
replset.minvalid
slaves
system.indexes
system.replset
```

`replset.minvalid` contains information for the initial sync of a given replica set member, and `system.replset` stores the replica set config document. `me` and `slaves` are used to implement write concern, described at the end of this chapter, and `system.indexes` is the standard index spec container.

First we'll focus on the oplog. Let's query for the oplog entry corresponding to the book document you added in the previous section. To do so, enter the following query. The resulting document will have four fields, and we'll discuss each in turn:

```
> db.oplog.rs.findOne({op: "i"})
{ "ts" : { "t" : 1296864947000, "i" : 1 }, "op" : "i", "ns" :
  "bookstores.books", "o" : { "_id" : ObjectId("4d4c96b1ec5855af3675d7a1"),
  "title" : "Oliver Twist" }
}
```

---

[4] The BSON timestamp is a unique identifier comprising the number of seconds since the epoch and an incrementing counter.

The first field, ts, stores the entry's BSON timestamp. Pay particular attention here; the shell displays the timestamp as a subdocument with two fields, t for the seconds since epoch and i for the counter. This might lead you to believe that you could query for the entry like so:

```
db.oplog.rs.findOne({ts: {t: 1296864947000, i: 1}})
```

In fact, this query returns null. To query with a timestamp, you need to explicitly construct a timestamp object. All the drivers have their own BSON timestamp constructors, and so does JavaScript. Here's how to use it:

```
db.oplog.rs.findOne({ts: new Timestamp(1296864947000, 1)})
```

Returning to the oplog entry, the second field, op, specifies the opcode. This tells the secondary node which operation the oplog entry represents. Here you see an i, indicating an insert. After op comes ns to signify the relevant namespace (database and collection) and o, which for insert operations contains a copy of the inserted document.

As you examine oplog entries, you may notice that operations affecting multiple documents are analyzed into their component parts. For multi-updates and mass deletes, a separate entry is created in the oplog for each document affected. For example, suppose you add a few more Dickens books to the collection:

```
> use bookstore
db.books.insert({title: "A Tale of Two Cities"})
db.books.insert({title: "Great Expectations"})
```

Now with four books in the collection, let's issue a multi-update to set the author's name:

```
db.books.update({}, {$set: {author: "Dickens"}}, false, true)
```

How does this appear in the oplog?

```
> use local
> db.oplog.$main.find({op: "u"})
{ "ts" : { "t" : 1296944149000, "i" : 1 }, "op" : "u",
"ns" : "bookstore.books",
"o2" : { "_id" : ObjectId("4d4dcb89ec5855af365d4283") },
"o" : { "$set" : { "author" : "Dickens" } } }

{ "ts" : { "t" : 1296944149000, "i" : 2 }, "op" : "u",
"ns" : "bookstore.books",
"o2" : { "_id" : ObjectId("4d4dcb8eec5855af365d4284") },
"o" : { "$set" : { "author" : "Dickens" } } }

{ "ts" : { "t" : 1296944149000, "i" : 3 }, "op" : "u",
"ns" : "bookstore.books",
"o2" : { "_id" : ObjectId("4d4dcbb6ec5855af365d4285") },
"o" : { "$set" : { "author" : "Dickens" } } }
```

As you can see, each updated document gets its own oplog entry. This normalization is done as part of the more general strategy of ensuring that secondaries always end up with the same data as the primary. To guarantee this, every applied operation must be idempotent—it can't matter how many times a given oplog entry is applied; the result must always be the same. Other multidocument operations, like deletes, will exhibit the same behavior. You're encouraged to try different operations and see how they ultimately appear in the oplog.

To get some basic information about the oplog's current status, you can run the shell's db.getReplicationInfo() method:

```
> db.getReplicationInfo()
{
    "logSizeMB" : 50074.10546875,
    "usedMB" : 302.123,
    "timeDiff" : 294,
    "timeDiffHours" : 0.08,
    "tFirst" : "Thu Jun 16 2011 21:21:55 GMT-0400 (EDT)",
    "tLast" : "Thu Jun 16 2011 21:26:49 GMT-0400 (EDT)",
    "now" : "Thu Jun 16 2011 21:27:28 GMT-0400 (EDT)"
}
```

Here you see the timestamps of the first and last entries in this oplog. You can find these oplog entries manually by using the $natural sort modifier. For example, the following query fetches the latest entry: db.oplog.rs.find().sort({$natural: -1}).limit(1)

The only important thing left to understand about replication is how the secondaries keep track of their place in the oplog. The answer lies in the fact that secondaries also keep an oplog. This is a significant improvement upon master-slave replication, so it's worth taking a moment to explore the rationale.

Imagine you issue a write to the primary node of a replica set. What happens next? First, the write is recorded and then added to the primary's oplog. Meanwhile, all secondaries have their own oplogs that replicate the primary's oplog. So when a given secondary node is ready to update itself, it does three things. First, it looks at the timestamp of the latest entry in its own oplog. Next, it queries the primary's oplog for all entries greater than that timestamp. Finally, it adds each of those entries to its own oplog and applies the entries to itself.[5] This means that, in case of failover, any secondary promoted to primary will have an oplog that the other secondaries can replicate from. This feature essentially enables replica set recovery.

Secondary nodes use long polling to immediately apply new entries from the primary's oplog. Thus secondaries will usually be almost completely up to date. When they do fall behind, because of network partitions or maintenance on secondaries themselves, the latest timestamp in each secondary's oplog can be used to monitor any replication lag.

HALTED REPLICATION

Replication will halt permanently if a secondary can't find the point it's synced to in the primary's oplog. When that happens, you'll see an exception in the secondary's log that looks like this:

---

[5]   When journaling is enabled, documents are written to the core data files and to the oplog simultaneously in an atomic transaction.

```
repl: replication data too stale, halting
Fri Jan 28 14:19:27 [replsecondary] caught SyncException
```

Recall that the oplog is a capped collection. This means that entries in the collection eventually age out. Once a given secondary fails to find the point at which it's synced in the primary's oplog, there's no longer any way of ensuring that the secondary is a perfect replica of the primary. Because the only remedy for halted replication is a complete resync of the primary's data, you'll want to strive to avoid this state. To do that, you'll need to monitor secondary delay, and you'll need to have a large enough oplog for your write volume. You'll learn more about monitoring in chapter 10. Choosing the right oplog size is what we'll cover next.

SIZING THE REPLICATION OPLOG

The oplog is a capped collection and as such, it can't be resized once it's been created (at least, as of MongoDB v2.0).[6] This makes it important to choose an initial oplog size carefully.

The default oplog sizes vary somewhat. On 32-bit systems, the oplog will default to 50 MB, whereas on 64-bit systems, the oplog will be the larger of 1 GB or 5% of free disk space.[7] For many deployments, 5% of free disk space will be more than enough. One way to think about an oplog of this size is to recognize that once it overwrites itself 20 times, the disk will likely be full.

That said, the default size won't be ideal for all applications. If you know that your application will have a high write volume, you should do some empirical testing before deploying. Set up replication and then write to the primary at the rate you'll have in production. You'll want to hammer the server in this way for at least an hour. Once done, connect to any replica set member and get the current replication info:

```
db.getReplicationInfo()
```

Once you know how much oplog you're generating per hour, you can then decide how much oplog space to allocate. You should probably shoot for being able to withstand at least eight hours of secondary downtime. You want to avoid having to completely resync any node, and increasing the oplog size will buy you time in the event of network failures and the like.

If you want to change the default oplog size, you must do so the first time you start each member node using mongod's --oplogSize option. The value is in megabytes. Thus you can start mongod with a 1 GB oplog like so:

```
mongod --replSet myapp --oplogSize 1024
```

HEARTBEAT AND FAILOVER

The replica set heartbeat facilitates election and failover. By default, each replica set member pings all the other members every two seconds. In this way, the system can

---

[6] The option to increase the size of a capped collection is a planned feature. See https://jira.mongodb.org/browse/SERVER-1864.

[7] Unless you're running on OS X, in which case the oplog will be 192 MB. This smaller size is due to the assumption that OSX machines are development machines.

ascertain its own health. When you run `rs.status()`, you see the timestamp of each node's last heartbeat along with its state of health (1 means healthy and 0 means unresponsive).

As long as every node remains healthy and responsive, the replica set will hum along its merry way. But if any node becomes unresponsive, action may be taken. What every replica set wants is to ensure that exactly one primary node exists at all times. But this is possible only when a majority of nodes is visible. For example, look back at the replica set you built in the previous section. If you kill the secondary, then a majority of nodes still exists, so the replica set doesn't change state but simply waits for the secondary to come back online. If you kill the primary, then a majority still exists, but there's no primary. Therefore, the secondary is automatically promoted to primary. If more than one secondary happens to exist, then the most current secondary will be the one elected.

But there are other possible scenarios. Imagine that both the secondary and the arbiter are killed. Now the primary remains, but there's no majority—only one of the three original nodes remains healthy. In this case, you'll see a message like this in the primary's log:

```
Tue Feb  1 11:26:38 [rs Manager] replSet can't see a majority of the set,
    relinquishing primary
Tue Feb  1 11:26:38 [rs Manager] replSet relinquishing primary state
Tue Feb  1 11:26:38 [rs Manager] replSet SECONDARY
```

With no majority, the primary actually demotes itself to a secondary. This may seem puzzling, but think about what might happen if this node were allowed to remain primary. If the heartbeats fail due to some kind of network partition, then the other nodes will still be online. If the arbiter and secondary are still up and able to see each other, then according to the rule of the majority, the remaining secondary will become a primary. If the original primary doesn't step down, then you're suddenly in an untenable situation: a replica set with two primary nodes. If the application continues to run, then it might write to and read from two different primaries, a sure recipe for inconsistency and truly bizarre application behavior. Therefore, when the primary can't see a majority, it must step down.

COMMIT AND ROLLBACK

One final important point to understand about replica sets is the concept of a *commit*. In essence, you can write to a primary node all day long, but those writes won't be considered committed until they've been replicated to a majority of nodes. What do I mean by *committed* here? The idea can best be explained by example. Imagine again the replica set you built in the previous section. Suppose you issue a series of writes to the primary that don't get replicated to the secondary for some reason (connectivity issues, secondary is down for backup, secondary is lagging, and so forth). Now suppose further that the secondary is suddenly promoted to primary. You write to the new primary, and eventually the old primary comes back online and tries to replicate from the new primary. The problem here is that the old primary has a series of writes that don't exist in the new primary's oplog. This situation triggers a rollback.

In a rollback, all writes that were never replicated to a majority are undone. This means that they're removed from both the secondary's oplog and the collection where they reside. If a secondary has registered a delete, then the node will look for the deleted document in another replica and restore it to itself. The same is true for dropped collections and updated documents.

The reverted writes are stored in the `rollback` subdirectory of the relevant node's data path. For each collection with rolled-back writes, a separate BSON file will be created whose filename includes the time of the rollback. In the event that you need to restore the reverted documents, you can examine these BSON files using the `bsondump` utility and manually restore them, possibly using `mongorestore`.

If you ever find yourself having to restore rolled-back data, you'll realize that this is a situation you want to avoid, and fortunately you can to some extent. If your application can tolerate the extra write latency, you can use write concern, described later, to ensure that your data is replicated to a majority of nodes on each write (or perhaps after every several writes). Being smart about write concern and about monitoring of replication lag in general will help you mitigate or even avoid the problem of rollback altogether.

In this section you learned perhaps a few more replication internals than expected, but the knowledge should come in handy. Understanding how replication works goes a long way in helping you to diagnose any issues you may have in production.

8.2.3 Administration

For all the automation they provide, replica sets have some potentially complicated configuration options. In what follows, I'll describe these options in detail. In the interest of keeping things simple, I'll also suggest which options can be safely ignored.

CONFIGURATION DETAILS

Here I present the `mongod` startup options pertaining to replica sets, and I describe the structure of the replica set configuration document.

Replication options

Earlier, you learned how to initiate a replica set using the shell's `rs.initiate()` and `rs.add()` methods. These methods are convenient, but they hide certain replica set configuration options. Here you'll see how to use a configuration document to initiate and update a replica set's configuration.

A configuration document specifies the configuration of the replica set. To create one, first add a value for `_id` that matches the name you passed to the `--replSet` parameter:

```
> config = {_id: "myapp", members: []}
{ "_id" : "myapp", "members" : [ ] }
```

The individual `members` can be defined as part of the configuration document as follows:

```
config.members.push({_id: 0, host: 'arete:40000'})
config.members.push({_id: 1, host: 'arete:40001'})
config.members.push({_id: 2, host: 'arete:40002', arbiterOnly: true})
```

Your configuration document should now look like this:

```
> config
{
  "_id" : "myapp",
  "members" : [
    {
      "_id" : 0,
      "host" : "arete:40000"
    },
    {
      "_id" : 1,
      "host" : "arete:40001"
    },
    {
      "_id" : 2,
      "host" : "arete:40002",
      "arbiterOnly" : true
    }
  ]
}
```

You can then pass the document as the first argument to rs.initiate() to initiate the replica set.

Technically, the document consists of an _id containing the name of the replica set, an array specifying between 3 and 12 members, and an optional subdocument for specifying certain global settings. This sample replica set uses the minimum required configuration parameters, plus the optional arbiterOnly setting.

The document requires an _id that matches the replica set's name. The initiation command will verify that each member node has been started with the --replSet option with that name. Each replica set member requires an _id consisting of increasing integers starting from 0. Members also require a host field with a host name and optional port.

Here you initiate the replica set using the rs.initiate() method. This is a simple wrapper for the replSetInitiate command. Thus you could've started the replica set like so:

```
db.runCommand({replSetInitiate: config});
```

config is simply a variable holding your configuration document. Once initiated, each set member stores a copy of this configuration document in the local database's system.replset collection. If you query the collection, you'll see that the document now has a version number. Whenever you modify the replica set's configuration, you must also increment this version number.

To modify a replica set's configuration, there's a separate command, replSet-Reconfig, which takes a new configuration document. The new document can specify the addition or removal of set members along with alterations to both member-specific and global configuration options. The process of modifying a configuration document, incrementing the version number, and passing it as part of the replSetReconfig can be laborious, so there exist a number of shell helpers to ease the way. To see a list of them all, enter rs.help() at the shell. You've already seen rs.add().

Bear in mind that whenever a replica set reconfiguration results in the election of a new primary node, all client connections will be closed. This is done to ensure that clients won't attempt to send fire-and-forget writes to a secondary node.

If you're interested in configuring a replica set from one of the drivers, you can see how by examining the implementation of rs.add(). Enter rs.add (the method without the parentheses) at the shell prompt to see how the method works.

Configuration document options

Until now, we've limited ourselves to the simplest replica set configuration document. But these documents support several options for both replica set members and for the replica set as a whole. We'll begin with the member options. You've seen _id, host, and arbiterOnly. Here are these plus the rest, in all their gritty detail:

- _id *(required)*—A unique incrementing integer representing the member's ID. These _id values begin at 0 and must be incremented by one for each member added.

- host *(required)*—A string storing the host name of this member along with an optional port number. If the port is provided, it should be separated from the host name by a colon (for example, arete:30000). If no port number is specified, the default port, 27017, will be used.

- arbiterOnly—A Boolean value, true or false, indicating whether this member is an arbiter. Arbiters store configuration data only. They're lightweight members that participate in primary election but not in the replication itself.

- priority—An integer from 0 to 1000 that helps to determine the likelihood that this node will be elected primary. For both replica set initiation and failover, the set will attempt to elect as primary the node with the highest priority, as long as it's up to date.

  There are also cases where you might want a node never to be primary (say, a disaster recovery node residing in a secondary data center). In those cases, set the priority to 0. Nodes with a priority of 0 will be marked as passive in the results to the isMaster() command and will never be elected primary.

- votes—All replica set members get one vote by default. The votes setting allows you to give more than one vote to an individual member.

  This option should be used with extreme care, if at all. For one thing, it's difficult to reason about replica set failover behavior when not all members have the same number of votes. Moreover, the vast majority of production deployments will be perfectly well served with one vote per member. So if you do choose to alter the number of votes for a given member, be sure to think through and simulate the various failure scenarios very carefully.

- hidden—A Boolean value that, when `true`, will keep this member from show-ing up in the responses generated by the `isMaster` command. Because the MongoDB drivers rely on `isMaster` for knowledge of the replica set topology, hiding a member keeps the drivers from automatically accessing it. This set-ting can be used in conjunction with `buildIndexes` and must be used with `slaveDelay`.

- buildIndexes—A Boolean value, defaulting to `true`, that determines whether this member will build indexes. You'll want to set this value to `false` only on members that will never become primary (those with a priority of 0).

  This option was designed for nodes used solely as backups. If backing up indexes is important, then you shouldn't use this option.

- slaveDelay—The number of seconds that a given secondary should lag behind the primary. This option can be used only with nodes that will never become pri-mary. So to specify a `slaveDelay` greater than 0, be sure to also set a priority of 0.

  You can use a delayed slave as insurance against certain kinds of user errors. For example, if you have a secondary delayed by 30 minutes and an administra-tor accidentally drops a database, then you have 30 minutes to react to this event before it's propagated.

- tags—A document containing an arbitrary set of key-value pairs, usually used to identify this member's location in a particular data center or server rack. Tags are used for specifying granular write concern and read settings, and they're discussed in section 8.4.9.

That sums up the options for individual replica set members. There are also two global replica set configuration parameters scoped under a `settings` key. In the rep-lica set configuration document, they appear like this:

```
{
  settings: {
    getLastErrorDefaults: {w: 1},
    getLastErrorModes: {
      multiDC: { dc: 2 }
    }
  }
}
```

- getLastErrorDefaults—A document specifying the default arguments to be used when the client calls `getLastError` with no arguments. This option should be treated with care because it's also possible to set global defaults for `getLast-Error` within the drivers, and you can imagine a situation where application developers call `getLastError` not realizing that an administrator has specified a default on the server.

  For more details on `getLastError`, see section 3.2.3 on write concern. Briefly, to specify that all writes are replicated to at least two members with a timeout of 500 ms, you'd specify this value in the config like so: `settings: { getLastError-Defaults: {w: 2, wtimeout: 500} }`.

- getLastErrorModes—A document defining extra modes for the getLastError command. This feature is dependent on replica set tagging and is described in detail in section 8.4.4.

REPLICA SET STATUS

You can see the status of a replica set and its members by running the replSetGet-Status command. To invoke this command from the shell, run the rs.status() helper method. The resulting document indicates the extant members and their respective states, uptime, and oplog times. It's important to understand replica set member state; you can see a complete list of possible values in table 8.1.

You can consider a replica set stable and online when all its nodes are in any of states 1, 2, or 7 and when at least one node is running as the primary. You can use the replSetGetStatus command from an external script to monitor overall state, replication lag, and uptime, and this is recommended for production deployments.[8]

Table 8.1 Replica set states

State	State string	Notes
0	STARTUP	Indicates that the replica set is negotiating with other nodes by pinging all set members and sharing config data.
1	PRIMARY	This is the primary node. A replica set will always have *at most* one primary node.
2	SECONDARY	This is a secondary, read-only node. This node may become a primary in the event of a failover if and only if its priority is greater than 0 and it's not marked as hidden.
3	RECOVERING	This node is unavailable for reading and writing. You usually see this state after a failover or upon adding a new node. While recovering, a data file sync is often in progress; you can verify this by examine the recovering node's logs.
4	FATAL	A network connection is still established, but the node isn't responding to pings. This usually indicates a fatal error on the machine hosting the node marked *FATAL*.
5	STARTUP2	An initial data file sync is in progress.
6	UNKNOWN	A network connection has yet to be made.
7	ARBITER	This node is an arbiter.
8	DOWN	The node was accessible and stable at some point but isn't currently responding to heartbeat pings.
9	ROLLBACK	A rollback is in progress.

---

[8] Note that in addition to running the status command, you can get a useful visual through the web console. Chapter 10 discusses the web console and shows an example of its use with replica sets.

FAILOVER AND RECOVERY

You saw in the sample replica set a couple examples of failover. Here I summarize the rules of failover and provide some suggestions on handling recovery.

A replica set will come online when all members specified in the configuration can communicate with each other. Each node is given one vote by default, and those votes are used to form a majority and elect a primary. This means that a replica set can be started with as few as two nodes (and votes). But the initial number of votes also decides what constitutes a majority in the event of a failure.

Let's assume that you've configured a replica set of three complete replicas (no arbiters) and thus have the recommended minimum for automated failover. If the primary fails, and the remaining secondaries can see each other, then a new primary can be elected. As for deciding which one, the secondary with the most up-to-date oplog (or higher priority) will be elected primary.

Failure modes and recovery

Recovery is the process of restoring the replica set to its original state following a failure. There are two overarching failure categories to be handled. The first comprises what is called *clean failures*, where a given node's data files can still be assumed to be intact. One example of this is a network partition. If a node loses its connections to the rest of the set, then you need only wait for connectivity to be restored, and the partitioned node will resume as a set member. A similar situation occurs when a given node's mongod process is terminated for any reason but can be brought back online cleanly.[9] Again, once the process is restarted, it can rejoin the set.

The second type of failure comprises all *categorical failures*, where either a node's data files no longer exist or must be presumed corrupted. Unclean shutdowns of the mongod process without journaling enabled and hard drive crashes are both examples of this kind of failure. The only ways to recover a categorically failed node are to completely replace the data files via a resync or to restore from a recent backup. Let's look a both strategies in turn.

To completely resync, start a mongod with an empty data directory on the failed node. As long as the host and port haven't changed, the new mongod will rejoin the replica set and then resync all the existing data. If either the host or port has changed, then after bringing the mongod back online, you'll also have to reconfigure the replica set. As an example, suppose the node at arete:40001 is rendered unrecoverable and you bring up a new node at foobar:40000. You can reconfigure the replica set by grabbing the configuration document, modifying the host for the second node, and then passing that to the rs.reconfig() method:

```
> use local
> config = db.system.replset.findOne()
{
    "_id" : "myapp",
```

---

[9] For instance, if MongoDB is shut down cleanly then you know that the data files are okay. Alternatively, if running with journaling, the MongoDB instance should be recoverable regardless of how it's killed.

```
    "version" : 1,
    "members" : [
      {
        "_id" : 0,
        "host" : "arete:30000"
      },
      {
        "_id" : 1,
        "host" : "arete:30001"
      },
      {
        "_id" : 2,
        "host" : "arete:30002"
      }
    ]
}
> config.members[1].host = "foobar:40000"
arete:40000
> rs.reconfig(config)
```

Now the replica set will identify the new node, and the new node should start to sync from an existing member.

In addition to restoring via a complete resync, you also have the option of restoring from a recent backup. You'll typically perform backups from one of the secondary nodes by making snapshots of the data files and then storing them offline.[10] Recovery via backup is possible only if the oplog within the backup isn't stale relative to the oplogs of the current replica set members. This means that the latest operation in the backup's oplog must still exist in the live oplogs. You can use the information provided by db.getReplicationInfo() to see right away if this is the case. When you do, don't forget to take into account the time it'll take to restore the backup. If the backup's latest oplog entry is likely to go stale in the time it takes to copy the backup to a new machine, then you're better off performing a complete resync.

But restoring from backup can be faster, in part because the indexes don't have to be rebuilt from scratch. To restore from a backup, copy the backed-up data files to a mongod data path. The resync should begin automatically, and you can check the logs or run rs.status() to verify this.

DEPLOYMENT STRATEGIES

You now know that a replica set can consist of up to 12 nodes, and you've been presented with a dizzying array of configuration options and considerations regarding failover and recovery. There are a lot of ways you might configure a replica set, but in this section I'll present a couple that will work for the majority of cases.

The most minimal replica set configuration providing automated failover is the one you built earlier consisting of two replicas and one arbiter. In production, the arbiter can run on an application server while each replica gets its own machine. This configuration is economical and sufficient for many production apps.

---

[10] Backups are discussed in detail in chapter 10.

But for applications where uptime is critical, you'll want a replica set consisting of *three* complete replicas. What does the extra replica buy you? Think of the scenario where a single node fails completely. You still have two first-class nodes available while you restore the third. As long as a third node is online and recovering (which may take hours), the replica set can still fail over automatically to an up-to-date node.

Some applications will require the redundancy afforded by two data centers, and the three-member replica set can also work in this case. The trick is to use one of the data centers for disaster recovery only. Figure 8.2 shows an example of this. Here, the primary data center houses a replica set primary and secondary, and a backup data center keeps the remaining secondary as a passive node (with priority 0).

In this configuration, the replica set primary will always be one of the two nodes living in data center A. You can lose any one node or any one data center and still keep the application online. Failover will usually be automatic, except in the cases where both of A's nodes are lost. Because it's rare to lose two nodes at once, this would likely represent the complete failure or partitioning of data center A. To recover quickly, you could shut down the member in data center B and restart it without the --repl-Set flag. Alternatively, you could start two new nodes in data center B and then force a replica set reconfiguration. You're not supposed to reconfigure a replica set when a majority of nodes is unreachable, but you can do so in emergencies using the force option. For example, if you've defined a new configuration document, config, then you can force reconfiguration like so:

```
> rs.reconfig(config, {force: true})
```

As with any production system, testing is key. Make sure that you test for all the typical failover and recovery scenarios in a staging environment comparable to what you'll be

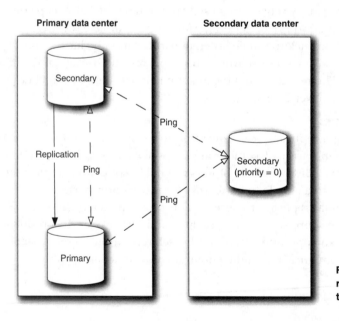

Figure 8.2 A three-node replica set with members in two data centers

running in production. Knowing from experience how your replica set will behave in these failures cases will secure some peace of mind and give you the wherewithal to calmly deal with emergencies as they occur.

8.3 *Master-slave replication*

Master-slave replication is the original replication paradigm in MongoDB. This flavor of replication is easy to configure and has the advantage of supporting any number of slave nodes. But master-slave replication is no longer recommended for production deployments. There are a couple reasons for this. First, failover is completely manual. If the master node fails, then an administrator must shut down a slave and restart it as a master node. Then the application must be reconfigured to point to the new master. Second, recovery is difficult. Because the oplog exists only on the master node, a failure requires that a new oplog be created on the new master. This means that any other existing nodes will need to resync from the new master in the event of a failure.

In short, there are few compelling reasons to use master-slave replication. Replica sets are the way forward, and they're the flavor of replication you should use.

8.4 *Drivers and replication*

If you're building an application and using MongoDB's replication, then you need to know about three application-specific topics. The first concerns connections and failover. Next comes write concern, which allows you to decide to what degree a given write should be replicated before the application continues. The final topic, read scaling, allows an application to distribute reads across replicas. I'll discuss these topics one by one.

8.4.1 *Connections and failover*

The MongoDB drivers present a relatively uniform interface for connecting to replica sets.

SINGLE-NODE CONNECTIONS

You'll always have the option of connecting to a single node in a replica set. There's no difference between connecting to a node designated as a replica set primary and connecting to one of the vanilla standalone nodes we've used for the examples throughout the book. In both cases, the driver will initiate a TCP socket connection and then run the `isMaster` command. This command then returns a document like the following:

```
{ "ismaster" : true, "maxBsonObjectSize" : 16777216, "ok" : 1 }
```

What's most important to the driver is that the `isMaster` field be set to `true`, which indicates that the given node is either a standalone, a master running master-slave replication, or a replica set primary.[11] In all of these cases, the node can be written to, and the user of the driver can perform any CRUD operation.

---

[11] The `isMaster` command also returns a value for the maximum BSON object size for this version of the server. The drivers then validate that all BSON objects are within this limit prior to inserting them.

But when connecting directly to a replica set secondary, you must indicate that you *know* you're connecting to such a node (for most drivers, at least). In the Ruby driver, you accomplish this with the :slave_ok parameter. Thus to connect directly to the first secondary you created earlier in the chapter, the Ruby code would look like this:

```
@con = Mongo::Connection.new('arete', 40001, :slave_ok => true)
```

Without the :slave_ok argument, the driver will raise an exception indicating that it couldn't connect to a primary node. This check is in place to keep you from inadvertently writing to a secondary node. Though such attempts to write will always be rejected by the server, you won't see any exceptions unless you're running the operations with safe mode enabled.

The assumption is that you'll usually want to connect to a primary node master; the :slave_ok parameter is enforced as a sanity check.

REPLICA SET CONNECTIONS

You can connect to any replica set member individually, but you'll normally want to connect to the replica set as a whole. This allows the driver to figure out which node is primary and, in the case of failover, reconnect to whichever node becomes the new primary.

Most of the officially supported drivers provide ways of connecting to a replica set. In Ruby, you connect by creating a new instance of ReplSetConnection, passing in a list of seed nodes:

```
Mongo::ReplSetConnection.new(['arete', 40000], ['arete', 40001])
```

Internally, the driver will attempt to connect to each seed node and then call the isMaster command. Issuing this command to a replica set returns a number of important set details:

```
> db.isMaster()
{
  "setName" : "myapp",
  "ismaster" : true,
  "secondary" : false,
  "hosts" : [
    "arete:40000",
    "arete:40001"
  ],
  "arbiters" : [
    "arete:40002"
  ],
  "maxBsonObjectSize" : 16777216,
  "ok" : 1
}
```

Once a seed node responds with this information, the driver has everything it needs. Now it can connect to the primary member, again verify that this member is still primary, and then allow the user to read and write through this node. The response object also allows the driver to cache the addresses of the remaining secondary and arbiter nodes. If an operation on the primary fails, then on subsequent requests, the driver can attempt to connect to one of the remaining nodes until it can reconnect to a primary.

It's important to keep in mind that although replica set failover is automatic, the drivers don't attempt to hide the fact that a failover has occurred. The course of events goes something like this: First, the primary fails or a new election takes place. Subsequent requests will reveal that the socket connection has been broken, and the driver will then raise a connection exception and close any open sockets to the database. It's now up to the application developer to decide what happens next, and this decision will depend on both the operation being performed and the specific needs of the application.

Keeping in mind that the driver will automatically attempt to reconnect on any subsequent request, let's imagine a couple of scenarios. First, suppose that you only issue reads to the database. In this case, there's little harm in retrying a failed read since there's no possibility of changing database state. But now imagine that you also regularly write to the database. As stated many times before, you can write to the database with and without safe mode enabled. With safe mode, the driver appends to each write a call to the `getlasterror` command. This ensures that the write has arrived safely and reports any server errors back to the application. Without safe mode, the driver simply writes to the TCP socket.

If your application writes without safe mode and a failover occurs, then you're left in an uncertain state. How many of the recent writes made it to the server? How many were lost in the socket buffer? The indeterminate nature of writing to a TCP socket makes answering these questions practically impossible. How big of a problem this is depends on the application. For logging, non-safe-mode writes are probably acceptable, since losing writes hardly changes the overall logging picture; but for users creating data in the application, non-safe-mode writes can be a disaster.

With safe mode enabled, only the most recent write is in question; it may have arrived on the server, or it may not have. At times it'll be appropriate to retry the write, and at other times an application error should be thrown. The drivers will always raise an exception; developers can then decide how these exceptions are handled.

In any case, retrying an operation will cause the driver to attempt to reconnect to the replica set. But since drivers will differ somewhat in their replica set connection behavior, you should always consult your driver's documentation for specifics.

8.4.2 *Write concern*

It should be clear now that running in safe mode by default is reasonable for most applications, as it's important to know that writes have arrived error-free at the primary server. But greater levels of assurance are frequently desired, and *write concern* addresses this by allowing developers to specify the extent to which a write should be replicated before allowing the application to continue on. Technically, you control write concern via two parameters on the `getlasterror` command: `w` and `wtimeout`.

The first value, w, admits a few possible values, but usually indicates the total number of servers that the latest write should be replicated to; the second is a timeout that causes the command to return an error if the write can't be replicated in the specified number of milliseconds.

For example, if you want to make sure that a given write is replicated to at least one server, then you can indicate a w value of 2. If you want the operation to time out if this level of replication isn't achieved in 500 ms, you include a wtimeout of 500. Note that if you don't specify a value for wtimeout, and the replication for some reason never occurs, then the operation will block indefinitely.

When using a driver, you enable write concern not by calling getLastError explicitly but rather by creating a write concern object or by setting the appropriate safe mode option; it depends on the specific driver's API.[12] In Ruby, you can specify a write concern on a single operation like so:

```
@collection.insert(doc, :safe => {:w => 2, :wtimeout => 200})
```

Sometimes you simply want to ensure that a write is replicated to a majority of available nodes. For this case, you can set a w value of majority:

```
@collection.insert(doc, :safe => {:w => "majority"})
```

Even fancier options exist. For instance, if you've enabled journaling, then you can also force that the journal be synced to disk by adding the j option:

```
@collection.insert(doc, :safe => {:w => 2, :j => true})
```

Many drivers also support setting default write concern values for a given connection or database. To find out how to set write concern in your particular case, check your driver's documentation. A few more language examples can be found in appendix D.

Write concern works with both replica sets and master-slave replication. If you examine the local databases, you'll see a couple collections, me on secondary nodes and slaves on the primary node, that are used to implement write concern. Whenever a secondary polls a primary, the primary makes a note of the latest oplog entry applied to each secondary in its slaves collection. Thus, the primary knows what each secondary has replicated at all times and can therefore reliably answer the getlasterror command's write requests.

Keep in mind that using write concern with values of w greater than 1 will introduce extra latency. Configurable write concern essentially allows *you* to make the trade-off between speed and durability. If you're running with journaling, then a write concern with w equal to 1 should be fine for most applications. On the other hand, for logging or analytics, you might elect to disable journaling and write concern altogether and rely solely on replication for durability, allowing that you may lose some writes in the event of a failure. Consider these trade-offs carefully and test the different scenarios when designing your application.

---

[12] There are examples of setting write concern in Java, PHP, and C++ in appendix D.

8.4.3 Read scaling

Replicated databases are great for read scaling. If a single server can't handle the application's read load, then you have the option to route queries to more than one replica. Most of the drivers have built-in support for sending queries to secondary nodes. With the Ruby driver, this is provided as an option on the ReplSetConnection constructor:

```
Mongo::ReplSetConnection.new(['arete', 40000],
        ['arete', 40001], :read => :secondary )
```

When the :read argument is set to :secondary, the connection object will choose a random, nearby secondary to read from.

Other drivers can be configured to read from secondaries by setting a slaveOk option. When the Java driver is connected to a replica set, setting slaveOk to true will enable secondary load balancing on a per-thread basis. The load balancing implementations found in the drivers are designed to be generally applicable, so they may not work for all apps. When that's the case, users frequently customize their own. As usual, consult your driver's documentation for specifics.

Many MongoDB users scale with replication in production. But there are three cases where this sort of scaling won't be sufficient. The first concerns the number of servers needed. As of MongoDB v2.0, replica sets support a maximum of 12 members, 7 of which can vote. If you need even more replicas for scaling, you *can* use master-slave replication. But if you don't want to sacrifice automated failover and you need to scale beyond the replica set maximum, then you'll need to migrate to a sharded cluster.

The second case involves applications with a high write load. As mentioned at the beginning of the chapter, secondaries must keep up with this write load. Sending reads to write-laden secondaries may inhibit replication.

A third situation that replica scaling can't handle is consistent reads. Because replication is asynchronous, replicas aren't always going to reflect the latest writes to the primary. Therefore, if your application reads arbitrarily from secondaries, then the picture presented to end users isn't always guaranteed to be fully consistent. For applications whose main purpose is to display content, this almost never presents a problem. But other apps, where users are actively manipulating data, will require consistent reads. In these cases, you have two options. The first is to separate the parts of the application that need consistent reads from the parts that don't. The former can always be read from the primary, and the latter can be distributed to secondaries. When this strategy is either too complicated or simply doesn't scale, sharding is the way to go.[13]

---

[13] Note that to get consistent reads from a sharded cluster, you must always read from the primary nodes of each shard, and you must issue safe writes.

8.4.4   *Tagging*

If you're using either write concern or read scaling, you may find yourself wanting more granular control over exactly which secondaries receive writes or reads. For example, suppose you've deployed a five-node replica set across two data centers, *NY* and *FR*. The primary data center, NY, contains three nodes, and the secondary data center, FR, contains the remaining two. Let's say that you want to use write concern to block until a certain write has been replicated to at least one node in data center FR. With what you know about write concern right now, you'll see that there's no good way to do this. You can't use a w value of majority, since this will translate into a value of 3, and the most likely scenario is that the three nodes in NY will acknowledge first. You could use a value of 4, but this won't hold up well if, say, you lose one node from each data center.

Replica set tagging solves this problem by allowing you to define special write concern modes that target replica set members with certain tags. To see how this works, you first need to learn how to tag a replica set member. In the config document, each member can have a key called tags pointing to an object containing key-value pairs. Here's an example:

```
{
    "_id" : "myapp",
    "version" : 1,
    "members" : [
        {
            "_id" : 0,
            "host" : "ny1.myapp.com:30000",
            "tags": { "dc": "NY", "rackNY": "A" }
        },
        {
            "_id" : 1,
            "host" : "ny2.myapp.com:30000",
            "tags": { "dc": "NY", "rackNY": "A" }
        },
        {
            "_id" : 2,
            "host" : "ny3.myapp.com:30000",
            "tags": { "dc": "NY", "rackNY": "B" }
        },
        {
            "_id" : 3,
            "host" : "fr1.myapp.com:30000",
            "tags": { "dc": "FR", "rackFR": "A" }
        },
        {
            "_id" : 4,
            "host" : "fr2.myapp.com:30000",
            "tags": { "dc": "FR", "rackFR": "B" }
        }
    ],

    settings: {
```

```
    getLastErrorModes: {
      multiDC: { dc: 2 } },
      multiRack: { rackNY: 2 } },
    }
  }
}
```

This is a tagged configuration document for the hypothetical replica set spanning two data centers. Note that each member's tag document has two key-value pairs: the first identifies the data center and the second names the local server rack for the given node. Keep in mind that the names used here are completely arbitrary and only meaningful in the context of this application; you can put anything in a tag document. What's most important is how you use it.

That's where `getLastErrorModes` come into play. These allow you to define modes for the `getLastError` command that implement specific write concern requirements. In the example, you've defined two of these. The first, `multiDC`, is defined as { `"dc"`: 2 }, which indicates that a write should be replicated to nodes tagged with at least two different values for `dc`. If you examine the tags, you'll see this will necessarily ensure that the write has been propagated to both data centers. The second mode specifies that at least two server racks in NY should have received the write. Again the tags should make this clear.

In general, a `getLastErrorModes` entry consists of a document with one or more keys (in this case, `dc` and `rackNY`) whose values are integers. These integers indicate the number of different tagged values for the key that must be satisfied for the `getLastError` command to complete successfully. Once you've define these modes, you can use them as values for `w` in your application. For example, using the first mode in Ruby looks like this:

```
@collection.insert(doc, :safe => {:w => "multiDC"})
```

In addition to making write concern more sophisticated, tagging promises to provide more granular control over which replicas are used for read scaling. Unfortunately, at the time of this writing, the semantics for reading against tags haven't been defined or implemented in the official MongoDB drivers. For updates, follow the issue for the Ruby driver at https://jira.mongodb.org/browse/RUBY-326.

8.5 Summary

It should be clear from all that we've discussed that replication is incredibly useful and that it's also essential for most deployments. MongoDB's replication is supposed to be easy, and setting it up usually is. But when it comes to backing up and failing over, there are bound to be hidden complexities. For these complex cases, let experience, and some help from this chapter, breed familiarity.

Sharding 9

MongoDB was designed from the start to support sharding. This has always been an ambitious goal because building a system that supports automatic range-based partitioning and balancing, with no single point of failure, is hard. Thus the initial support for production-level sharding was first made available in August 2010 with the release of MongoDB v1.6. Since then, numerous improvements have been made to the sharding subsystem. Sharding effectively enables users to keep large volumes of data evenly distributed across nodes and to add capacity as needed. In this chapter, I'll present the layer that makes this possible in all its glory.

We'll begin with a sharding overview, discussing what sharding is, why it's important, and how it's implemented in MongoDB. Although this will give you a basic working knowledge of sharding, you won't fully understand it until you set up your own sharded cluster. That's what you'll do in the second section, where you'll build a sample cluster to host data from a massive Google Docs-like application. We'll then discuss some sharding mechanics, describing how queries and indexing work across shards. We'll look at the ever-important choice of shard key. And I'll end the chapter with a lot of specific advice on running sharding in production.

Sharding is complicated. To get the most out of this chapter, you should run the examples. You'll have no trouble running the sample cluster entirely on one machine; once you do, start experimenting with it. There's nothing like having a live sharded deployment on hand for understanding MongoDB as a distributed system.

9.1 Sharding overview

Before you build your first sharded cluster, it's useful to understand what sharding is and why it's sometimes appropriate. The explanation about why sharding matters gets to one of the core justifications for the MongoDB project as a whole. Once you understand why sharding is important, you'll appreciate learning about the core components that make up a sharded cluster and the key concepts that underlie MongoDB's sharding machinery.

9.1.1 What sharding is

Up until this point, you've used MongoDB as a single server, where each `mongod` instance contains a complete copy of your application's data. Even when using replication, each replica clones every other replica's data entirely. For the majority of applications, storing the complete data set on a single server is perfectly acceptable. But as the size of the data grows, and as an application demands greater read and write throughput, commodity servers may not be sufficient. In particular, these servers may not be able to address enough RAM, or they might not have enough CPU cores, to process the workload efficiently. In addition, as the size of the data grows, it may become impractical to store and manage backups for such a large data set all on one disk or RAID array. If you're to continue to use commodity or virtualized hardware to host the database, then the solution to these problems is to distribute the database across more than one server. The method for doing this is sharding.

Numerous large web applications, notably Flickr and LiveJournal, have implemented manual sharding schemes to distribute load across MySQL databases. In these implementations, the sharding logic lives entirely inside the application. To understand how this works, imagine that you had so many users that you needed to distribute your Users table across multiple database servers. You could do this by designating one database as the lookup database. This database would contain the metadata mapping each user ID (or some range of user IDs) to a given shard. Thus a query for a user would actually involve two queries: the first query would contact the lookup database to get the user's shard location and then a second query would be directed to the individual shard containing the user data.

For these web applications, manual sharding solves the load problem, but the implementation isn't without its faults. The most notable of these is the difficulty involved in migrating data. If a single shard is overloaded, the migration of that data to other shards is an entirely manual process. A second problem with manual sharding is the difficulty of writing reliable application code to route reads and writes and manage the database as a whole. Recently, frameworks for managing manual sharding have been released, most notably Twitter's Gizzard (see http://mng.bz/4qvd).

But as anyone who's manually sharded a database will tell you, getting it right isn't easy. MongoDB was built in large part to address this problem. Because sharding is at the heart of MongoDB, users need not worry about having to design an external sharding framework when the time comes to scale horizontally. This is especially important for handling the hard problem of balancing data across shards. The code that makes balancing work isn't the sort of thing that most people can cook up over a weekend.

Perhaps most significantly, MongoDB has been designed to present the same interface to the application before and after sharding. This means that application code needs little if any modification when the database must be converted to a sharded architecture.

You should now have some sense for the rationale behind automated sharding. Still, before describing the MongoDB sharding process in more detail, we should pause for a moment to answer another obvious first question: when is sharding necessary?

WHEN TO SHARD

The question of when to shard is more straightforward than you might expect. We've talked about the importance of keeping indexes and the working data set in RAM, and this is the primary reason to shard. If an application's data set continues to grow unbounded, then there will come a moment when that data no longer fits in RAM. If you're running on Amazon's EC2, then you'll hit that threshold at 68 GB because that's the amount of RAM available on the largest instance at the time of this writing. Alternatively, you may run your own hardware with much more than 68 GB of RAM, in which case you'll probably be able to delay sharding for some time. But no machine has infinite capacity for RAM; therefore, sharding eventually becomes necessary.

To be sure, there *are* some fudge factors here. For instance, if you have your own hardware and can store all your data on solid state drives (an increasingly affordable prospect), then you'll likely be able to push the data-to-RAM ratio without negatively affecting performance. It might also be the case that your working set is a fraction of your total data size and that, therefore, you can operate with relatively little RAM. On the flip side, if you have an especially demanding write load, then you may want to shard *well before* data reaches the size of RAM, simply because you need to distribute the load across machines to get the desired write throughput.

Whatever the case, the decision to shard an existing system will always be based on regular analyses of disk activity, system load, and the ever-important ratio of working set size to available RAM.

9.1.2 *How sharding works*

To understand how MongoDB's sharding works, you need to know about the components that make up a sharded cluster, and you need to understand the software processes that coordinate those components. These are the subjects of the next two sections.

SHARDING COMPONENTS

A sharded cluster consists of shards, mongos routers, and config servers. Refer to the diagram in figure 9.1 as we discuss each of these components.

Shards

A MongoDB shard cluster distributes data across one or more shards. Each shard is deployed as a MongoDB replica set, and this set stores some portion of the cluster's total data. Because each shard is a replica set, each shard has its own replication mechanism and can fail over automatically. You can connect directly to an individual shard just as you would to a standalone replica set. But if you connect to a replica set that's part of a sharded cluster, you'll see just a portion of the cluster's total data.

Mongos routers

If each shard contains part of the cluster's data, then you still need an interface to the cluster as a whole. That's where mongos comes in. The mongos process is a router that directs all reads and writes to the appropriate shard. In this way, mongos provides clients with a coherent view of the system.

mongos processes are lightweight and nonpersistent. They typically reside on the same machines as the application servers, ensuring that only one network hop is

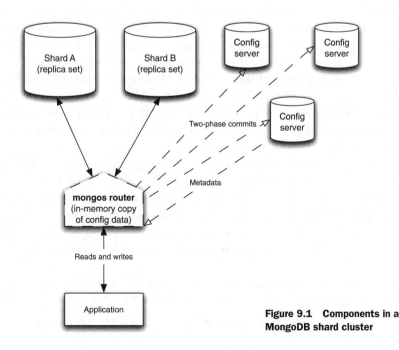

Figure 9.1 Components in a MongoDB shard cluster

required for requests to any given shard. In other words, the application connects locally to a mongos, and the mongos manages connections to the individual shards.

Config servers

If mongos processes are nonpersistent, then something must durably store the shard cluster's canonical state; that's the job of the config servers. The config servers persist the shard cluster's metadata. This data includes the global cluster configuration; the locations of each database, collection, and the particular ranges of data therein; and a change log preserving a history of the migrations of data across shards.

The metadata held by the config servers is central to the proper functioning and upkeep of the cluster. For instance, every time a mongos process is started, the mongos fetches a copy of the metadata from the config servers. Without this data, no coherent view of the shard cluster is possible. The importance of this data, then, informs the design and deployment strategy for the config servers.

If you examine figure 9.1, you'll see that there are three config servers, but that they're not deployed as a replica set. They demand something stronger than asynchronous replication; when the mongos process writes to them, it does so using a two-phase commit. This guarantees consistency across config servers. You must run exactly three config servers in any production deployment of sharding, and these servers must reside on separate machines for redundancy.[1]

You now know what a shard cluster consists of, but you're probably still wondering about the sharding machinery itself. How is data actually distributed? I'll explain that in the next section by introducing the core sharding operations.

CORE SHARDING OPERATIONS

A MongoDB shard cluster distributes data across shards on two levels. The coarser of these is by database. As you create new databases in the cluster, each database is assigned to a different shard. If you do nothing else, a database and all its collections will live forever on the shard where they were created.

Because most applications will keep all their data in the same physical database, this distribution isn't very helpful. You need to distribute on a more granular level, and the collection satisfies this requirement. MongoDB's sharding is designed specifically to distribute individual collections across shards. To understand this better, let's imagine how this might work in a real application.

Suppose you're building a cloud-based office suite for managing spreadsheets and that you're going to store all the data in MongoDB.[2] Users will be able to create as many documents as they want, and you'll store each one as a separate MongoDB document in a single spreadsheets collection. Assume that over time, your application grows to a million users. Now imagine your two primary collections: users and spreadsheets. The users collection is manageable. Even with a million users, at 1 KB

---

[1] You can also run just a single config server, but only as a way of more easily testing sharding. Running with just one config server in production is like taking a transatlantic flight in a single-engine jet: it might get you there, but lose an engine and you're hosed.

[2] Think something like Google Docs, which, among other things, allows users to create spreadsheets and presentations.

per user document, the collection is roughly 1 GB and can easily be served by a single machine. But the `spreadsheets` collection is a different story. If you assume that each user owns an average of 50 spreadsheets, and that each averages 50 KB in size, then you're talking about a 1 TB `spreadsheets` collection. If this is a highly active application, then you'll want to keep the data in RAM. To keep this data in RAM and distribute reads and writes, you must shard the collection. That's where sharding comes into play.

Sharding a collection

MongoDB's sharding is range-based. This means that every document in a sharded collection must fall within some range of values for a given key. MongoDB uses a so-called *shard key* to place each document within one of these ranges.[3] You can understand this better by looking at a sample document from the theoretical spreadsheet management application:

```
{
  _id: ObjectId("4d6e9b89b600c2c196442c21")
  filename: "spreadsheet-1",
  updated_at: ISODate("2011-03-02T19:22:54.845Z"),
  username: "banks",
  data: "raw document data"
}
```

When you shard this collection, you must declare one or more of these fields as the shard key. If you choose `_id`, then documents will be distributed based on ranges of object IDs. But for reasons that will become clear later, you're going to declare a compound shard key on `username` and `_id`; therefore, each range will usually represent some series of user names.

You're now in a position to understand the concept of a *chunk*. A chunk is a contiguous range of shard key values located on a single shard. As an example, you can imagine the `docs` collection being divided across two shards, A and B, into the chunks you see in table 9.1. Each chunk's range is marked by a start and end value.

A cursory glance at this table reveals one of the main, sometimes counterintuitive, properties of chunks: that although each individual chunk represents a contiguous range of data, those ranges can appear on any shard.

A second important point about chunks is that they're not *physical* but *logical*. In other words, a chunk doesn't represent a contiguous series of document on disk. Rather, to say that the chunk beginning with *harris* and ending with *norris* exists on shard A is simply to say that any document with a shard key falling within this range can be found in shard A's `docs` collection. This implies nothing about the *arrangement* of those documents within the collection.

Table 9.1 Chunks and shards

Start	End	Shard
-∞	abbot	B
abbot	dayton	A
dayton	harris	B
harris	norris	A
norris	∞	B

---

[3] Alternate distributed databases might use the terms *partition key* or *distribution key* instead.

Splitting and migrating

At the heart of the sharding mechanism are the splitting and migration of chunks.

First, consider the idea of splitting chunks. When you initially set up a sharded cluster, just one chunk exists. That one chunk's range encompasses the entire sharded collection. How then do you arrive at a sharded cluster with multiple chunks? The answer is that chunks are split once they reach a certain size threshold. The default max chunk size is 64 MB or 100,000 documents, whichever comes first. As data is added to a new sharded cluster, the original chunk eventually reaches one of these thresholds, triggering a chunk split. Splitting a chunk is a simple operation; it basically involves dividing the original range into two ranges so that two chunks, each representing the same number of documents, are created.

Note that chunk splitting is *logical*. When MongoDB splits a chunk, it merely modifies the chunk metadata so that one chunk becomes two. Splitting a chunk, therefore, does not affect the physical ordering of the documents in a sharded collection. This means that splitting is simple and fast.

But as you'll recall, one of the biggest difficulties in designing a sharding system is ensuring that data is always evenly balanced. MongoDB's sharded clusters balance by moving chunks between shards. We call this *migrating*, and unlike splitting, it's a real, physical operation.

Migrations are managed by a software process known as the *balancer*. The balancer's job is to ensure that data remains evenly distributed across shards. It accomplishes this by keeping track of the number of chunks on each shard. Though the heuristic varies somewhat depending on total data size, the balancer will usually initiate a balancing round when the difference between the shard with the greatest number of chunks and the shard with the least number of chunks is greater than eight. During the balancing round, chunks are migrated from the shard with the greater number of chunks to the shard with fewer chunks until the two shards are roughly even.

Don't worry too much if this doesn't make sense yet. The next section, where I'll demonstrate sharding with a sample cluster, will bring the concepts of the shard key and chunking into the light of practice.

9.2   *A sample shard cluster*

The best way to get a handle on sharding is to see how it works in action. Fortunately, it's possible to set up a sharded cluster on a single machine, and that's exactly what we'll do now.[4] We'll then simulate the behavior of the sample cloud-based spreadsheet application described in the previous section. Along the way, we'll examine the global shard configuration and see first-hand how data is partitioned based on the shard key.

---

[4] The idea is that you can run every mongod and mongos process on a single machine for testing. Later in the chapter, we'll look at production sharding configurations and the minimum number of machines required for a viable deployment.

9.2.1 Setup

You set up a shard cluster in two phases. In the first, you start all the required mongod and mongos processes. In the second, the easier of the two, you issue a series of commands to initiate the cluster. The shard cluster you'll build will consist of two shards and three config servers. You'll also start a single mongos to communicate with the cluster. Figure 9.2 shows a map of all the processes that you'll launch with their port numbers in parentheses.

You'll be running a bunch of commands to bring the cluster online, so if you find yourself losing the forest for the trees, refer back to this figure.

STARTING THE SHARDING COMPONENTS

Let's start by creating the data directories for the two replica sets that will serve as our shards.

```
$ mkdir /data/rs-a-1
$ mkdir /data/rs-a-2
$ mkdir /data/rs-a-3
$ mkdir /data/rs-b-1
$ mkdir /data/rs-b-2
$ mkdir /data/rs-b-3
```

Next, start each mongod. Because you're running so many processes, you'll use the --fork option to run them in the background.[5] The commands for starting the first replica set are shown next.

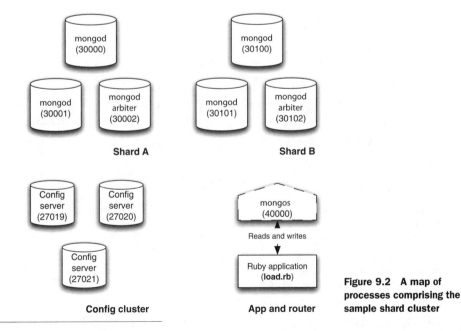

Shard A

Shard B

Config cluster

App and router

Figure 9.2 A map of processes comprising the sample shard cluster

---

[5] If you're running Windows, note that fork won't work for you. Because you'll have to open a new terminal window for each process, you're best off omitting the logpath option as well.

```
$ mongod --shardsvr --replSet shard-a --dbpath /data/rs-a-1 \
  --port 30000 --logpath /data/rs-a-1.log --fork --nojournal
$ mongod --shardsvr --replSet shard-a --dbpath /data/rs-a-2 \
  --port 30001 --logpath /data/rs-a-2.log --fork --nojournal
$ mongod --shardsvr --replSet shard-a  --dbpath /data/rs-a-3 \
  --port 30002 --logpath /data/rs-a-3.log --fork --nojournal
```

And here are the commands for the second one:

```
$ mongod --shardsvr --replSet shard-b --dbpath /data/rs-b-1 \
  --port 30100 --logpath /data/rs-b-1.log --fork --nojournal
$ mongod --shardsvr --replSet shard-b --dbpath /data/rs-b-2 \
  --port 30101 --logpath /data/rs-b-2.log --fork --nojournal
$ mongod --shardsvr --replSet shard-b --dbpath /data/rs-b-3 \
  --port 30102 --logpath /data/rs-b-3.log --fork --nojournal
```

As usual, you now need to initiate these replica sets. Connect to each one individually, run rs.initiate(), and then add the remaining nodes. The first should look like this:[6]

```
$ mongo arete:30000
> rs.initiate()
```

You'll have to wait a minute or so before the initial node becomes primary. Once it does, you can add the remaining nodes:

```
> rs.add("arete:30000")
> rs.add("arete:30001", {arbiterOnly: true})
```

Initiating the second replica set is similar. Again, wait a minute after running rs .initiate():

```
$ mongo arete:30100
> rs.initiate()
> rs.add("arete:30100")
> rs.add("arete:30101", {arbiterOnly: true})
```

Finally, verify that both replica sets are online by running the rs.status() command from the shell on each one. If everything checks out, you're ready to start the config servers.[7] Now you create each config server's data directory and then start a mongod for each one using the configsvr option:

```
$ mkdir /data/config-1
$ mongod --configsvr --dbpath /data/config-1 --port 27019 \
  --logpath /data/config-1.log --fork --nojournal

$ mkdir /data/config-2
$ mongod --configsvr --dbpath /data/config-2 --port 27020 \
  --logpath /data/config-2.log --fork --nojournal

$ mkdir /data/config-3
$ mongod --configsvr --dbpath /data/config-3 --port 27021 \
  --logpath /data/config-3.log --fork --nojournal
```

---

[6] arete is the name of the local host.

[7] Again, if running on Windows, omit the --fork and --logpath options, and start each mongod in a new window.

Ensure that each config server is up and running by connecting with the shell or by tailing the log file and verifying that each process is listening on the configured port. Looking at the logs for any one config server, you should see something like this:

```
Wed Mar  2 15:43:28 [initandlisten] waiting for connections on port 27020
Wed Mar  2 15:43:28 [websvr] web admin interface listening on port 28020
```

If each config server is running, you can go ahead and start the mongos. The mongos must be started with the configdb option, which takes a comma-separated list of config database addresses:[8]

```
$ mongos --configdb arete:27019,arete:27020,arete:27021 \
  --logpath /data/mongos.log --fork --port 40000
```

CONFIGURING THE CLUSTER

You have all the sharding components in place. Now it's time to configure the cluster. Start by connecting to the mongos. To simplify the task, you'll use the sharding helper methods. These are methods run on the global sh object. To see a list of all available helper methods, run sh.help().

You'll enter a series of configuration commands beginning with the addshard command. The helper for this command is sh.addShard(). This method takes a string consisting of the name of a replica set followed by the addresses of two or more seed nodes for connecting. Here you specify the two replica sets you created along with the addresses of the two non-arbiter members of each set:

```
$ mongo arete:40000
> sh.addShard("shard-a/arete:30000,arete:30001")
  { "shardAdded" : "shard-a", "ok" : 1 }
> sh.addShard("shard-b/arete:30100,arete:30101")
  { "shardAdded" : "shard-b", "ok" : 1 }
```

If successful, the command response will include the name of the shard just added. You can examine the config database's shards collection to see the effect of your work. Instead of using the use command, you'll use the getSiblingDB() method to switch databases:

```
> db.getSiblingDB("config").shards.find()
{ "_id" : "shard-a", "host" : "shard-a/arete:30000,arete:30001" }
{ "_id" : "shard-b", "host" : "shard-b/arete:30100,arete:30101" }
```

As a shortcut, the listshards command returns the same information:

```
> use admin
> db.runCommand({listshards: 1})
```

While we're on the topic of reporting on sharding configuration, the shell's sh.status() method nicely summarizes the cluster. Go ahead and try running it now.

---

[8] Be careful not to put spaces between the config server addresses when specifying them.

The next configuration step is to enable sharding on a database. This is a prerequisite for sharding any collection. Your application's database will be called `cloud-docs`, and so you enable sharding like so:

```
> sh.enableSharding("cloud-docs")
```

Like before, you can check the config data to see the change you just made. The config database holds a collection called `databases` that contains a list of databases. Each document specifies the database's primary shard location and whether it's partitioned (whether sharding is enabled):

```
> db.getSiblingDB("config").databases.find()
{ "_id" : "admin", "partitioned" : false, "primary" : "config" }
{ "_id" : "cloud-docs", "partitioned" : true, "primary" : "shard-a" }
```

Now all you need to do is shard the `spreadsheets` collection. When you shard a collection, you define a shard key. Here you'll use the compound shard key {username: 1, _id: 1} because it's good for distributing data and makes it easy to view and comprehend chunk ranges:

```
> sh.shardCollection("cloud-docs.spreadsheets", {username: 1, _id: 1})
```

Again, you can verify the configuration by checking the config database for sharded collections:

```
> db.getSiblingDB("config").collections.findOne()
{
  "_id" : "cloud-docs.spreadsheets",
  "lastmod" : ISODate("1970-01-16T00:50:07.268Z"),
  "dropped" : false,
  "key" : {
    "username" : 1,
    "_id" : 1
  },
  "unique" : false
}
```

This sharded collection definition may remind you of something; it looks a bit like an index definition, especially with its `unique` key. When you shard an empty collection, MongoDB creates an index corresponding to the shard key on each shard.[9] Verify this for yourself by connecting directly to a shard and running the `getIndexes()` method. Here you connect to your first shard, and the output contains the shard key index, as expected:

```
$ mongo arete:30000
> use cloud-docs
> db.spreadsheets.getIndexes()
[
  {
    "name" : "_id_",
```

---

[9] If you're sharding an existing collection, you'll have to create an index corresponding to the shard key *before* you run the `shardcollection` command.

```
    "ns" : "cloud-docs.spreadsheets",
    "key" : {
      "_id" : 1
    },
    "v" : 0
  },
  {
    "ns" : "cloud-docs.spreadsheets",
    "key" : {
      "username" : 1,
      "_id" : 1
    },
    "name" : "username_1__id_1",
    "v" : 0
  }
]
```

Once you've sharded the collection, then at last, sharding is ready to go. You can now write to the cluster and data will distribute. We'll see how that works in the next section.

9.2.2 *Writing to a sharded cluster*

We'll write to the sharded collection so that you can observe the formation and movement of chunks, which is the essence of MongoDB's sharding. The sample documents, each representing a single spreadsheet, will look like this:

```
{
  _id: ObjectId("4d6f29c0e4ef0123afdacaeb"),
  filename: "sheet-1",
  updated_at: new Date(),
  username: "banks",
  data: "RAW DATA"
}
```

Note that the data field will contain a 5 KB string to simulate the raw data.

This book's source code includes a Ruby script you can use to write documents to the cluster. The script takes a number of iterations as its argument, and for each iteration, it inserts one 5 KB document for each of 200 users. The script's source is here:

```ruby
require 'rubygems'
require 'mongo'
require 'names'

@con  = Mongo::Connection.new("localhost", 40000)
@col  = @con['cloud']['spreadsheets']
@data = "abcde" * 1000

def write_user_docs(iterations=0, name_count=200)
  iterations.times do |n|
    name_count.times do |n|
      doc = { :filename => "sheet-#{n}",
              :updated_at => Time.now.utc,
              :username => Names::LIST[n],
              :data => @data
            }
```

```
      @col.insert(doc)
    end
  end
end

if ARGV.empty? || !(ARGV[0] =~ /^d+$/)
  puts "Usage: load.rb [iterations] [name_count]"
else
  iterations = ARGV[0].to_i

  if ARGV[1] && ARGV[1] =~ /^d+$/
    name_count = ARGV[1].to_i
  else
    name_count = 200
  end

  write_user_docs(iterations, name_count)
end
```

If you have the script on hand, you can run it from the command line with no arguments to insert the initial iteration of 200 values:

```
$ ruby load.rb
```

Now connect to mongos via the shell. If you query the spreadsheets collection, you'll see that it contains exactly 200 documents and that they total around 1 MB. You can also query a document, but be sure to exclude the sample data field (since you don't want to print 5 KB of text to the screen).

```
$ mongo arete:40000
> use cloud-docs
> db.spreadsheets.count()
200
> db.spreadsheets.stats().size
1019496
> db.spreadsheets.findOne({}, {data: 0})
{
  "_id" : ObjectId("4d6d6b191d41c8547d0024c2"),
  "username" : "Cerny",
  "updated_at" : ISODate("2011-03-01T21:54:33.813Z"),
  "filename" : "sheet-0"
}
```

Now you can check out what's happened sharding-wise. Switch to the config database and check the number of chunks:

```
> use config
> db.chunks.count()
1
```

There's just one chunk so far. Let's see how it looks:

```
> db.chunks.findOne()
{
  "_id" : "cloud-docs.spreadsheets-username_MinKey_id_MinKey",
  "lastmod" : {
```

```
    "t" : 1000,
    "i" : 0
  },
  "ns" : "cloud-docs.spreadsheets",
  "min" : {
    "username" : { $minKey : 1 },
    "_id" : { $minKey : 1 }
  },
  "max" : {
    "username" : { $maxKey : 1 },
    "_id" : { $maxKey : 1 }
  },
  "shard" : "shard-a"
}
```

Can you figure out what range this chunk represents? If there's just one chunk, then it spans the entire sharded collection. That's borne out by the min and max fields, which show that the chunk's range is bounded by $minKey and $maxKey.

MINKEY AND MAXKEY $minKey and $maxKey are used in comparison operations as the boundaries of BSON types. $minKey always compares lower than all BSON types, and $maxKey compares greater than all BSON types. Because the value for any given field can contain any BSON type, MongoDB uses these two types to mark the chunk endpoints at the extremities of the sharded collection.

You can see a more interesting chunk range by adding more data to the spreadsheets collection. You'll use the Ruby script again, but this time you'll run 100 iterations, which will insert an extra 20,000 documents totaling 100 MB:

```
$ ruby load.rb 100
```

Verify that the insert worked:

```
> db.spreadsheets.count()
20200
> db.spreadsheets.stats().size
103171828
```

Sample insert speed

Note that it may take several minutes to insert this data into the shard cluster. There are three reasons for the slowness. First, you're performing a round trip for each insert, whereas you might be able to perform bulk inserts in a production situation. Second, you're inserting using Ruby, whose BSON serializer is slower than that of certain other drivers. Finally, and most significantly, you're running all of the shard's nodes on a single machine. This places a huge burden on the disk, as four of your nodes are being written to simultaneously (two replica set primaries, and two replicating secondaries). Suffice it to say that in a proper production installation, this insert would run much more quickly.

Having inserted this much data, you'll definitely have more than one chunk. You can check the chunk state quickly by counting the number of documents in the chunks collection:

```
> use config
> db.chunks.count()
10
```

You can see more detailed information by running `sh.status()`. This method prints all of the chunks along with their ranges. For brevity, I'll only show the first two chunks:

```
> sh.status()
sharding version: { "_id" : 1, "version" : 3 }
 shards:
  { "_id": "shard-a", "host": "shard-a/arete:30000,arete:30001" }
  { "_id": "shard-b", "host": "shard-b/arete:30100,arete:30101" }

 databases:
  { "_id": "admin", "partitioned": false, "primary": "config" }
  { "_id": "test",  "partitioned": false, "primary": "shard-a" }
  { "_id": "cloud-docs", "partitioned": true,  "primary": "shard-b" }
     shard-a 5
     shard-b 5
   { "username": { $minKey : 1 }, "_id" : { $minKey : 1 } } --
     >>   { "username": "Abdul",
     "_id": ObjectId("4e89ffe7238d3be9f0000012") }
  on: shard-a { "t" : 2000, "i" : 0 }

    { "username" : "Abdul",
      "_id" : ObjectId("4e89ffe7238d3be9f0000012") } -->> {
      "username" : "Buettner",
      "_id" : ObjectId("4e8a00a0238d3be9f0002e98") }
   on : shard-a { "t" : 3000, "i" : 0 }
```

The picture has definitely changed. You now have 10 chunks. Naturally, each chunk represents a contiguous range of data. You can see that the first chunk with data is composed of documents from $minKey to Abdul and that the second chunk runs from Abdul to Buettner.[10] But not only do you have more chunks—the chunks have migrated to the second shard. You could visually scan the `sh.status()` output to see this, but there's an easier way:

```
> db.chunks.count({"shard": "shard-a"})
5
> db.chunks.count({"shard": "shard-b"})
5
```

As long as the cluster's data size is small, the splitting algorithm dictates that splits happen often. That's what you see now. This gives you a good distribution of data and chunks early on. From now on, as long as writes remain evenly distributed across the existing chunk ranges, few migrates will occur.

---

[10] If you're following along, note that your chunk distributions may differ somewhat.

> **Early chunk splitting**
>
> A sharded cluster will split chunks aggressively early on to expedite the migration of data across shards. Specifically, when the number of chunks is less than 10, chunks will split at one quarter of the max chunk size (16 MB), and when the number of chunks is between 10 and 20, they'll split at half the maximum chunk size (32 MB).
>
> This has two nice benefits. First, it creates a lot of chunks up front, which initiates a migration round. Second, that migration round occurs fairly painlessly, as the small chunk size ensures that the total amount of migrated data is small.

Now the split threshold will increase. You can see how the splitting slows down, and how chunks start to grow toward their max size, by doing a more massive insert. Try adding another 800 MB to the cluster:

```
$ ruby load.rb 800
```

This will take a lot time to run, so you may want to step away and grab a snack after starting this load process. By the time it's done, you'll have increased the total data size by a factor of eight. But if you check the chunking status, you'll see that there are only around twice as many chunks:

```
> use config
> db.chunks.count()
21
```

Given that there are more chunks, the average chunk ranges will be smaller, but each chunk will include more data. So for example, the first chunk in the collection spans from Abbott to Bender but it's already nearly 60 MB in size. Because the max chunk size is currently 64 MB, you'd soon see this chunk split if you were to continue inserting data.

Another thing to notice is that the distribution still looks pretty much even, as it was before:

```
> db.chunks.count({"shard": "shard-a"})
11
> db.chunks.count({"shard": "shard-b"})
10
```

Although the number of chunks has increased during the last 800 MB insert round, you can probably assume that no migrates occurred; a likely scenario is that each of the original chunks split in two, with a single extra split somewhere in the mix. You can verify this by querying the config database's changelog collection:

```
> db.changelog.count({what: "split"})
20
> db.changelog.find({what: "moveChunk.commit"}).count()
6
```

This is in line with these assumptions. A total of 20 splits have occurred, yielding 20 chunks, but only 6 migrates have taken place. For an extra-deep look at what's going on here, you can scan the change log entries. For instance, here's the entry recording the first chunk move:

```
> db.changelog.findOne({what: "moveChunk.commit"})
{
  "_id" : "arete-2011-09-01T20:40:59-2",
  "server" : "arete",
  "clientAddr" : "127.0.0.1:55749",
  "time" : ISODate("2011-03-01T20:40:59.035Z"),
  "what" : "moveChunk.commit",
  "ns" : "cloud-docs.spreadsheets",
  "details" : {
    "min" : {
      "username" : { $minKey : 1 },
      "_id" : { $minKey : 1 }
    },
    "max" : {
      "username" : "Abbott",
      "_id" : ObjectId("4d6d57f61d41c851ee000092")
    },
    "from" : "shard-a",
    "to" : "shard-b"
  }
}
```

Here you see the movement of chunks from shard-a to shard-b. In general, the documents you find in the change log are quite readable. As you learn more about sharding and begin prototyping your own shard clusters, the config change log makes an excellent live reference on split and migrate behavior. Refer to it often.

9.3   *Querying and indexing a shard cluster*

From the application's perspective, there's no difference between querying a sharded cluster and querying a single mongod. In both cases, the query interface and the process of iterating over the result set are the same. But behind the scenes, things are different, and it's worthwhile to understand exactly what's going on.

9.3.1   *Shard query types*

Imagine you're querying a shard cluster. How many shards does mongos need to contact to return a proper query response? If you give it some thought, you'll see that it depends on whether the shard key is present in the query selector. Remember that the config servers (and thus mongos) maintain a mapping of ranges to shards. These mappings are none other than the chunks that we examined earlier in the chapter. If a query includes the shard key, then mongos can quickly consult the chunk data to determine exactly which shard contains the query's result set. This is called a *targeted query*.

But if the shard key isn't part of the query, the query planner will have to visit all shards to fulfill the query completely. This is known as a *global* or *scatter/gather query*. The diagram in figure 9.3 illustrates both query types.

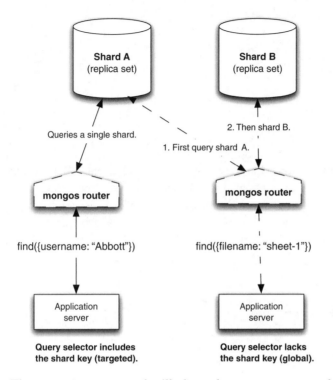

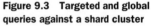

Figure 9.3 Targeted and global queries against a shard cluster

The `explain` command will show the exact query path taken by any given query against a sharded cluster. Let's start with a targeted query. Here you query for a document located in the first chunk, order-wise, of your collection.

```
> selector = {username: "Abbott",
  "_id" : ObjectId("4e8a1372238d3bece8000012")}
> db.spreadsheets.find(selector).explain()
{
  "shards" : {
    "shard-b/arete:30100,arete:30101" : [
      {
        "cursor" : "BtreeCursor username_1__id_1",
        "nscanned" : 1,
        "n" : 1,
        "millis" : 0,
        "indexBounds" : {
          "username" : [
            [
              "Abbott",
              "Abbott"
            ]
          ],
          "_id" : [
            [
              ObjectId("4d6d57f61d41c851ee000092"),
              ObjectId("4d6d57f61d41c851ee000092")
            ]
```

```
              ]
          }
        }
      ]
    },
    "n" : 1,
    "nscanned" : 1,
    "millisTotal" : 0,
    "numQueries" : 1,
    "numShards" : 1
}
```

The explain plan clearly shows that the query hit one shard, shard B, to return a single document.[11] The query planner is also sophisticated enough to use any prefix subset of the shard key for routing queries. This means you can also query by username alone:

```
> db.spreadsheets.find({username: "Abbott"}).explain()
{
  "shards" : {
    "shard-b/arete:30100,arete:30101" : [
      {
        "cursor" : "BtreeCursor username_1__id_1",
        "nscanned" : 801,
        "n" : 801,
      }
    ]
  },
  "n" : 801,
  "nscanned" : 801,
  "numShards" : 1
}
```

This query returns all 801 user documents but still goes to just one shard.

But what about global queries? These too are easily explained. Here's an example of a query by the filename field, which is neither an index nor part of the shard key:

```
> db.spreadsheets.find({filename: "sheet-1"}).explain()
{
  "shards" : {
    "shard-a/arete:30000,arete:30002,arete:30001" : [
      {
        "cursor" : "BasicCursor",
        "nscanned" : 102446,
        "n" : 117,
        "millis" : 85,
      }
    ],
    "shard-b/arete:30100,arete:30101" : [
      {
        "cursor" : "BasicCursor",
        "nscanned" : 77754,
```

---

[11] Note that in this and in the explain plans that follow, I've omitted several fields for the sake of brevity.

```
            "nscannedObjects" : 77754,
            "millis" : 65,
        }
    ]
  },
  "n" : 2900,
  "nscanned" : 180200,
  "millisTotal" : 150,
  "numQueries" : 2,
  "numShards" : 2
}
```

As you should expect, this global query performs a table scan on both shards. If this query were relevant to your application, you'd definitely want an index on `filename`. But in either case, the query will search the entire cluster to return a complete result.

Some queries require that you fetch an entire result set in parallel. For example, suppose you want to sort spreadsheets by update time. This requires merging the results within the `mongos` routing process. Without an index, a query like this is especially inefficient and frequently prohibited. So in the following example, where you query for the most recently created documents, you first create the necessary index:

```
> db.spreadsheets.ensureIndex({updated_at: 1})
> db.spreadsheets.find({}).sort({updated_at: 1}).explain()
{
  "shards" : {
    "shard-a/arete:30000,arete:30002" : [
      {
        "cursor" : "BtreeCursor updated_at_1",
        "nscanned" : 102446,
        "n" : 102446,
        "millis" : 191,
      }
    ],
    "shard-b/arete:30100,arete:30101" : [
      {
        "cursor" : "BtreeCursor updated_at_1",
        "nscanned" : 77754,
        "n" : 77754,
        "millis" : 130,
      }
    ]
  },
  "n" : 180200,
  "nscanned" : 180200,
  "millisTotal" : 321,
  "numQueries" : 2,
  "numShards" : 2
}
```

As expected, the cursor scans each shard's `updated_at` index to return the most recently updated documents.

A more likely query is to return the latest documents updated by a given user. Again, you'll create the necessary index and issue the query:

```
> db.spreadsheets.ensureIndex({username: 1, updated_at: -1})
> db.spreadsheets.find({username: "Wallace"}).sort(
  {updated_at: -1}).explain()
{
  "clusteredType" : "ParallelSort",
  "shards" : {
    "shard-1-test-rs/arete:30100,arete:30101" : [
      {
        "cursor" : "BtreeCursor username_1_updated_at_-1",
        "nscanned" : 801,
        "n" : 801,
        "millis" : 1,
      }
    ]
  },
  "n" : 801,
  "nscanned" : 801,
  "numQueries" : 1,
  "numShards" : 1
}
```

There are a couple of things to notice about this explain plan. The first is that the query is directed to just a single shard. Since you've specified part of the shard key, the query router can figure out which shard contains the relevant chunk. Realize then that a sort doesn't necessarily imply a trip to all shards; when the shard key is included in a sort query, the number of shards to query can often be pared down. In this case you hit just one shard, but you can imagine similar queries hitting some number of shards fewer than the total.

The second thing to notice from the explain plan is that the shard uses the {username: 1, updated_at: -1} index to serve the query. This illustrates an important point about how queries are processed in a sharded cluster. The shard key is used to route the query to a given shard, but once there, each shard itself determines which index to use to serve the query. Keep this in mind when designing queries and indexes for your application.

9.3.2 Indexing

You just saw some examples of how indexed queries work in a sharded cluster. If you're ever unsure about how a given query will resolve, use explain() to get the answer. This is usually straightforward, but a few more points about indexes should be kept in mind when running a sharded cluster. I'll enumerate them here:

1 Each shard maintains its own indexes. This should be obvious, but to be clear, know that when you declare an index on a sharded collection, each shard builds a separate index for its portion of the collection. For example, when you issued the db.spreasheets.ensureIndex() command via mongos in the previous section, each individual shard processed the index creation command individually.

2 It follows that the sharded collections on each shard should have the same indexes. If this ever isn't the case, you'll see inconsistent query performance.

3 Sharded collections permit unique indexes on the `_id` field and on the shard key only. Unique indexes are prohibited elsewhere because enforcing them would require intershard communication, which is complicated and still deemed too slow to be worth implementing.

Once you understand how queries are routed and how indexing works, you should be in a good position to write smart queries and indexes for your sharded cluster. Most all the advice on indexing and query optimization from chapter 7 will apply, and you have a powerful `explain()` tool to use when an empirical investigation proves necessary.

9.4   *Choosing a shard key*

So much depends upon the right choice of shard key. A poorly chosen shard key will prevent your application from taking advantage of many of the benefits provided by the sharded cluster. In the pathological case, both insert and query performance will be significantly impaired. Adding to the gravity of the decision is that once you've chosen a shard key, you're stuck with it. Shard keys are immutable.[12]

Part of having a good experience with sharding is knowing what makes a good shard key. Because this isn't immediately intuitive, I'll start by describing the kinds of shard keys that *don't* work well. This will naturally lead to a discussion of the ones that do.

9.4.1   *Ineffective shard keys*

Some shard keys distribute poorly. Others make it impossible to take advantage of the principle of locality. Still others potentially prevent chunks from splitting. Here we take a look at the kinds of shard keys that generate these sub-optimal states.

POOR DISTRIBUTION

The BSON object ID is the default primary key for every MongoDB document. A data type so close to the heart of the MongoDB would at first appear a promising candidate for a shard key. Alas, this appearance is deceiving. Recall that the most significant bits of all object IDs form a timestamp. This means that object IDs are always ascending. And, unfortunately, ascending values make for terrible shard keys.

To see the problem with ascending shard keys, you need to remember that sharding is range-based. With an ascending shard key, all the most recent inserts will fall within some narrow continuous range. In sharding terms, this means that these inserts will be routed to a single chunk, and thus to a single shard. This effectively nullifies one of sharding's greatest benefits: the automatic distribution of the insert load across machines.[13] It should be clear that if you want the insert load to be distributed across shards, you can't use an ascending shard key. You need something more random.

---

[12] Note that there's no good way to alter the shard key once you've created it. Your best bet is to create a new sharded collection with the proper key, export the data from the old sharded collection, and then restore the data to the new one.

[13] Note that an ascending shard key shouldn't affect updates as long as documents are updated randomly.

LACK OF LOCALITY

An ascending shard key has a clear direction; a completely random shard key has no direction at all. The former fails to distribute inserts; the latter might distribute them too well. This may have a counterintuitive ring to it, as the whole point of sharding is to distribute reads and writes. But we can illustrate with a simple thought experiment.

Imagine that each of the documents in your sharded collection contains an MD5 and that the MD5 field is the shard key. Because the value of an MD5 will vary randomly across documents, this shard key will ensure that inserts distribute evenly across all shards in the cluster. This is desirable. But take a second to imagine how inserts into each shard's *index* on the MD5 fields will work. Because the MD5 is totally random, each virtual memory page in the index is equally likely to be accessed on every insert. Practically speaking, this means that the index must always fit in RAM and that if the indexes and data ever grow beyond the limits of physical RAM, page faults, and thus decreased performance, will be inevitable.

This is basically a problem of *locality of reference.* The idea of locality, at least here, is that data accessed within any given time interval is frequently related; this closeness can be exploited for optimization. For example, although object IDs make for poor shard keys, they do provide excellent locality because they're ascending. This means that successive inserts into the index will always occur within recently used virtual memory pages; so only a small portion of the index need be in RAM at any one time.

To take a less abstract example, imagine your application allows users to upload photos and that each photo's metadata is stored in a single document within a sharded collection. Now suppose that a user performs a batch upload of 100 photos. If the shard key is totally random, the database won't be able to take advantage of the locality here; inserts into the index will occur at 100 random locations. But let's say the shard key is the user's ID. In this case, each write to the index will occur at roughly the *same* location because every inserted document will have the same user ID value. Here you take advantage of locality, and you realize potentially significant gains in performance.

Random shard keys present one more problem: any meaningful range query on such a key will have to be sent to all shards. Think again about the sharded photos collection just described. If you want your app to be able to display a user's 10 most recently created photos (normally a trivial query), a random shard key will still require that this query be distributed to all shards. As you'll see in the next section, a coarser-grained shard key will permit a range query like this to take place on a single shard.

UNSPLITTABLE CHUNKS

If random and ascending shard keys don't work well, then the next obvious option is a coarse-grained shard key. A user ID is a good example of this. If you shard your photos collection on a user ID, then you can expect to see inserts distributed across shards, if only because it's impossible to tell which users will insert data when. Thus the coarse-grained shard key takes the element of randomness and uses that to the shard cluster's advantage.

The second benefit of a coarse-grained shard key is that it lets the system ride out the efficiency gains provided by locality of reference. When a user inserts 100 photo metadata documents, a shard key on the user ID field ensures that these inserts go to the same shard and are written to roughly the same parts of the index. This is efficient.

Distribution and locality are great benefits, but with a coarse-grained shard key comes one intractable problem: the potential for uninhibited chunk growth. How is that possible? Think for a moment about the sample shard key on user ID. What's the smallest possible chunk range permitted by this shard key? The smallest range will span a single user ID; no smaller range is possible. This is problematic because every data set has outliers. Suppose that you have a few outlier users whose number of photos stored exceeds the average user's number by millions. Will the system ever be able to split any one user's photos into more than one chunk? The answer is, no. This is an unsplittable chunk, and it's a danger to a shard cluster because it can create an imbalance of data across shards.

Clearly, the ideal would be a shard key that combines the benefits of a coarse-grained key with those of a fine-grained one. You'll see what that looks like in the next section.

9.4.2 Ideal shard keys

From the preceding, it should be clear that you want to choose a shard key that will

1. Distribute inserts evenly across shards
2. Ensure that CRUD operations can take advantage of locality
3. Be granular enough to allow chunks to split

Shard keys that fit these requirements are generally composed of two fields, the first being coarse-grained and the second more fine-grained. A good example of this is the shard key in the spreadsheets example. There, you declared a compound shard key on {username: 1, _id: 1}. As various users insert into the cluster, you can expect that most, if not all, of any one user's spreadsheets will live on a single shard. Even when a user's documents reside on more than one shard, the presence of the unique _id field in the shard key guarantees that queries and updates to any one document will always be directed to a single shard. And if you need to perform a more sophisticated query on a user's data, you can be sure that the query will be routed only to those shards containing that user's data.

Most importantly, the shard key on {username: 1, _id: 1} guarantees that chunks will always be splittable, even if a given user creates a huge number of documents.

Let's take another example. Suppose you're building a website analytics system. As you'll see in appendix B, a good data model for such a system would store one document per page per month. Then, within that document, you'd store the data for each day of the month, incrementing various counter fields for each page hit, and so on. Here are the fields of a sample analytics document relevant to your shard key choice:

```
{ _id: ObjectId("4d750a90c35169d10fc8c982"),
  domain: "org.mongodb",
  url: "/downloads",
  period: "2011-12"
}
```

The simplest shard key for a sharded collection containing documents like this would consist of each page's domain followed by its url: {domain: 1, url: 1}. All pages from a given domain would generally live on a single shard, but the outlier domains with massive numbers of pages would still be split across shards when necessary.

9.5   *Sharding in production*

When deploying a shard cluster to production, you're presented with a number of choices and challenges. Here I describe a couple of recommended deployment topologies and provide some answers to common deployment questions. We'll then consider matters of server administration, including monitoring, backups, failover, and recovery.

9.5.1   *Deployment and configuration*

Deployment and configuration are hard to get right the first time around. The following are some guidelines for organizing the cluster and configuring with ease.

DEPLOYMENT TOPOLOGIES

To launch the sample MongoDB shard cluster, you had to start a total of nine processes (three mongods for each replica set, plus three config servers). That's a potentially frightening number. First-time users might assume that running a two-shard cluster in production would require nine separate machines. Fortunately, many fewer are needed. You can see why by looking at the expected resource requirements for each component of the cluster.

Consider first the replica sets. Each replicating member contains a complete copy of the data for its shard and may run as a primary or secondary node. These processes will always require enough disk space to store their copy of the data, and enough RAM to serve that data efficiently. Thus replicating mongods are the most resource-intensive processes in a shard cluster and must be given their own machines.

What about replica set arbiters? These processes store replica set config data only, which is kept in a single document. Hence, arbiters incur little overhead and certainly *don't* need their own servers.

Next are the config servers. These also store a relatively small amount of data. For instance, the data on the config servers managing the sample replica set totaled only about 30 KB. If you assume that this data will grow linearly with shard cluster data size, then a 1 TB shard cluster might swell the config servers' data size to a mere 30 MB.[14] This means that config servers don't necessarily need their own machines, either. But

---

[14] That's a highly conservative estimate. The real value will likely be far smaller.

given the critical role played by the config servers, some users prefer to place them on a few modestly provisioned machines (or virtual instances).

From what you already know about replica sets and shard clusters, you can construct a list of minimum deployment requirements:

1 Each member of a replica set, whether it's a complete replica or an arbiter, needs to live on a distinct machine.
2 Every replicating replica set member needs its own machine.
3 Replica set arbiters are lightweight enough to share a machine with another process.
4 Config servers can optionally share a machine. The only hard requirement is that all config servers in the config cluster reside on distinct machines.

Satisfying these rules might feel like tackling a logic problem. Fortunately, we'll apply them right now by looking at two reasonable deployment topologies for the sample two-shard cluster. The first requires just four machines. The process layout is illustrated in figure 9.4.

This configuration satisfies all the deployment rules just mentioned. Predominant on each machine are the replicating nodes of each shard. The remaining processes are arranged so that all three config servers and all members of each replica set live on different machines. To speak of fault tolerance, this topology will tolerate the failure of any one machine. No matter which machine fails, the cluster will continue to process reads and writes. If the failing machine happens to host one of the config

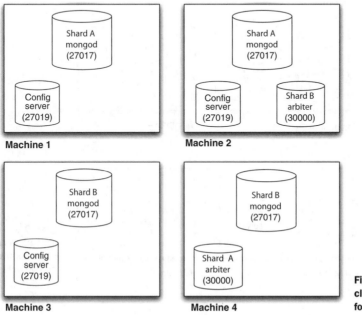

Figure 9.4 A two-shard cluster deployed across four machines

servers, then all chunk splits and migrations will be suspended.[15] Fortunately, suspending sharding operations rarely affects the working of a shard cluster; splitting and migrating can wait until the lost machine is recovered.

That's the *minimum* recommend setup for a two-shard cluster. But applications demanding the highest availability and the fastest paths to recovery will need something more robust. As discussed in the previous chapter, a replica set consisting of two replicas and one arbiter is vulnerable while recovering. Having three nodes reduces the fragility of the set during recovery and also allows you to keep a node in a secondary data center for disaster recovery. Figure 9.5 shows a robust two-shard cluster topology. Each shard consists of a three-node replica set, where each node contains a complete copy of the data. For disaster recovery, one config server and one node from each shard are located in a secondary data center; to ensure that those nodes never become primary, they're given a priority of 0.

With this configuration, each shard is replicated twice, not just once. Additionally, the secondary data center has all the data necessary for a user to completely reconstruct the shard cluster in the event of the failure of the first data center.

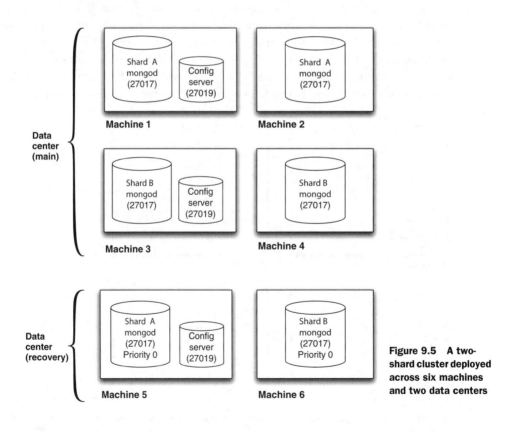

Figure 9.5   A two-shard cluster deployed across six machines and two data centers

---

[15] All three config servers need to be online for any sharding operations to take place.

Data center failures

The most likely data center failure is a power outage. When not running your MongoDB servers without journaling enabled, a power outage will mean unclean shutdowns of the MongoDB servers, potentially corrupting the data files. The only reliable recovery from such a failure is a database repair, a lengthy process that guarantees downtime.

Most users will run their entire cluster within a single data center only, and this is fine for plenty of applications. The main precaution to take in this case is to ensure that at least one node from each shard, and one config server, is running with journaling enabled. This will greatly expedite recovery once power is restored. Journaling is covered in chapter 10.

Still, some failures are more severe. Power outages can sometimes last for days. Floods, earthquakes, and other natural disasters can physically destroy a data center. Users who want to be able to recover quickly from these kinds of failure must deploy their shard clusters across multiple data centers.

The decision about which sharding topology is best for your application should always be based on serious considerations about how much downtime you can tolerate, as measured by your mean time to recovery (MTR). Think about the potential failure scenarios and simulate them. Consider the consequences for your application (and business) if a data center should fail.

CONFIGURATION NOTES
The following are a few useful notes on configuring a sharded cluster.

Estimating cluster size
Users frequently want to know how many shards to deploy and how large each shard should be. The answer, of course, depends on the circumstances. If you're deploying on Amazon's EC2, you shouldn't shard until you've maxed out the largest available instances. At the time of this writing, the largest EC2 nodes have 68 GB of RAM. If you're running on your own hardware, you can easily go larger. It wouldn't be unreasonable to wait until you've reached 100 GB of data before going to shard.

Naturally, each additional shard introduces extra complexity, and each shard also requires replicas. Thus it's better to have a small number of large shards than a large number of small ones.

Sharding an existing collection
You can shard existing collections, but don't be surprised if it takes some time to distribute the data across shards. Only one balancing round can happen at a time, and the migrations will move only around 100-200 MB of data per minute. Thus, sharding a 50 GB collection will take around eight hours, and this will likely involve some moderate disk activity. In addition, when you initially shard a large collection like this, you may have to split manually to expedite the sharding process, since splitting is triggered by inserts.

Given this, it should be clear that sharding a collection at the last minute isn't a good response to a performance problem. If you plan on sharding a collection at some point in the future, you should do so well in advance of any anticipated performance degradation.

Presplitting chunks for initial load

If you have a large data set that you need to load into a sharded collection, and you know something about the distribution of the data, then you can save a lot of time by presplitting and then premigrating chunks. For example, suppose you wanted to import the spreadsheet data into a fresh MongoDB shard cluster. You can ensure that the data distributes evenly upon import by first splitting and then migrating chunks across shards. You can use the split and moveChunk commands to accomplish this. These are aliased by the sh.splitAt() and sh.moveChunks() helpers, respectively.

Here's an example of a manual chunk split. You issue the split command, specify the collection you want, and then indicate a split point:

```
> sh.splitAt( "cloud-docs.spreadsheets",
    { "username" : "Chen", "_id" : ObjectId("4d6d59db1d41c8536f001453") })
```

When run, this command will locate the chunk that logically contains the document where username is Chen and _id is ObjectId("4d6d59db1d41c8536f001453").[16] It then splits the chunk at that point, which results in two chunks. You can continue splitting like this until you have a set of chunks that nicely distribute the data. You'll want to make sure that you've created enough chunks to keep the average chunk size well within the 64 MB split threshold. Thus if you expect to load 1 GB of data, you should plan to create around 20 chunks.

The second step is to ensure that all shards have roughly the same number of chunks. Since all chunks will initially reside on the same shard, you'll need to move them. Each chunk can be moved using the moveChunk command. The helper method simplifies this:

```
> sh.moveChunk("cloud-docs.spreadsheets", {username: "Chen"}, "shardB")
```

This says that you want to move the chunk that logically would contain the document {username: "Chen"} to shard B.

9.5.2 Administration

I'll round out this chapter with a few words about sharding administration.

MONITORING

A shard cluster is a complex piece of machinery; as such, you should monitor it closely. The serverStatus and currentOp() commands can be run on any mongos, and their output will reflect aggregate statistics across shards. I'll discuss these commands in more detail in the next chapter.

---

[16] Note that such a document need not exist. That should be clear from the fact that you're splitting chunks on an empty collection.

In addition to aggregating server statistics, you'll want to keep an eye on the distribution of chunks and on individual chunk sizes. As you saw in the sample cluster, all of this information is stored in the config database. If you ever detect unbalanced chunks or unchecked chunk growth, you can use the split and movechunk commands to address these issues. Alternatively, you can consult the logs to see whether the balancing operation has halted for some reason.

MANUAL PARTITIONING

There are a couple of cases where you may want to manually split and migrate chunks on a live shard cluster. For example, as of MongoDB v2.0, the balancer doesn't directly take into account the load on any one shard. Obviously, the more a shard is written to, the larger its chunks become, and the more likely they are to eventually migrate. Nevertheless, it's not hard to imagine situations where you'd be able to alleviate load on a shard by migrating chunks. This is another situation where the movechunk command can be helpful.

ADDING A SHARD

If you've determined that you the need more capacity, you can add a new shard to an existing cluster using the same method you used earlier:

```
sh.addShard("shard-c/rs1.example.net:27017,rs2.example.net:27017")
```

When adding capacity in this way, be realistic about how long it'll take to migrate data to the new shard. As stated earlier, you can expect data to migrate at a rate of 100–200 MB per minute. This means that if you need to add capacity to a sharded cluster, you should do so long before performance starts to degrade. To determine when you need to add a new shard, consider the rate at which your data set is growing. Obviously, you'll want to keep indexes and working set in RAM. So a good rule of thumb is to plan to add a new shard at least several weeks before the indexes and working set on your existing shards reach 90% of RAM.

If you're not willing to play it safe, as described here, then you open yourself up to a world of pain. Once your indexes and working set don't fit in RAM, your application can come to a halt, especially if the application demands high write and read throughput. The problem is that the database will have to page to and from the disk, which will slow reads and writes, backlogging operations that can't be served into a read/write queue. At that point, adding capacity is difficult because migrating chunks between shards adds read load to existing shards. Obviously, when a database is overloaded, the last thing you want to do is add load.

All of this is just to emphasize that you should monitor your cluster and add capacity well before you need to.

REMOVING A SHARD

You may, in rare cases, want to remove a shard. You can do so using the removeshard command:

```
> use admin
> db.runCommand({removeshard: "shard-1/arete:30100,arete:30101"})
```

```
{
  "msg" : "draining started successfully",
  "state" : "started",
  "shard" : "shard-1-test-rs",
  "ok" : 1 }
```

The command response indicates that chunks are now being drained from the shard to be relocated to other shards. You can check the status of the draining process by running the command again:

```
> db.runCommand({removeshard: "shard-1/arete:30100,arete:30101"})
{
  "msg" : "draining ongoing",
  "state" : "ongoing",
  "remaining" : {
    "chunks" : 376,
    "dbs" : 3
  },
  "ok" : 1 }
```

Once the shard is drained, you also need to make sure that no database's primary shard is the shard you're going to remove. You can check database shard membership by querying the config.databases collection:

```
> use config
> db.databases.find()
  { "_id" : "admin", "partitioned" : false, "primary" : "config" }
  { "_id" : "cloud-docs", "partitioned" : true, "primary" : "shardA" }
  { "_id" : "test", "partitioned" : false, "primary" : "shardB" }
```

What you see here is that the cloud-docs database is owned by shardB but the test database is owned by shardA. Since you're removing shardB, you need to change the test database's primary node. You can accomplish that with the moveprimary command:

```
> db.runCommand({moveprimary: "test", to: "shard-0-test-rs" });
```

Run this command for each database whose primary is the shard to be removed. Then run the removeshard command again to very the shard is completely drained:

```
> db.runCommand({removeshard: "shard-1/arete:30100,arete:30101"})
{ "msg": "remove shard completed successfully",
  "stage": "completed",
  "host": "arete:30100",
  "ok" : 1
}
```

Once you see that the removal is completed, it's safe to take the removed shard offline.

UNSHARDING A COLLECTION

Although you can remove a shard, there's no official way to unshard a collection. If you do need to unshard a collection, your best option is to dump the collection and then restore the data to a new collection with a different name.[17] You can then drop

---

[17] The utilities you use to dump and restore, mongodump and mongorestore, are covered in the next chapter.

the sharded collection you dumped. For example, suppose that foo is a sharded collection. You must dump foo by connecting to mongos with mongodump:

```
$ mongodump -h arete --port 40000 -d cloud-docs -c foo
connected to: arete:40000
DATABASE: cloud-docs    to    dump/cloud-docs
  cloud-docs.foo to dump/cloud-docs/foo.bson
      100 objects
```

This will dump the collection to a file called foo.bson. You can then restore that file using mongorestore:

```
$ mongorestore -h arete --port 40000 -d cloud-docs -c bar
Tue Mar 22 12:06:12 dump/cloud-docs/foo.bson
Tue Mar 22 12:06:12    going into namespace [cloud-docs.bar]
Tue Mar 22 12:06:12    100 objects found
```

Once you've moved the data into an unsharded collection, you're now free to drop the old sharded collection, foo.

BACKING UP A SHARDED CLUSTER

To back up a sharded cluster, you need a copy of the config data, and you need a copy of the data from each shard. There are two ways to get this data. The first is to use the mongodump utility. Dump the data from one of the config servers and then dump the data from each individual shard. Alternatively, you can run mongodump through the mongos router and dump the entire sharded collection, including the config database, at once. The main problem with this strategy is that the sharded cluster's total data might be too large to dump to a single machine.

Another common way to back up a sharded cluster is to copy the data files from one member of each shard and from one config server. This backup procedure is described in the next chapter for an individual mongod process and replica set. You merely need to apply that process to each shard and to one config server.

Regardless of the backup procedure you decide upon, you need to ensure that chunks aren't in the process of moving when you back up the system. This means stopping the balancer process.

Stopping the balancer

At the moment, disabling the balancer is a matter of upserting a document into the config database's settings collection:

```
> use config
> db.settings.update({_id: "balancer"}, {$set: {stopped: true}}, true);
```

Do be careful here: once you've updated the config, the balancer still might not be done working. Before you proceed to back up the cluster, you'll need to make sure that the balancer has completed the latest balancing round. The best way to do this is to check the locks collection for the entry with an _id value of balancer and ensure that its state is 0. Here's a sample entry from that collection:

```
> use config
> db.locks.find({_id: "balancer"})
```

```
{ "_id" : "balancer", "process" : "arete:40000:1299516887:1804289383",
  "state" : 1,
  "ts" : ObjectId("4d890d30bd9f205b29eda79e"),
  "when" : ISODate("2011-03-22T20:57:20.249Z"),
  "who" : "arete:40000:1299516887:1804289383:Balancer:846930886",
  "why" : "doing balance round"
}
```

Any state greater than 0 indicates that balancing is happening. The `process` field shows the host name and port of the computer running the `mongos` that's orchestrating the balancing round. In this case, the host is `arete:40000`. If balancing ever fails to stop after you modify the settings collection, you should examine the logs from the balancing `mongos` for errors.

Once you know that the balancer has stopped, it's safe to run your backups. After taking your backups, don't forget to restart the balancer. You can do so by resetting the `stopped` value:

```
> use config
> db.settings.update({_id: "balancer"}, {$set: {stopped: false}}, true);
```

To simplify some of these operations with the balancer, MongoDB v2.0 has introduced a couple shell helpers. For example, you can start and stop the balancer with `sh.setBalancerState()`:

```
> sh.setBalancerState(false)
```

This is equivalent to adjusting the `stopped` value in the `settings` collection. Once you've disabled the balancer in this way, you make repeated calls to `sh.isBalancerRunning()` until the balancer stops.

FAILOVER AND RECOVERY

Although we've covered general replica set failures, it's also important to note a sharded cluster's potential points of failure along with best practices for recovery.

Failure of a shard member

Each shard consists of a replica set. Thus if any member of one of these replica sets fails, a secondary member will be elected primary, and the `mongos` process will automatically connect to it. Chapter 8 describes the specific steps to take in restoring a failed replica set member. The method you choose depends on how the member has failed, but regardless, the instructions are the same whether the replica set is part of a sharded cluster or not.

If you see anomalous behavior after a replica set failover, you can reset the system by restarting all `mongos` processes. This will ensure proper connections to the new replica sets. In addition, if you notice that balancing isn't working, you should check the config database's `locks` collection for entries whose `process` fields point to former primary nodes. If you see such an entry, the lock document is stale, and you're safe manually deleting it.

Failure of a config server

A sharded cluster requires three config servers for normal operation, but up to two of these can fail. Whenever you have fewer than three config servers, your remaining config servers will become read-only, and all splitting and balancing operations will be suspended. Note that this won't negatively affect the cluster as a whole. Reads and writes to the cluster will still work, and the balancer will start from where it left off once all three config servers are restored.

To restore a config server, copy the data files from an existing config server to the failed config server's machine. Then restart the server.[18]

Failure of a mongos

The failure of a mongos process is nothing to worry about. If you're hosting mongos on an application server, and mongos fails, then it's likely that your application server has failed, too. Recovery in this case simply means restoring the server.

Regardless of how mongos fails, the process has no state of its own. This means that recovering a mongos is a simple matter of restarting the mongos process and pointing it at the config servers.

9.6   *Summary*

Sharding is an effective strategy for maintaining high read and write performance on large data sets. MongoDB's sharding works well in numerous production deployments, and can work for you, too. Instead of having to worry about implementing your own half-baked, custom sharding solution, you can take advantage of all the effort that's been put into MongoDB's sharding mechanism. If you follow the advice in this chapter, paying particular attention to the recommend deployment topologies, the strategies for choosing a shard key, and the importance of keeping data in RAM, then sharding will serve you well.

---

[18] As always, before you copy any data files, make sure you either lock the mongod (as described in chapter 10) or shut it down cleanly. Never copy data files while the server is live.

Deployment and administration

This book would be incomplete without a few notes on deployment and administration. After all, it's one thing to use MongoDB but another to keep it running smoothly in production. The goal of this final chapter, then, is to prepare you to make good decisions when deploying and administering MongoDB. You can think of this chapter as providing the wisdom required to keep to you from experiencing the unpleasantness of a production database meltdown.

I'll begin by addressing general deployment issues, including hardware requirements, security, and data imports and exports. Then I'll outline methods for monitoring MongoDB. We'll discuss maintenance responsibilities, the most important of which is backups. And we'll end the chapter with a general plan for addressing performance issues.

10.1 Deployment

To deploy MongoDB for success, you need to choose the right hardware and the appropriate server topology. If you have preexisting data, then you need to know how to effectively import (and export) it. And finally, you need to make sure that your deployment is secure. We'll address all of these issues in the sections to come.

10.1.1 Deployment environment

Here I'll present considerations for choosing good deployment environments for MongoDB. I'll discuss specific hardware requirements, such as CPU, RAM, and disks, and provide recommendations for optimizing the operating system environment. I'll also provide some advice for deploying in the cloud.

ARCHITECTURE

Two notes on hardware architecture are in order.

First, because MongoDB maps all data files to a virtual address space, all production deployments should be run on 64-bit machines. As stated elsewhere, a 32-bit architecture limits MongoDB to about 2 GB of storage. With journaling enabled, the limit is reduced to around 1.5 GB. This is dangerous in production because, if these limits are ever surpassed, MongoDB will behave unpredictably. Feel free to run on 32-bit machines for unit testing and staging, but in production and for load testing, stick to 64-bit architectures.

Next, MongoDB must be run on little-endian machines. This usually isn't difficult to comply with, but users running SPARC, PowerPC, PA-RISC, and other big-endian architectures will have to hold off.[1] Most of the drivers support both little- and big-endian byte orderings, so clients of MongoDB can usually run on either architecture.

CPU

MongoDB isn't particularly CPU-intensive; database operations are rarely CPU-bound. Your first priority when optimizing for MongoDB is to ensure that operations aren't I/O-bound (see the next two sections on RAM and disks).

But once your indexes and working set fit entirely in RAM, you may see some CPU-boundedness. If you have a single MongoDB instance serving tens (or hundreds) of thousands of queries per second, you can realize performance increases by providing more CPU cores. For reads that don't use JavaScript, MongoDB can utilize all available cores.

If you do happen to see CPU saturation on reads, check your logs for slow query warnings. You may be lacking the proper indexes, thereby forcing table scans. If you have a lot of open clients and each client is running table scans, then the scanning plus the resultant context switching will be CPU-intensive. The solution to this problem is to add the necessary indexes.

---

[1] If you're interested in big-endian support for the core server, see https://jira.mongodb.org/browse/SERVER-1625.

For writes, MongoDB will use only one core at a time. This is because of the global write lock. Thus the only way to scale write load is ensure that writes aren't I/O-bound, and from there scale horizontally with sharding. This is mitigated somewhat in MongoDB v2.0 because generally writes won't take the lock around a page fault but will instead allow another operation to complete. Still, a number of concurrency optimizations are in the works. Among the possible options to be implemented are collection-level locking and extent-based locking. Consult JIRA and the latest release notes for the status of these improvements.

RAM

As with any database, MongoDB performs best with lots of RAM. Be sure to select hardware (virtual or otherwise) with enough RAM to contain your frequently used indexes plus your working data set. Then as your data grows, keep a close eye on the ratio of RAM to working set size. If you allow working set size to grow beyond RAM, you may start to see significant performance degradation. Paging from disk in and of itself isn't a problem, as it's a necessary step in loading data into memory. But if you're unhappy with performance, excessive paging may be your problem. Chapter 7 discusses the relationship between working set, index size, and RAM in great detail. At the end of this chapter, you read about ways of identifying RAM deficiencies.

There are a few use cases where you can safely let data size grow well beyond available RAM, but they're the exception, not the rule. One example is using MongoDB as an archive, where reads and writes seldom happen and where you don't need fast responses. In this case, having as much RAM as data might be prohibitively expensive with little benefit, since the application won't ever utilize so much RAM. For all data sets, the key is testing. Test a representative prototype of your application to ensure that you get the necessary baseline performance.

DISKS

When choosing disks, you need to consider IOPS (input/output operations per second) and seek time. The differences between running on a single consumer-grade hard drive, running in the cloud in a virtual disk (say, EBS), and running against a high-performance SAN can't be overemphasized. Some applications will perform acceptably against a single network-attached EBS volume, but demanding applications will require something more.

Disk performance is important for a few reasons. The first is that, as you're writing to MongoDB, the server by default will force a sync to disk every 60 seconds. This is known as a *background flush*. With a write-intensive app and a slow disk, the background flushing may be slow enough to negatively affect overall system performance. Second, a fast disk will allow you to warm up the server much more quickly. Any time you need to restart a server, you also have to load your data set into RAM. This happens lazily; each successive read or write to MongoDB will load a new virtual memory page into RAM until the physical memory is full. A fast disk will make this process much faster, which will increase MongoDB's performance following a cold restart. Finally, a fast disk can alter the required ratio of working set size to RAM for your application. Using, say, a solid state drive, you may be able to run with much less RAM (or much greater capacity) than you would otherwise.

Regardless of the type of disk used, serious deployments will generally use, not a single disk, but a redundant array of disks (RAID) instead. Users typically manage a RAID cluster using Linux's logical volume manager, LVM, with a RAID level of 10. RAID 10 provides redundancy while maintaining acceptable performance, and is commonly used in MongoDB deployments.[2]

If your data is spread across multiple databases within the same MongoDB server, then you can also ensure capacity by using the server's --directoryperdb flag. This will create a separate directory in the data file path for each database. Using this, you can conceivably mount a separate volume (RAIDed or not) for each database. This may allow you to take advantage of some performance increases, since you'll be able to read from separate sets of spindles (or solid state drives).

FILE SYSTEMS

You'll get the best performance from MongoDB if you run it on the right file system. Two file systems in particular, ext4 and xfs, feature fast, contiguous disk allocation. Using these file systems will speed up MongoDB's frequent preallocations.

Once you mount your fast file system, you can achieve another performance gain by disabling updates to files' last access time (atime). Normally, the operating system will update a file's atime every time the file is read or written. In a database environment, this amounts to a lot of unnecessary work. Disabling atime on Linux is relatively easy. First, make a backup of the file system config file. Then open the original file in your favorite editor:

```
sudo mv /etc/fstab /etc/fstab.bak
sudo vim /etc/fstab
```

For each mounted volume, you'll see a list of settings aligned by column. Under the options column, add the noatime directive:

```
# file-system         mount  type    options  dump  pass
UUID=8309beda-bf62-43  /ssd   ext4    noatime  0     2
```

Then save your work. The new settings should take effect immediately.

FILE DESCRIPTORS

Some Linux systems cap the number of allowable open file descriptors at 1,024. This is occasionally too low for MongoDB and may result in errors opening connections (which you'll see clearly in the logs). Naturally, MongoDB requires a file descriptor for each open file and network connection. Assuming you store your data files in a folder with the word *data* in it, you can see the number of data file descriptors using lsof and a few well-placed pipes:

```
lsof | grep mongo | grep data | wc -l
```

---

[2] For an overview of RAID levels, see http://en.wikipedia.org/wiki/Standard_RAID_levels.

Counting the number of network connection descriptors is just as easy:

```
lsof | grep mongo | grep TCP | wc -l
```

When it comes to file descriptors, the best strategy is to start with a high limit so that you never run out in production. You can check the current limit temporarily with the `ulimit` utility:

```
ulimit -Hn
```

To raise the limit permanently, open your `limits.conf` file with your editor of choice:

```
sudo vim /etc/security/limits.conf
```

Then set the soft and hard limits. These are specified on a per-user basis. This example assumes that the `mongodb` user will be running the `mongod` process:

```
mongod hard nofile 2048
mongod hard nofile 10240
```

The new settings will take effect when that user logs in again.

CLOCKS

It turns out that replication is susceptible to *clock skew.* If the clocks on the machines hosting the various nodes of a replica set ever diverge, then replication may not function properly. This isn't ideal, but fortunately there's a solution. You need to ensure that each of your servers uses *NTP (Network Time Protocol)* to keep their clocks synchronized. On Unix variants, this means running the `ntpd` daemon. On Windows, the Windows Time Services fulfills this role.

THE CLOUD

More and more users are running MongoDB in virtualized environments, collectively known as *the cloud.* Among these, Amazon's EC2 has become a deployment environment of choice because of its ease of use, wide geographic availability, and competitive pricing. EC2, and other environments like it, can be adequate for deploying MongoDB, but you should keep in mind the drawbacks, especially if your application will be pushing MongoDB to its limits.

The first problem with EC2 is that you're forced to choose from a limited set of instance types. At the time of this writing, you can't get a virtual instance with more than 68 GB of RAM. A limit like this forces you to shard your database once your working set grows beyond those 68 GB, and this might not be appropriate for every application. If you can run on real hardware, you can run with more RAM; the cost of hardware being equal, this can affect the decision to shard.

Another potential problem is that EC2 is essentially a black box. You may experience service blips or instance slowdowns and have no way of diagnosing or remedying them.

The third issue concerns storage. EC2 allows you to mount virtual block devices known as *EBS volumes.* EBS volumes provide a great deal of flexibility, allowing you to add storage and move volumes across machines as needed. EBS also allows you to take snapshots, which you can use for backups. The problem with EBS volumes is that they don't provide a high level of throughput, especially when compared to what's possible with physical disks. For this reason, most MongoDB users hosting serious applications on EC2 run EBS with a RAID 10 for increased read throughput. This is all but required for high-performance applications.

For these reasons, rather than dealing with some of EC2's limitations and unpredictability, many users prefer to run MongoDB on their own physical hardware. Then again, EC2 and the cloud in general are convenient and perfectly acceptable for a wide variety of users. The lesson is to consider your application and test it in the cloud before committing to cloud-based storage.

10.1.2 Server configuration

Once you've settled on a deployment environment, you need to decide on an overall server configuration. This involves choosing a server topology and deciding whether, and how, to use journaling.

CHOOSING A TOPOLOGY

The minimum recommended deployment topology is a three-member replica set. At least two members of the set must be data-storing (non-arbiter) replicas residing on separate machines. The third member may be yet another replica or it can be an arbiter, which doesn't necessarily need its own machine; you can run an arbiter on an application server, for instance. Two reasonable replica set deployment configurations are presented in chapter 8.

If you expect your working set size to exceed RAM from the start, then you may want to begin with a sharded cluster, which consists of at least two replica sets. Detailed recommendation on sharded deployments, along with advice on when to start sharding, are presented in chapter 9.

You can deploy a single server to support testing and staging environments. But for production deployments, a single server isn't recommended, even if journaling is enabled. Having just one machine complicates backup and recovery, and when there's a server failure, there's nothing to fail over to.

But you can make an exception in certain rare cases. If an application doesn't need high availability or quick recovery, and has a relatively small data set (say, < 1 GB), then running on a single server may be permissible. Still, considering the ever-decreasing costs of hardware, and the numerous benefits of running with replication, the arguments for foregoing a second machine are weak indeed.

JOURNALING

MongoDB v1.8 introduced journaling, and MongoDB v2.0 enables journaling by default. When journaling is enabled, MongoDB will commit all writes to a journal before writing to the core data files. This allows the MongoDB server to come back online quickly and cleanly in the event of an unclean shutdown.

Prior to v1.8, no such feature existed, and thus unclean shutdowns often led to disaster. How was this possible? I've mentioned several times that MongoDB maps each data file to virtual memory. This means that when MongoDB writes, it writes to a virtual memory address and not directly to disk. The OS kernel periodically syncs these writes from virtual memory to disk, but the frequency and completeness of these kernel syncs are indeterminate. So MongoDB forcibly syncs all data files every 60 seconds using the fsync system call. The problem here is that if the MongoDB process is killed with unsynced writes, there's no way of knowing what state the data files are in. They may be corrupted.

In the event of an unclean shutdown of a nonjournaled mongod process, restoring the data files to a consistent state requires running a repair. The repair process rewrites the data files, discarding anything it can't understand (corrupted data). Because downtime and data loss are generally frowned upon, repairing in this way is usually part of a last-ditch recovery effort. Resyncing from an existing replica is almost always easier and more reliable. Being able to recover in this way is one of the reasons why it's so important to run with replication.

Journaling obviates the need for database repairs because MongoDB can use the journal to restore the data files to a consistent state. In MongoDB v2.0, journaling is enabled by default, but you can disable it with the --nojournal flag:

```
$ mongod --nojournal
```

When enabled, the journal files will be kept in a directory called journal located just below the main data path.

If you run your MongoDB server with journaling enabled, keep a of couple points in mind. First, journaling impairs write performance. Users wanting the highest write performance and the assurance of a journal have a couple of options. One is to enable journaling only on passive replicas. As long as these replicas can keep up with the primary, there'll be no sacrifice in performance. Another, perhaps complementary, solution is to mount a separate disk just for the journal. Then create a symlink between the journal directory and the auxiliary volume. The auxiliary volume need not be large; a 120 GB disk is more than sufficient, and a solid state drive (SSD) of this size is affordable. Mounting a separate SSD for the journal files will ensure that journaling runs with the smallest possible performance penalty.

The second point is that journaling, by itself, does *not* guarantee that no write will be lost. It guarantees only that MongoDB will always come back online in a consistent state. Journaling works by syncing a write buffer to disk every 100 ms. So an unclean shutdown can result in the loss of up to the last 100 ms of writes. If this isn't acceptable for any part of your application, you can use the j option on the getlasterror command to instruct the server to wait until the journal is synced before returning:

```
db.runCommand({getlasterror: 1, j: true})
```

On the application level, you'd run this as a safe mode option (just like w and wtimeout). In Ruby, you might use the j option like this:

```
@collection.insert(doc, :safe => {:j => true})
```

Do be aware that running this after every write is unwise, because it'll force every write to wait for the next journal sync. This means that all writes may take up to 100 ms to return. So use this feature with care.[3]

10.1.3 *Data imports and exports*

If you're migrating an existing system to MongoDB, or if you need to seed the database with information from, say, a data warehouse, then you'll need an efficient import method. You might also need a good export strategy, since you may have to export data from MongoDB to external processing jobs. For example, exporting data to Hadoop for batch processing has become a common practice.[4]

There are two ways to import and export data with MongoDB. You can use the included tools, `mongoimport` and `mongoexport`, or you can write a simple program using one of the drivers.[5]

MONGOIMPORT AND MONGOEXPORT

Bundled with MongoDB are two utilities for importing and exporting data: `mongoimport` and `mongoexport`. You can use `mongoimport` to import JSON, CSV, and TSV files. This is frequently useful for loading data from relational databases into MongoDB:

```
$ mongoimport -d stocks -c values --type csv --headerline stocks.csv
```

In the example, you import a CSV file called `stocks.csv` into the `values` collection of the `stocks` database. The `--headerline` flag indicates that the first line of the CSV contains the field names. You can see all the import options by running `mongoimport --help`.

Use `mongoexport` to export all of a collection's data to a JSON or CSV file:

```
$ mongoexport -d stocks -c values -o stocks.csv
```

This command exports data to the file stocks.csv. As with its counterpart, you can see the rest of `mongoexport`'s command options by starting it with the `--help` flag.

CUSTOM IMPORT AND EXPORT SCRIPTS

You're likely to use MongoDB's import and export tools when the data you're dealing with is relatively flat; once you introduce sub-documents and arrays, the CSV format becomes awkward because it's not designed to represent nested data. When you need to export a rich document to CSV or import a CSV to a rich MongoDB document, it may be easier to build a custom tool instead. You can do this using any of the drivers. For example, MongoDB users commonly write scripts that connect to a relational database and then combine the data from two tables into a single collection.

---

[3] Future releases of MongoDB promise finer-grained control over journal syncing. Consult the latest release notes for details.

[4] For this particular use case, an officially supported MongoDB-Hadoop adapter is available at http://github.com/mongodb/mongo-hadoop.

[5] Note that importing and exporting data is distinct from backups, which are covered later in the chapter.

That's the tricky part about moving data in and out of MongoDB: the way the data is modeled may differ between systems. In these cases, be prepared to use the drivers as your conversion tools.

10.1.4 Security

Most RDBMSs feature elaborate security subsystems, allowing authorization of users and groups with fine-grained control over permissions. By contrast, MongoDB v2.0 supports only a simple, per-database authentication mechanism. This makes the security of the machines on which MongoDB is run all the more important. Here we'll discuss a few considerations for running MongoDB in a secure environment and you'll show how authentication works.

SECURE ENVIRONMENTS

MongoDB, like all databases, should be run in a secure environment. Production users of MongoDB must take advantage of the security features of modern operating systems to ensure the safety of their data. Probably the most important of these features is the firewall. The only potential difficulty in using a firewall with MongoDB is knowing which machines need to communicate with each other. Fortunately, the communication rules are simple. With a replica set, each node must be able to reach every other node. In addition, all database clients must be able to connect with every replica set node that the client might conceivably talk to.

A shard cluster consists in part of replica sets. So all the replica set rules apply; the client in the case of sharding is the `mongos` router. Additionally:

- All shards must be able to communicate directly with one another.
- Both the shards and the `mongos` routers must be able to talk to the config servers.

A related security concern is the *bind address*. By default, MongoDB will listen on all addresses on the machine. But you may want MongoDB to listen on one or more specific addresses instead. For this you can start `mongod` and `mongos` with the `--bind_ip` option, which takes a list of one or more comma-separated IP addresses. For example, to listen on the loopback interface as well as on the internal IP address 10.4.1.55, you'd start `mongod` like this:

```
mongod --bind_ip 127.0.0.1,10.4.1.55
```

Do note that data between machines will be sent in the clear. Official SSL support is scheduled to be release in MongoDB v2.2.

AUTHENTICATION

MongoDB's authentication was originally built for users hosting MongoDB servers in shared environments. It's not feature-rich, but it's useful when a little extra security is required. Here we'll first discuss the authentication API and then describe how to use it with replica sets and sharding.

The authentication API

To get started with authentication, first create an admin user by switching to the `admin` database and running `db.addUser()`. This method takes two arguments: a username and a password:

```
> use admin
> db.addUser("boss", "supersecret")
```

Admin users can create other users and access all databases on the server. With an admin user in place, you can enable authentication. To do so, restart the `mongod` instance with the `--auth` option:

```
$ mongod --auth
```

Now only authorized users will be able to access the database. Restart the shell, and then log in as the admin user with the `db.auth()` method:

```
> use admin
> db.auth("boss", "supersecret")
```

You can now create users for individual databases. If you want to create read-only users, add `true` as the last argument to the `db.addUser()` method. Here you add two users for the `stocks` database. The first has all permissions; the second can only read from the database:

```
> use stocks
> db.addUser("trader", "moneyfornuthin")
> db.addUser("read-only-trader", "foobar", true)
```

Now, just three users—boss, trader, and read-only-trader—can access the `stocks` database. If you ever want to see a list of all users with access to a given database, query the `system.users` collection:

```
> db.system.users.find()
{ "_id" : ObjectId("4d82100a6dfa7bb906bc4df7"),
  "user" : "trader", "readOnly" : false,
  "pwd" : "e9ee53b89ef976c7d48bb3d4ea4bffc1" }
{ "_id" : ObjectId("4d8210176dfa7bb906bc4df8"),
  "user" : "read-only-trader", "readOnly" : true,
  "pwd" : "c335fd71fb5143d39698baab3fdc2b31" }
```

Deleting a user from this collection will revoke the user's access to the database. If you prefer a helper, you can use the shell's `db.removeUser()` method, which does the same thing.

You don't need to explicitly log out; terminating the connection (closing the shell) will accomplish that just fine. But there *is* a command for logging out if you need it:

```
> db.runCommand({logout: 1})
```

Naturally, you can leverage all of the authentication logic we've been exploring here using the drivers. Check your driver's API for the details.

Replica set authentication

Replica sets support the same authentication API just described, but enabling authentication for a replica set requires a couple of extra steps. To start, create a file containing at least six characters from the Base64 character set.[6] The contents of the file will serve as a kind of password that each replica set member uses to authenticate with the others. As an example, you might create a file called `secret.txt` and fill it with the following:

```
tOps3cr3tpa55word
```

Place the file on each replica set member's machine and adjust the permissions so that it's accessible only by the owner:

```
sudo chmod 600 /home/mongodb/secret.txt
```

Finally, start each replica set member by specifying the location of the password file using the `--keyFile` option:

```
mongod --keyFile /home/mongodb/secret.txt
```

Authentication will now be enabled for the set. You'll want to create an admin user in advance, as you did in the previous section.

Sharding authentication

Sharding authentication is an extension of replica set authentication. Each replica set in the cluster is secured as just described, by using a key file. In addition, all the config servers and every `mongos` instance also use a key file containing the same password. Start each of these processes with the `--keyFile` option pointing to the a file containing a password to be used by the entire shard cluster. Once you've done this, the whole cluster can use authentication.

10.2 *Monitoring and diagnostics*

Once you've deployed MongoDB in production, you'll want to keep an eye on it. If performance is slowly degrading or if failures are occurring frequently, you'll want to be apprised of these. That's where monitoring comes in. Let's start with the simplest kind of monitoring: logging. Then we'll explore the built-in commands that provide the most information about the running MongoDB server; these commands underlie the `mongostat` utility and the web console, both of which I'll describe in brief. I'll make a couple of recommendations on external monitoring tools. And then I'll end the section by presenting two diagnostic utilities: `bsondump` and `mongosniff`.

10.2.1 *Logging*

Logging is the first level of monitoring; as such, you should plan on keeping logs for all your deployments.[7] This usually isn't a problem because MongoDB requires that

---

[6] The Base64 character set consists of all uppercase and lowercase letters in the English alphabet, the digits 0-9, and the + and / characters.

[7] Never simply pipe logs to /dev/null or stdout.

you specify the --logpath option when running it in the background. But there are a few extra settings to be aware of. To enable verbose logging, start the mongod process with the -vvvvv option (the more v's, the more verbose the output). This is handy if, for instance, you need to debug some code and want to log every query. But do be aware that verbose logging will make your logs quite large and may affect server performance.

Next you can start mongod with the --logappend option. This will append to an existing log rather than overwriting it.

Finally, if you have a long-running MongoDB process, you may want to write a script that periodically rotates the log files. MongoDB provides the logrotate command for this purpose. Here's how to run it from the shell:

```
> use admin
> db.runCommand({logrotate: 1})
```

Sending the SIGUSR1 signal to the process also runs the logrotate command. Here's how to send that signal to process number 12345:

```
$ kill -SIGUSR1 12345
```

10.2.2 *Monitoring tools*

Here I describe the monitoring commands and tools that ship with MongoDB.

DATABASE COMMANDS

Three database commands reveal MongoDB's internal state. These underlie all MongoDB monitoring applications.

serverStatus

The output to the serverStatus command is a veritable embarrassment of riches. Among the statistics tracked are page faults, B-tree access rates, open connections, and total inserts, updates, queries, and deletes. An abridged sample of the server-Status command output is shown next:

```
> use admin
> db.runCommand({serverStatus: 1})
{
  "host" : "ubuntu",
  "version" : "1.8.0",
  "process" : "mongod",
  "uptime" : 246562,
  "localTime" : ISODate("2011-03-13T17:01:37.189Z"),

  "globalLock" : {
    "totalTime" : 246561699894,
    "lockTime" : 243,
    "ratio" : 9.855545289656455e-10,
    "currentQueue" : {
      "total" : 0,
      "readers" : 0,
      "writers" : 0
    },
  },
```

```
    "mem" : {
      "bits" : 64,
      "resident" : 3580,
      "virtual" : 9000,
      "mapped" : 6591
    }

"ok" : 1 }
```

The globalLock section is important because it indicates the total amount of time the server has spent in a write lock. A high ratio may indicate a write bottleneck. The currentQueue is perhaps a more concrete representation of bottlenecks. If a large number of writes or reads are waiting in the queue, then some kind of optimization may be in order.

The mem section shows how the mongod process is using memory. The bits field indicates that this is a 64-bit machine. resident is the amount of physical memory occupied by MongoDB. virtual is the number of megabytes the process has mapped to virtual memory, and mapped, a subset of virtual, indicates how much of that memory is mapped for the data files alone. In this case, about 6.5 GB of data files are mapped to virtual memory, with 3.5 GB of that in physical memory. I've repeatedly stated that the working set should ideally fit in RAM. The mem section can provide an approximate indication of whether this is the case.

The serverStatus output changes and improves with each MongoDB release, and thus documenting it in a semi-permanent medium like this book isn't always helpful. You can see a detailed and up-to-date interpretation of this output at http://www.mongodb.org/display/DOCS/serverStatus.

top

The top command displays operation counters on a per-database level. If your application uses multiple physical databases, or if you'd like to see how long on average operations are taking, then this is a useful command. Here's some sample output:

```
> use admin
> db.runCommand({top: 1}) {
"totals" : { "cloud-docs" :
{ "total" : { "time" : 194470, "count" : 20 },
  "readLock" : { "time" : 324, "count" : 12 },
  "writeLock" : { "time" : 194146, "count" : 8 },
  "queries" : { "time" : 194470, "count" : 20 },
  "getmore" : { "time" : 0, "count" : 0 } },
"ok" : 1}
```

Here you see that a lot of time is being spent in a write lock. It may be worthwhile to investigate this further to see whether writes are unnecessarily slow.

db.currentOp()

It's frequently useful to know what MongoDB is doing *right now*. The db.currentOp() method exposes this information by returning a list of all the operations currently running along with any other operations waiting to run. Here's an example of the method's output, run against the shard cluster you set up in the previous chapter:

```
db.currentOp()
[ {
      "opid" : "shard-1-test-rs:1232866",
      "active" : true,
      "lockType" : "read",
      "waitingForLock" : false,
      "secs_running" : 11,
      "op" : "query",
      "ns" : "docs.foo",
      "query" : {
        "$where" : "this.n > 1000"
      },
      "client_s" : "127.0.0.1:38068",
      "desc" : "conn"
  } ]
```

A particularly slow query is at work here. You can see that the query has been running for a whopping eleven seconds and that like all queries, it's taken a read lock. If this operation is problematic, you might want to investigate its source by looking at the client field. Alas, this is a sharded cluster, so the source is a mongos process, as indicated by the field name client_s. If you need to kill the operation, you can pass the opid to the db.killOp() method:

```
db.killOp("shard-1-test-rs:1232866")
{
  "op" : "shard-1-test-rs:1233339",
  "shard" : "shard-1-test-rs",
  "shardid" : 1233339
}
```

If you'd like to see a verbose listing of all the operations running on the current MongoDB server, you can issue the following virtual command:

```
db['$cmd.sys.inprog'].find({$all: 1})
```

MONGOSTAT

The db.currentOp() method shows only the operations queued or in progress at a particular moment in time. Similarly, the serverStatus command provides a point-in-time snapshot of various system fields and counters. But sometimes you need a view of the system's real-time activity, and that's where mongostat comes in. Modeled after iostat and other similar tools, mongostat polls the server at a fixed interval and displays an array of statistics, from the number of inserts per second to the amount of resident memory, to the frequency of B-tree page misses.

You can invoke the mongostat command on localhost, and the polling will occur once a second:

```
$ mongostat
```

It's also highly configurable, and you can start it with --help to see all the options. One of the more notable features is cluster discovery; when you start mongostat with the --discover option, you can point it to a single node, and it'll discover the

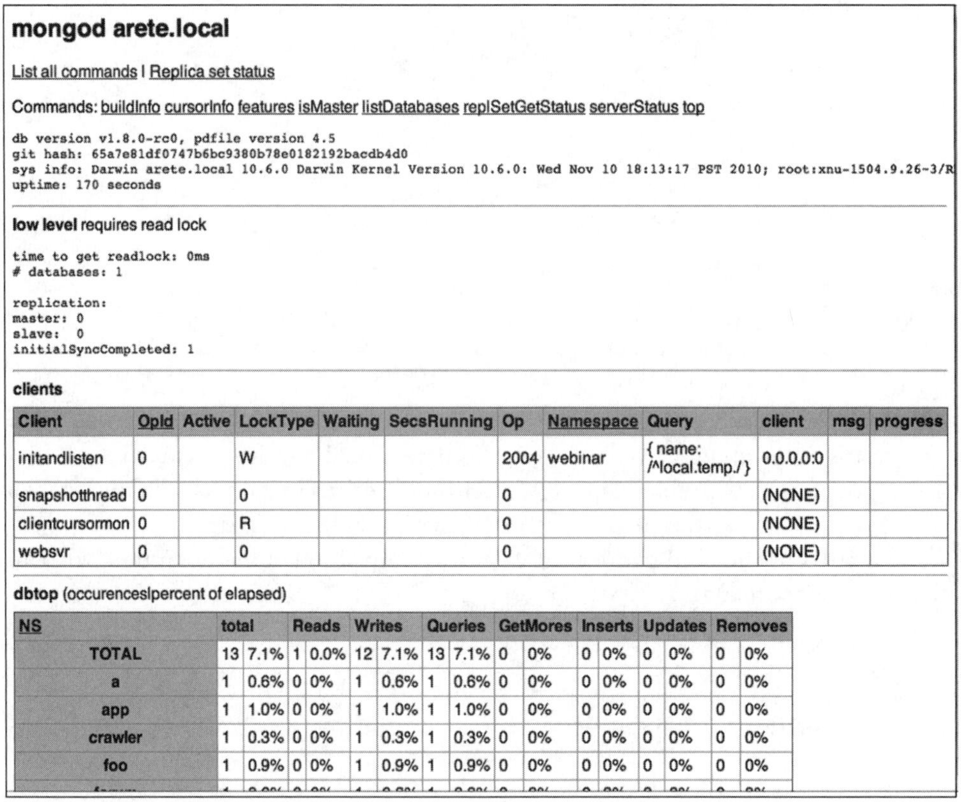

mongod arete.local

List all commands I Replica set status

Commands: buildInfo cursorInfo features isMaster listDatabases replSetGetStatus serverStatus top

```
db version v1.8.0-rc0, pdfile version 4.5
git hash: 65a7e81df0747b6bc9380b78e0182192bacdb4d0
sys info: Darwin arete.local 10.6.0 Darwin Kernel Version 10.6.0: Wed Nov 10 18:13:17 PST 2010; root:xnu~1504.9.26-3/R
uptime: 170 seconds
```

low level requires read lock

```
time to get readlock: 0ms
# databases: 1

replication:
master: 0
slave:  0
initialSyncCompleted: 1
```

clients

Client	OpId	Active	LockType	Waiting	SecsRunning	Op	Namespace	Query	client	msg	progress
initandlisten	0		W			2004	webinar	{ name: /^local.temp./ }	0.0.0.0:0		
snapshotthread	0		0			0			(NONE)		
clientcursormon	0		R			0			(NONE)		
websvr	0		0			0			(NONE)		

dbtop (occurencesIpercent of elapsed)

NS	total		Reads		Writes		Queries		GetMores		Inserts		Updates		Removes	
TOTAL	13	7.1%	1	0.0%	12	7.1%	13	7.1%	0	0%	0	0%	0	0%	0	0%
a	1	0.6%	0	0%	1	0.6%	1	0.6%	0	0%	0	0%	0	0%	0	0%
app	1	1.0%	0	0%	1	1.0%	1	1.0%	0	0%	0	0%	0	0%	0	0%
crawler	1	0.3%	0	0%	1	0.3%	1	0.3%	0	0%	0	0%	0	0%	0	0%
foo	1	0.9%	0	0%	1	0.9%	1	0.9%	0	0%	0	0%	0	0%	0	0%

Figure 10.1   The MongoDB web console

remaining nodes in a replica set or sharded cluster. It then displays the entire cluster's statistics in aggregate.

THE WEB CONSOLE

You can get a slightly more visual window into a running mongod process through the web console. Every mongod listens for HTTP requests on the thousandth port above the server port. Thus if you're running a mongod on port 27017, the web console will be available on port 28017. If running on localhost, you can point your web browser to http://localhost:28017, and you'll see a page like the one in figure 10.1.

Yet more status information is available by enabling the server's basic REST interface. If you start mongod with the --rest flag, you'll enable a number of extra web console commands that are linked to from the main web console landing page.

10.2.3 *External monitoring applications*

Most serious deployments will require an external monitoring application. Nagios and Munin are two popular open source monitoring systems used to keep an eye on many MongoDB deployments. You can use each of these with MongoDB by installing a simple open source plug-in.

Writing a plug-in for any arbitrary monitoring application isn't difficult. It mostly involves running various statistics commands against a live MongoDB database. The serverStatus, dbstats, and collstats commands usually provide all the information you might need, and you can get all of them straight from the HTTP REST interface, avoiding the need for a driver.

10.2.4 Diagnostic tools (mongosniff, bsondump)

MongoDB includes two diagnostic utilities. The first is mongosniff, which sniffs packets from a client to the MongoDB server and prints them intelligibly. If you happen to be writing a driver or debugging an errant connection, then this is your hammer. You can start it up like this to listen on the local network interface at the default port:

```
sudo mongosniff --source NET I0
```

Then when you connect with any client, say the MongoDB shell, you'll get an easy-to-read stream of network chatter:

```
127.0.0.1:58022  -->> 127.0.0.1:27017 test.$cmd 61 bytes
  id:89ac9c1d 2309790749 query: { isMaster: 1.0 }  ntoreturn: -1
127.0.0.1:27017 <<-- 127.0.0.1:58022  87 bytes
  reply n:1 cursorId: 0 { ismaster: true, ok: 1.0 }
```

You can see all the mongosniff options by running it with --help.

Another useful utility is bsondump, which allows you to examine raw BSON files. BSON files are generated by the mongodump utility (discussed later) and by replica set rollbacks.[8] For instance, let's say you've dumped a collection with a single document. If that collection ends up in a file called users.bson, then you can examine the contents pretty easily:

```
$ bsondump users.bson
{ "_id" : ObjectId( "4d82836dc3efdb9915012b91" ), "name" : "Kyle" }
```

As you can see, bsondump prints the BSON as JSON by default. If you're doing serious debugging, you'll want to see the real composition of BSON types and sizes. For that, run the utility in debug mode:

```
$ bsondump --type=debug users.bson
--- new object ---
  size : 37
    _id
      type:  7 size: 17
    name
      type:  2 size: 15
```

This gives you the total size of the object (37 bytes), the types of the two fields (7 and 2), and those fields' sizes.

---

[8] There may be other situations where you'll find raw BSON, but MongoDB's data files aren't one of them, so don't try to view them with bsondump.

10.3   *Maintenance*

Here I'll describe the three most common MongoDB maintenance tasks. First, I'll discuss backups. As with any database, prudence dictates a regular backup policy. Then, I'll describe compaction, as the data files may require it under rare circumstances. Finally, I'll briefly mention upgrades, as you'll want to run the latest stable MongoDB release when possible.

10.3.1   *Backups and recovery*

Part of running a production database deployment is being prepared for disasters. Backups play an important role in this. When disaster strikes, a good backup can save the day, and in these cases, you'll never regret having invested time and diligence in a regular backup policy. Yet some users still decide that they can live without backups. These users have only themselves to blame when they can't recover their databases. Don't be one of these users.

There are two general strategies for backing up a MongoDB database. The first is to use the mongodump and mongorestore utilities. The second, and probably the more common, is to copy the raw data files.

MONGODUMP AND MONGORESTORE

mongodump writes the contents of a database as BSON files. mongorestore reads these files and restores them. These tools are useful for backing up individual collections and databases as well as the whole server. They can be run against a live server (you don't have to lock or shut down the server) or you can point them to a set of data files, but only when the server is locked or shut down. The simplest way to run mongodump is like so:

```
$ mongodump -h localhost --port 27017
```

This will dump each database and collection from the server at localhost to a directory called dump. The dump will include all the documents from each collection, including the system collections that define users and indexes. But significantly, the indexes themselves won't be included in the dump. The means that when you restore, any indexes will have to be rebuilt. If you have an especially large data set, or a large number of indexes, this will take time.

To restore BSON files, run mongorestore, and point it at the dump folder:

```
$ mongorestore -h localhost --port 27017 dump
```

Note that when restoring, mongorestore won't drop data by default. So if you're restoring to an existing database, be sure to run with the --drop flag.

DATAFILE-BASED BACKUPS

Most users opt for a file-based backup, where the raw data files are copied to a new location. This approach is often faster than mongodump, since the backups and restorations require no transformation of the data.[9] The only potential problem with a file-

---

[9]   As an example, this strategy preserves all indexes—no need to rebuild them on restore.

based backup is that it requires locking the database, but generally you'll lock a secondary node, and thus should be able to keep your application online for the duration of the backup.

> **COPYING THE DATA FILES** Users frequently make the mistake of copying the data files or taking a snapshot without first locking the database. With journaling disabled, this will result in corruption of the copied files. When journaling is enabled, it's safe to take a snapshot, but copying the files themselves is tricky, and easy to botch.
>
> So regardless of whether journaling is enabled, the recommendation of this book is to always lock the database before copying data files or taking a disk snapshot. The resulting peace of mind and guaranteed file integrity are well worth the minor delay incurred by locking.

To copy the data files, you first need to make sure that they're in a consistent state. So you either have to shut down the database or lock it. Since shutting down the database might be too involved for some deployments, most users opt for the locking approach. Here's the command for syncing and locking:

```
> use admin
> db.runCommand({fsync: 1, lock: true})
```

At this point, the database is locked against writes and the data files are synced to disk. This means that it's now safe to copy the data files. If you're running on a file system or storage system that supports snapshots, then it's best to take a snapshot and copy later. This allows you to unlock quickly.

If you can't run a snapshot, then you'll have to keep the database locked while you copy the data files. If you're copying data files from a secondary node, be sure that the node is current with the primary and has enough oplog to remain offline for the duration of the backup.

Once you've finished making a snapshot or backing up, you can unlock the database. The somewhat arcane unlock command can be issued like so:

```
> db.$cmd.sys.unlock.findOne()
> { "ok" : 1, "info" : "unlock requested" }
```

Do note that this is merely a *request* to unlock; the database may not unlock right away. Run the db.currentOp() method to verify that the database is no longer locked.

10.3.2 Compaction and repair

MongoDB includes a facility for repairing a database. You can initiate it from the command line to repair all databases on the server:

```
$ mongod --repair
```

Or you can run the repairDatabase command to repair a single database:

```
> use cloud-docs
> db.runCommand({repairDatabase: 1})
```

Repair is an offline operation. While it's running, the database will be locked against reads and writes. The repair process works by reading and rewriting all data files, discarding any corrupted documents in the process. It also rebuilds each index. This means that to repair a database, you need enough free disk space to store the rewrite of its data. To say repairs are expensive is an understatement, as repairing a very large database can take days.

MongoDB's repair was originally used as a kind of last-ditch effort for recovering a corrupted database. In the event of an unclean shutdown, without journaling enabled, a repair is the only way to return the data files to a consistent state. Fortunately, if you deploy with replication, run at least one server with journaling enabled, and perform regular off-site backups, you should never have to recover by running a repair. Relying on repair for recovery is foolish. Avoid it.

What then might a database repair be good for? Running a repair will compact the data files and rebuild the indexes. As of the v2.0 release, MongoDB doesn't have great support for data file compaction. So if you perform lots of random deletes, and especially if you're deleting small documents (< 4 KB), it's possible for total storage size to remain constant or grow despite these regularly occurring deletes. Compacting the data files is a good remedy for this excess use of space.

If you don't have the time or resources to run a complete repair, there are two options, both of which operate on a single collection. You can either rebuild indexes or compact the collection. To rebuild indexes, use the reIndex() method:

```
> use cloud-docs
> db.spreadsheets.reIndex()
```

This might be useful, but generally speaking, index space is efficiently reused; the data file space is what can be a problem. So the compact command is usually a better choice. compact will rewrite the data files and rebuild all indexes for one collection. Here's how you run it from the shell:

```
> db.runCommand({ compact: "spreadsheets" })
```

This command has been designed to be run on a live secondary, obviating the need for downtime. Once you've finished compacting all the secondaries in a replica set, you can step down the primary and then compact that node. If you must run the compact command on the primary, you can do so by adding {force: true} to the command key. Note that if you go this route, the command will write lock the system:

```
> db.runCommand({ compact: "spreadsheets", force: true })
```

10.3.3 Upgrading

MongoDB is still a relatively young project, which means that new releases generally contain lots of important bug fixes and performance improvements. For this reason, you should try to run the latest stable version of the software when possible. Upgrading, at least until v2.0, has been a simple process of shutting down the old mongod process and starting the new one with the old data files. Subsequent versions of MongoDB are likely to make small changes to the index and data file formats, and this will require a slightly more lengthy upgrade process. Always check the latest release notes for accurate recommendations.

Of course, when upgrading MongoDB, you're probably going to be upgrading a replicated cluster. In the case of a replica set, the general strategy is to upgrade one node at a time, starting with the secondary nodes.

10.4   *Performance troubleshooting*

In this final section, I outline a heuristic for diagnosing and resolving performance issues.

Most of the performance issues in MongoDB deployments can be traced to a single source: the hard disk. In essence, the more pressure placed on the disk, the slower MongoDB runs. Thus the goal of most performance optimizations is to reduce reliance on disk. There are several ways to accomplish this, but before we look at them, it's useful to know how to ascertain disk performance in the first place. On Unix derivatives, the `iostat` tool is ideal for this. In the following example, I use the `-x` option to show extended statistics, and you specify 2 to display those stats at two-second intervals:[10]

```
$ iostat -x 2
Device:    rsec/s    wsec/s avgrq-sz avgqu-sz    await  svctm  %util
sdb          0.00   3101.12    10.09    32.83   101.39   1.34  29.36

Device:    rsec/s    wsec/s avgrq-sz avgqu-sz    await  svctm  %util
sdb          0.00   2933.93     9.87    23.72   125.23   1.47  34.13
```

For a detailed description of each of these fields, consult your system's man pages. For a quick diagnostic, you'll be most interested in the last three columns. `await` indicates the average time in milliseconds for serving I/O requests. This average includes time spent in the I/O queue and time spent actually servicing I/O requests. `svctime` indicates the average time spent serving requests alone. And `%util` is the percentage of CPU time spent issuing I/O requests to the disk.

The preceding `iostat` snippet shows moderate disk usage. The average time waiting on I/O is around 100 ms (hint: that's a lot!), the average service time is about 1 ms, and the percent utilization is about 30%. If you were to investigate the MongoDB logs on this machine, you'd likely see numerous slow operations (queries, inserts, or otherwise). In fact, it's those slow operations that would initially alerts you to a potential problem. The `iostat` output can help you confirm the problem. Note that it's not uncommon to find MongoDB users whose systems approach 100% disk utilization; these users generally find themselves frustrated with MongoDB, though the heavy utilization is rarely MongoDB's fault alone. In the next five sections, I'll present some remedies that optimize database operations and ease the load off the disk.

---

[10] Note that this example is Linux-specific. On Mac OS X, the command is `iostat -w 2`.

10.4.1 *Check indexes and queries for efficiency*

When you discover a performance issue, indexes are the first place you should look. This assumes that your application issues queries and updates, which are the primary operations that can use indexes.[11] Chapter 7 outlines a procedure for identifying and fixing slow operations; this involves enabling the query profiler and then ensuring that every query and update uses an index efficiently. In general, this means that each operation scans as few documents as possible.

It's also important to make sure that there are no redundant indexes, since a redundant index will take up space on disk, require more RAM, and demand more work on each write. Chapter 7 mentions ways to eliminate these redundant indexes.

What then? After auditing your indexes and queries, you may discover inefficiencies that, when corrected, fix the performance problems altogether. You'll no longer see slow query warnings in the logs, and the iostat output will show reduced utilization. Adjusting indexes fixes performance issues more often than you might think; this should always be the first place you look when addressing a performance issue.

10.4.2 *Add RAM*

But altering the indexes doesn't always work. You might have the most optimized queries and a perfect set of indexes, and still see high disk utilization. When this is the case, you'll first want to look at the ratio of index size and working set to physical RAM. To start, run the stats() command on each of the databases used by your application:

```
> use app
> db.stats()
{
    "db" : "app",
    "collections" : 5,
    "objects" : 3932487,
    "avgObjSize" : 543.012,
    "dataSize" : 2135390324,
    "storageSize" : 2419106304,
    "numExtents" : 38,
    "indexes" : 4,
    "indexSize" : 226608064,
    "fileSize" : 6373244928,
    "nsSizeMB" : 16,
    "ok" : 1
}
```

Now look at the data size and index size. Here the data size is just over 2 GB, and the index size is around 230 MB. Assuming that the working set comprises all the data in the system, you'll want at least 3 GB on this machine to keep from going to disk too frequently. If this machine had just 1.5 GB RAM, then you'd expect to see high disk utilization.

---

[11] Certain database commands, like count, also use indexes.

When looking at the database stats, it's also worth noting the difference between `dataSize` and `storageSize`. If `storageSize` exceeds `dataSize` by more than a factor of two, then performance may suffer because of on-disk fragmentation. This fragmentation can force the machine to use much more RAM than is required; so in this case, you may want to try compacting your data files first before adding more RAM. See the section on compaction earlier in the chapter for instructions on how to do this.

10.4.3 Increase disk performance

There are a couple of issues with adding RAM. The first is that it isn't always possible; for example, if you're running on EC2, then the largest available virtual machine limits you to 68 GB RAM. The second issue is that adding RAM doesn't always solve the I/O problem. For instance, if your application is write intensive, then the background flushes or the paging of new data into RAM may overwhelm your disks anyway. Thus if you have efficient indexes and sufficient RAM and still see disk I/O slowness, then you may want to look into improving disk performance.

There are two ways to increase disk performance. One is to purchase faster disks. A 15 K RPM drive or an SSD might be worth the investment. Alternatively, or in addition, you can configure your disks in a RAID array, as this can increase both read and write throughput.[12] A RAID array may resolve I/O bottlenecks if configured properly. As mentioned, running a RAID 10 on EBS volumes increases read throughput significantly.

10.4.4 Scale horizontally

Horizontal scaling is the next obvious step to take in addressing a performance problem. Here there are two routes you can take. If your application is read intensive, it may be that a single node can't serve all the queries demanded of it, even with optimized indexes and data in RAM. This may call for distribution of reads across replicas. The official MongoDB drivers provide support for scaling across the members of a replica set, and this strategy is worth a try before escalating to a sharded cluster.

When all else fails, there's sharding. You should move to a sharded cluster when any of the following apply:

- You can't fit your working set entirely into the physical RAM of any one machine.
- The write load is too intensive for any one machine.

If you've set up a sharded cluster and still experience performance issues, then you should first go back and make sure that all your indexes are optimized, that data is fitting into RAM, and that your disks are performing effectively. To get the best hardware utilization, you may need to add more shards.

---

[12] The other nice thing about RAID is that with the right RAID level, you get disk redundancy.

10.4.5 Seek professional assistance

The sources of performance degradations are manifold and frequently idiosyncratic. Anything from poor schema design to sneaky server bugs can negatively affect performance. If you feel you've tried every possible remedy and still can't get results, then you should consider allowing someone experienced in the ways of MongoDB to audit your system. A book can take you far, but an experienced human being can make all the difference in the world. When you're at a loss for ideas and in doubt, seek professional assistance. The solutions to performance issues are sometimes entirely unintuitive.

10.5 Summary

This chapter has presented the most important considerations for deploying MongoDB in production. You should have the knowledge you need to select the right hardware for MongoDB, monitor your deployments, and maintain regular backups. In addition, you should have some idea about how to go about resolving performance issues. Ultimately, this knowledge will develop with experience. But MongoDB is predictable enough to be amenable to the simple heuristic presented here. Except for when it isn't. MongoDB tries to make life simple, but databases and their interactions with live applications are frankly complex. When this book's advice fails to scale, a knowledgeable expert can go a long way.

appendix A
Installation

In this appendix you'll learn how to install MongoDB on Linux, Mac OS X, and Windows, and you'll get at an overview of MongoDB's most commonly used configuration options. For developers, there are a few notes on compiling MongoDB from its source.

I'll conclude with some pointers on installing Ruby and RubyGems; this will aid those wanting to run the Ruby-based examples from the book.

A.1 Installation

Before we proceed to the installation instructions, a note on MongoDB versioning is in order. Briefly, you should run the latest stable version for your architecture. Stable releases of MongoDB are marked by an even minor version number. Thus, versions 1.8, 2.0, and 2.2 are stable; 1.9 and 2.1 are development versions and should not be used in production. The downloads page at http://mongodb.org provides statically linked binaries compiled for 32-bit and 64-bit systems. These binaries are available for the latest stable releases as well as for the development branches and nightly builds of the latest revision. The binaries provide the easiest way to install MongoDB across most platforms, including Linux, Mac OS X, Windows, and Solaris, and they're the method we'll prefer here.

A.1.1 MongoDB on Linux

There are three ways to install MongoDB on Linux. You can download the precompiled binaries directly from the mongodb.org website, use a package manager, or compile manually from source. We'll discuss the first two in the next sections, and then provide a few notes on compiling later in the appendix.

INSTALLING WITH PRECOMPILED BINARIES
First navigate to http://www.mongodb.org/downloads. There you'll see a grid with all the latest downloadable MongoDB binaries. Select the download URL for the latest stable version for your architecture. These examples use MongoDB v2.0 compiled for a 64-bit system.

Download the archive using your web browser or the `curl` utility. Then expand the archive using `tar`:

```
$ curl http://downloads.mongodb.org/linux/mongodb-linux-x86_64-2.0.0.tgz
    > mongo.tg
$ tar -xzvf mongo.tgz
```

To run MongoDB, you'll need a data directory. By default, the `mongod` daemon will store its data files in /data/db. Create that directory, and ensure that it has the proper permissions:

```
$ sudo mkdir -p /data/db/
$ sudo chown `id -u` /data/db
```

You're ready to start the server. Just change to the MongoDB bin directory and launch the `mongod` executable:

```
cd mongodb-linux-x86_64-2.0.0/bin
./mongod
```

If all goes well, you should see something like the following abridged startup log. Note the last lines, confirming that the server is listening on the default port of 27017:

```
Thu Mar 10 11:28:51 [initandlisten] MongoDB starting :
  pid=1773 port=27017 dbpath=/data/db/ 64-bit
Thu Mar 10 11:28:51 [initandlisten] db version v2.0.0, pdfile version 4.5
...
Thu Mar 10 11:28:51 [initandlisten] waiting for connections on port 27017
Thu Mar 10 11:28:51 [websvr] web admin interface listening on port 28017
```

If the server terminates unexpectedly, then refer to section A.5.

USING A PACKAGE MANAGER

Package managers can greatly simplify the installation of MongoDB. The only major downside is that package maintainers may not always keep up with the latest MongoDB releases. It's important to run the latest stable point release, so if you do choose to use a package manager, be sure that the version you're installing is a recent one.

If you happen to be running Debian, Ubuntu, CentOS, or Fedora, you'll always have access to the latest versions. This is because 10gen maintains and publishes its own packages for these platforms. You can find more information on installing these particular packages on the mongodb.org website. Instructions for Debian and Ubuntu can be found at http://mng.bz/ZffG. For CentOS and Fedora, see http://mng.bz/JSjC.

Packages are also available for FreeBSD and ArchLinux. See their respective package repositories for details.

A.1.2   *MongoDB on Mac OS X*

There are three ways to install MongoDB on Mac OS X. You can download the precompiled binaries directly from the mongodb.org website, use a package manager, or compile manually from source. We'll discuss the first two in the next sections, and then provide a few notes on compiling later in the appendix.

PRECOMPILED BINARIES

First navigate to http://www.mongodb.org/downloads. There you'll see a grid with all the latest downloadable MongoDB binaries. Select the download URL for the latest stable version for your architecture. The following example uses MongoDB v2.0 compiled for a 64-bit system.

Download the archive using your web browser or the `curl` utility. Then expand the archive using `tar`:

```
$ curl http://downloads.mongodb.org/osx/mongodb-osx-x86_64-2.0.0.tgz >
    mongo.tgz
$ tar xzf mongo.tgz
```

To run MongoDB, you'll need a data directory. By default, the `mongod` daemon will store its data files in `/data/db`. Go ahead and create that directory:

```
$ mkdir -p /data/db/
```

You're now ready to start the server. Just change to the MongoDB `bin` directory and launch the `mongod` executable:

```
$ cd mongodb-osx-x86_64-2.0.0/bin
$ ./mongod
```

If all goes well, you should see something like the following abridged startup log. Note the last lines, confirming that the server is listening on the default port of 27017:

```
Thu Mar 10 11:28:51 [initandlisten] MongoDB starting :
  pid=1773 port=27017 dbpath=/data/db/ 64-bit
Thu Mar 10 11:28:51 [initandlisten] db version v2.0.0, pdfile version 4.5
...
Thu Mar 10 11:28:51 [initandlisten] waiting for connections on port 27017
Thu Mar 10 11:28:51 [websvr] web admin interface listening on port 28017
```

If the server terminates unexpectedly, then refer to section A.5.

USING A PACKAGE MANAGER

Package managers can greatly simplify the installation of MongoDB. The only major downside is that package maintainers may not always keep up with the latest MongoDB releases. It's important to run the latest stable point release, so if you do choose to use a package manager, be sure that the version you're installing is a recent one.

MacPorts (http://www.macports.org) and Homebrew (http://mxcl.github.com/homebrew/) are two package managers for Mac OS X known to maintain up-to-date versions of MongoDB. To install via MacPorts, run the following:

```
sudo port install mongodb
```

Note that MacPorts will build MongoDB and all its dependencies from scratch. If you go this route, be prepared for a lengthy compile.

Homebrew, rather than compiling, merely downloads the latest binaries, so it's much faster than MacPorts. You can install MongoDB through Homebrew as follows:

```
$ brew update
$ brew install mongodb
```

After installing, Homebrew will provide instructions on how to start MongoDB using the Mac OS X launch agent.

A.1.3 *MongoDB on Windows*

There two ways to install MongoDB on Windows. The easier, preferred way is to download the precompiled binaries directly from the mongodb.org website. You can also compile from source, but this is recommended only for developers and advanced users. You can read about compiling from source in the next section.

PRECOMPILED BINARIES

First navigate to http://www.mongodb.org/downloads. There you'll see a grid with all the latest downloadable MongoDB binaries. Select the download URL for the latest stable version for your architecture. Here we'll install MongoDB v2.0 compiled for 64-bit Windows.

Download the appropriate distribution, and then unzip it. You can do this from the Windows Explorer by locating the MongoDB .zip file, right-clicking on it, and then selecting Extract All... You'll then be able to choose the folder where the contents will be unzipped.

Alternatively, you can use the command line. First navigate to your Downloads directory. Then use the unzip utility to extract the archive:

```
C:\> cd \Users\kyle\Downloads
C:\> unzip mongodb-win32-x86_64-2.0.0.zip
```

To run MongoDB, you'll need a data folder. By default, the mongod daemon will store its data files in C:\data\db. Open the Windows command prompt, and create the folder like so:

```
C:\> mkdir \data
C:\> mkdir \data\db
```

You're now ready to start the server. Just change to the MongoDB bin directory and launch the mongod executable:

```
C:\> cd \Users\kyle\Downloads
C:\Users\kyle\Downloads> cd mongodb-win32-x86_64-2.0.0\bin
C:\Users\kyle\Downloads\mongodb-win32-x86_64-2.0.0\bin> mongod.exe
```

If all goes well, you should see something like the following abridged startup log. Note the last lines, confirming that the server is listening on the default port of 27017:

```
Thu Mar 10 11:28:51 [initandlisten] MongoDB starting :
    pid=1773 port=27017 dbpath=/data/db/ 64-bit
Thu Mar 10 11:28:51 [initandlisten] db version v2.0.0, pdfile version 4.5
...
Thu Mar 10 11:28:51 [initandlisten] waiting for connections on port 27017
Thu Mar 10 11:28:51 [websvr] web admin interface listening on port 28017
```

If the server terminates unexpectedly, then refer to section A.5.

Finally, you'll want to start the MongoDB shell. To do that, open a second terminal window, and then launch mongo.exe:

```
C:\> cd \Users\kyle\Downloads\mongodb-win32-x86_64-2.0.0\bin
C:\Users\kyle\Downloads\mongodb-win32-x86_64-2.0.0\bin> mongo.exe
```

A.1.4 Compiling MongoDB from source

Compiling MongoDB from source is recommended only for advanced users and developers. If all you want to do is operate on the bleeding edge, without having to compile, you can always download the nightly binaries for the latest revisions from the mongodb.org website.

That said, you may want to compile yourself. The trickiest part about compiling MongoDB is managing the various dependencies. These include Boost, Spider-Monkey, and PCRE. The latest compilation instructions for each platform can be found at http://www.mongodb.org/display/DOCS/Building.

A.1.5 Troubleshooting

MongoDB is easy to install, but users occasionally experience minor problems. These usually manifest as error messages generated when trying to start the mongod daemon. Here I provide a list of the most common of these errors along with their resolutions.

WRONG ARCHITECTURE

If you try to run a binary compiled for a 64-bit system on a 32-bit machine, you'll see an error like the following:

```
-bash: ./mongod: cannot execute binary file
```

On Windows 7, the message is more helpful:

```
This version of
C:\Users\kyle\Downloads\mongodb-win32-x86_64-1.7.4\bin\mongod.exe
is not compatible with the version of Windows you're running.
Check your computer's system information to see whether you need
a x86 (32-bit) or x64 (64-bit) version of the program, and then
contact the software publisher.
```

The solution in both cases is to download and then run the 32-bit binary instead. Binaries for both architectures are available on the MongoDB download site (http://www.mongodb.org/downloads).

NONEXISTENT DATA DIRECTORY

MongoDB requires a directory for storing its data files. If the directory doesn't exist, you'll see an error like the following:

```
dbpath (/data/db/) does not exist, terminating
```

The solution is to create this directory. To see how, consult the preceding instructions for your operating system.

LACK OF PERMISSIONS

If you're running on a Unix variant, you'll need to make sure that the user running the mongod executable has permissions to write to the data directory. Otherwise, you'll see this error

```
Permission denied: "/data/db/mongod.lock", terminating
```

or possibly this one:

```
Unable to acquire lock for lockfilepath: /data/db/mongod.lock, terminating
```

In either case, you can solve the problem by opening up permissions in the data directory using chmod or chown.

UNABLE TO BIND TO PORT

MongoDB runs by default on port 27017. If another process, or another mongod, is bound to the same port, you'll see this error:

```
listen(): bind() failed errno:98
    Address already in use for socket: 0.0.0.0:27017
```

There are two possible solutions to this. The first is to find out what other process is running on port 27017 and then terminate it. Alternatively, run mongod on a different port using the --port flag. Here's how to run MongoDB on port 27018:

```
mongod --port 27018
```

A.2   *Basic configuration options*

Here I present a brief overview of the flags most commonly used when running MongoDB.

- --dbpath—The path to the directory where the data files are to be stored. This defaults to /data/db.
- --logpath—The path to the filename where log output should be directed. Log output will be printed to standard output (stdout) by default.
- --port—The port that MongoDB listens on. If not specified, this is set to 27017.
- --rest—This flag enables a simple REST interface that enhances the server's default web console. The web console is always available 1,000 port numbers above the port the server listens on. Thus if the server is listening at localhost on port 27017, then the web console will be available at http://localhost:28017/. Spend some time exploring the web console and the commands it exposes, as you can discover a lot about a live MongoDB server this way.
- --fork—Detaches the process to run as a daemon. Note that fork only works on Unix variants. Windows users seeking similar functionality should look at the instructions for running MongoDB as a proper Windows service. These are available at mongodb.org.

Those are the most important of the MongoDB startup flags. Here's an example of their use on the command line:

```
$ mongod --dbpath /var/local/mongodb --logpath /var/log/mongodb.log
--port 27018 --rest --fork
```

Note that it's also possible to specify all of these options in a config file. Simply create a new text file (we'll call it mongodb.conf) and you can specify all the preceding options, one per line:

```
dbpath=/var/local/mongodb
logpath=/var/log/mongodb.log
port=27018
rest=true
fork=true
```

You can then invoke mongod using the config file with the -f option:

```
$ mongod -f mongodb.conf
```

If you ever find yourself connected to a MongoDB and wondering which options were used at startup, you can get a list of them by running the getCmdLineOpts command:

```
> use admin
> db.runCommand({getCmdLineOpts: 1})
```

A.3 Installing Ruby

A number of the examples in this book are written in Ruby, so to run them yourself, you'll need a working Ruby installation. This means installing the Ruby interpreter as well as Ruby's package manager, RubyGems.

You should use a version of Ruby greater than or equal to 1.8.7. Versions 1.8.7 and 1.9.3 are the most common production versions at the time of this writing.

A.3.1 Linux and Mac OS X

Ruby comes installed by default on Max OS X and on a number of Linux distributions. You may want to check whether you have a recent version by running

```
ruby -v
```

If the command isn't found, or if you're running a version older than 1.8.7, you'll want to install or upgrade. There are detailed instructions for installing Ruby on Mac OS X as well as on a number of Unix variants at http://www.ruby-lang.org/en/downloads/ (you may have to scroll down the page to see the instructions for the various platforms). Most package managers (such as MacPorts and Aptitude) also maintain a recent version of Ruby, and they're likely to be the easiest avenue for getting a working Ruby installation.

In addition to the Ruby interpreter, you need the Ruby package manager, RubyGems, to install the MongoDB Ruby driver. Find out whether RubyGems is installed by running the gem command:

```
gem -v
```

You can install RubyGems through a package manager, but most users download the latest version and use the included installer. Instructions for doing this can be found at https://rubygems.org/pages/download.

A.3.2   *Windows*

By far the easiest way to install Ruby and RubyGems on Windows is to use the Windows Ruby Installer. The installer can be found here: http://rubyinstaller.org/downloads. When you run the executable, a wizard will guide you through the installation of both Ruby and RubyGems.

In additional to installing Ruby, you can also install the Ruby DevKit, which permits the easy compilation of Ruby C extensions. The MongoDB Ruby driver's BSON library may optionally use these extensions.

appendix B
Design patterns

B.1   Patterns

The early chapters of this book implicitly advocate a certain set of design patterns. Here I'll summarize those patterns and augment them with a few patterns that fall outside the flow of the text.

B.1.1   Embed versus reference

Suppose you're building a simple application in MongoDB that stores blog posts and comments. How do you represent this data? Do you embed the comments in their respective blog post documents? Or is it better to create two collections, one for posts and the other for comments, and then relate the comments to the posts with an object id reference?

This is the problem of embedding versus referencing, and it's a common source of confusion for new users of MongoDB. Fortunately, there's a simple rule of thumb that works for most schema design scenarios: Embed when the child objects always appear in the context of their parent. Otherwise, store the child objects in a separate collection.

What does this mean for blog posts and comments? It depends on the application. If the comments always appear within a blog post, and if they don't need to be ordered in arbitrary ways (by post date, comment rank, and so on), then embedding is fine. But if, say, you want to be able to display the most recent comments, regardless of which post they appear on, then you'll want to reference. Embedding may provide a slight performance advantage, but referencing is far more flexible.

B.1.2   One-to-many

As stated in the previous section, you can represent a one-to-many relationship by either embedding or referencing. You should embed when the *many* object intrinsically belongs with its parent and rarely changes. The schema for a how-to application illustrates this well. The steps in each guide can be represented as an array of sub-documents because these steps are an intrinsic part of the guide, and rarely change:

```
{ title: "How to soft-boil an egg",
        steps: [
```

```
      { desc: "Bring a pot of water to boil.",
        materials: ["water", "eggs"] },
      { desc: "Gently add the eggs a cook for four minutes.",
        materials: ["egg timer"]},
      { desc: "Cool the eggs under running water." },
    ]
}
```

When the two related entities will appear independently in the application, you'll want to relate. Many articles on MongoDB suggest that embedding comments in blog posts is a good idea. But relating is far more flexible. For one thing, you can easily show users a list of all their comments. You can also show all recent comments across all posts. These features, considered de rigueur for most sites, aren't possible with embedded documents at this time.[1] You typically relate documents using an object ID. Here's a sample post:

```
{ _id: ObjectId("4d650d4cf32639266022018d"),
  title: "Cultivating herbs",
  text: "Herbs require occasional watering..."
}
```

And here's a comment, related by the post_id field:

```
{ _id: ObjectId("4d650d4cf32639266022ac01"),
  post_id: ObjectId("4d650d4cf32639266022018d"),
  username: "zjones",
  text: "Indeed, basil is a hearty herb!"
}
```

The post and the comment live in their own collections, and it takes two queries to display a post with its comments. Because you'll be querying comments on their post_id field, you'll want an index there:

```
db.comments.ensureIndex({post_id: 1})
```

We used this one-to-many pattern extensively in chapters 4, 5, and 6; look there for more examples.

B.1.3 *Many-to-many*

In RDBMSs, you use a join table to represent many-to-many relationships; in MongoDB, you use *array keys*. You can see a clear example of this technique earlier in the book where we relate products and categories. Each product contains an array of category IDs, and both products and categories get their own collections. If you have two simple category documents

```
{ _id: ObjectId("4d6574baa6b804ea563c132a"),
  title: "Epiphytes"
}
```

---

[1] There's a popular feature request for *virtual collections*, which could provide the best of both worlds. See http://jira.mongodb.org/browse/SERVER-142 to track this issue.

```
{ _id: ObjectId("4d6574baa6b804ea563c459d"),
  title: "Greenhouse flowers"
}
```

then a product belonging to both categories will look like this:

```
{ _id: ObjectId("4d6574baa6b804ea563ca982"),
  name: "Dragon Orchid",
  category_ids: [ ObjectId("4d6574baa6b804ea563c132a"),
                  ObjectId("4d6574baa6b804ea563c459d") ]
}
```

For efficient queries, you should index the array of category IDs:

```
db.products.ensureIndex({category_ids: 1})
```

Then, to find all products in the Epiphytes category, simply match against the `category_id` field:

```
db.products.find({category_id: ObjectId("4d6574baa6b804ea563c132a")})
```

And to return all category documents related to the Dragon Orchid product, first get the list of that product's category IDs:

```
product = db.products.findOne({_id: ObjectId("4d6574baa6b804ea563c132a")})
```

And then query the `categories` collection using the `$in` operator:

```
db.categories.find({_id: {$in: product['category_ids']}})
```

You'll notice that finding the categories requires two queries, whereas the product search takes just one. This optimizes for the common case, as you're more likely to search for products in a category than the other way around.

B.1.4 *Trees*

Like most RDBMSs, MongoDB has no built-in facility for tree representation and traversal. Thus if you need tree-like behavior, then you've got to roll your own solution. I presented a solution to the category hierarchy problem in chapters 5 and 6. The strategy there was to store a snapshot of the category's ancestors within each category document. This denormalization makes updates more complicated but greatly simplifies reads.

Alas, the denormalized ancestor approach isn't great for all problems. Another common tree scenario is the online forum, where hundreds of messages are frequently nested many levels deep. There's too much nesting, and too much data, for the ancestor approach to work well here. A good alternative is the *materialized path.*

Following the materialized path pattern, each node in the tree contains a `path` field. This field stores the concatenation of each of the node's ancestor's IDs, and root-level nodes have a null `path` because they have no ancestors. Let's flesh out an example to see how this works. First, look at the comment thread in figure B.1. This represents a few questions and answers in thread about Greek history.

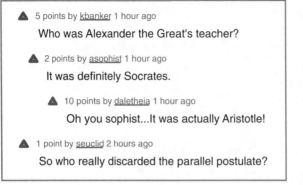

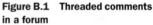

Figure B.1 **Threaded comments in a forum**

Let's see how these comments look as documents organized with a materialized path. The first is a root-level comment, so the path is null:

```
{ _id: ObjectId("4d692b5d59e212384d95001"),
  depth: 0,
  path: null,
  created: ISODate("2011-02-26T17:18:01.251Z"),
  username: "plotinus",
  body: "Who was Alexander the Great's teacher?",
  thread_id: ObjectId("4d692b5d59e212384d95223a")
}
```

The other root-level question, the one by user seuclid, will have the same structure. More illustrative are the follow-up comments to the question about Alexander the Great's teacher. Examine the first of these, and note that path contains the _id of the immediate parent:

```
{ _id: ObjectId("4d692b5d59e212384d951002"),
  depth: 1,
  path: "4d692b5d59e212384d95001",
  created: ISODate("2011-02-26T17:21:01.251Z"),
  username: "asophist",
  body: "It was definitely Socrates.",
  thread_id: ObjectId("4d692b5d59e212384d95223a")
}
```

The next deeper comment's path contains both the IDs of the original and immediate parents, in that order and separated by a colon:

```
{ _id: ObjectId("4d692b5d59e212384d95003"),
  depth: 2,
  path: "4d692b5d59e212384d95001:4d692b5d59e212384d951002",
  created: ISODate("2011-02-26T17:21:01.251Z"),
  username: "daletheia",
  body: "Oh you sophist...It was actually Aristotle!",
  thread_id: ObjectId("4d692b5d59e212384d95223a")
}
```

At a minimum, you'll want indexes on the thread_id and path fields, as you'll always be querying on exactly one of these fields:

```
db.comments.ensureIndex({thread_id: 1})
db.comments.ensureIndex({path: 1})
```

Now the question is how you go about querying and displaying the tree. One of the advantages of the materialized path pattern is that you query the database only once, whether you're displaying the entire comment thread or just a sub-tree within the thread. The query for the first of these is straightforward:

```
db.comments.find({thread_id: ObjectId("4d692b5d59e212384d95223a")})
```

The query for a particular sub-tree is more subtle because it uses a prefix query:

```
db.comments.find({path: /^4d692b5d59e212384d95001/})
```

This returns all comments with a path beginning with the specified string. This string represents the _id of the comment with the username plotinus, and if you examine the path field on each child comment, it's easy to see that they'll all satisfy the query. And they'll do so quickly because these prefix queries can use the index on path.

Getting the list of comments is easy, since it requires just one database query. Displaying them is trickier because you need a list that preserves thread order. This requires a bit of client-side processing, which you can achieve with the following Ruby methods.[2] The first method, threaded_list, builds a list of all root-level comments and a map that keys parent IDs to lists of child nodes:

```ruby
def threaded_list(cursor, opts={})
  list      = []
  child_map = {}
  start_depth = opts[:start_depth] || 0

  cursor.each do |comment|
    if comment['depth'] == start_depth
      list.push(comment)
    else
      matches = comment['path'].match(/([d|w]+)$/)
      immediate_parent_id = matches[1]
      if immediate_parent_id
        child_map[immediate_parent_id] ||= []
        child_map[immediate_parent_id] << comment
      end
    end
  end

  assemble(list, child_map)
end
```

The assemble method takes the list of root nodes and the child map and then builds a new list in display order:

---

[2] This book's source code includes a complete example of threaded comments with materialized paths using the display methods presented here.

```
def assemble(comments, map)
  list = []
  comments.each do |comment|
    list.push(comment)
    child_comments = map[comment['_id'].to_s]
    if child_comments
      list.concat(assemble(child_comments, map))
    end
  end

  list
end
```

To print the comments, you merely iterate over the list, indenting appropriately for each comment's depth:

```
def print_threaded_list(cursor, opts={})
  threaded_list(cursor, opts).each do |item|
    indent = "  " * item['depth']
    puts indent + item['body'] + " #{item['path']}"
  end
end
```

Querying for the comments and printing them is then straightforward:

```
cursor = @comments.find.sort("created")
print_threaded_list(cursor)
```

B.1.5   *Worker queues*

You can implement worker queues in MongoDB using either standard or capped collections. In both cases, the findAndModify command will permit you to process queue entries atomically.

A queue entry requires a state and a timestamp plus any remaining fields to contain the payload. The state can be encoded as a string, but an integer is more space-efficient. We'll use 0 and 1 to indicate *processed* and *unprocessed*, respectively. The timestamp is the standard BSON date. And the payload here is a simple plaintext message, but could be anything in principle:

```
{ state: 0,
  created: ISODate("2011-02-24T16:29:36.697Z"),
  message: "hello world" }
```

You'll need to declare an index that allows you to efficiently fetch the oldest unprocessed entry (FIFO). A compound index on state and created fits the bill:

```
db.queue.ensureIndex({state: 1, created: 1})
```

You then use findAndModify to return the next entry and mark it as processed:

```
q = {state: 0}
s = {created: 1}
u = {$set: {state: 1}}
db.queue.findAndModify({query: q, sort: s, update: u})
```

If you're using a standard collection, then you'll need to be sure to remove old queue entries. It's possible to remove them at processing time using findAndModify's {remove: true} option. But some applications may want to postpone removal for a later time, once the processing is complete.

Capped collections may also serve as the basis for a worker queue. Without the default index on _id, a capped collection has potentially faster insert speed, but the difference will be negligible for most applications. The other potential advantage is automatic deletion. But this feature is a double-edged sword: you'll have to make sure that the collection is large enough to prevent unprocessed entries from aging out. Thus if you do use a capped collection, make it extra large. The ideal collection size will depend on your queue write throughput and the average payload size.

Once you've decided on the size of capped collection to use, the schema, index, and findAndModify will be identical to those of the standard collection just described.

B.1.6 *Dynamic attributes*

MongoDB's document data model is useful for representing entities whose attributes vary. Products are the canonical example of this, and you saw some ways of modeling these attributes earlier in the book. One viable way to model these attributes is to scope them to a sub-document. In a single products collection, you can then store disparate product types. You might store a set of headphones

```
{ _id: ObjectId("4d669c225d3a52568ce07646")
  sku: "ebd-123"
  name: "Hi-Fi Earbuds",
  type: "Headphone",
  attrs: { color: "silver",
           freq_low: 20,
           freq_hi: 22000,
           weight: 0.5
         }
}
```

and an SSD drive:

```
{ _id: ObjectId("4d669c225d3a52568ce07646")
  sku: "ssd-456"
  name: "Mini SSD Drive",
  type: "Hard Drive",
  attrs: { interface: "SATA",
           capacity: 1.2 * 1024 * 1024 * 1024,
           rotation: 7200,
           form_factor: 2.5
         }
}
```

If you need to frequently query on these attributes, you can create sparse indexes for them. For example, you can optimize for range queries in headphone frequency response:

```
db.products.ensureIndex({"attrs.freq_low": 1, "attrs.freq_hi": 1},
  {sparse: true})
```

You can also efficiently search hard disks by rotation speed with the following index:

```
db.products.ensureIndex({"attrs.rotation": 1}, {sparse: true})
```

The overall strategy here is to scope your attributes for readability and app discoverability and to use sparse indexes to keep null values out of the indexes.

If your attributes are completely unpredictable, then you can't build a separate index for each one. You have to use a different strategy in this case as illustrated by the following sample document:

```
{ _id: ObjectId("4d669c225d3a52568ce07646")
  sku: "ebd-123"
  name: "Hi-Fi Earbuds",
  type: "Headphone",
  attrs: [ {n: "color", v: "silver"},
           {n: "freq_low", v: 20},
           {n: "freq_hi", v: 22000},
           {n: "weight", v: 0.5}
         ]
}
```

Here `attrs` points to an array of sub-documents. Each of these documents has two values, n and v, corresponding to each dynamic attribute's name and value. This normalized representation allows you to index these attributes using a single compound index:

```
db.products.ensureIndex({"attrs.n": 1, "attrs.v": 1})
```

You can then query using these attributes, but to do that, you must use the $elem-Match query operator:

```
db.products.find({attrs: {$elemMatch: {n: "color", v: "silver"}}})
```

Note that this strategy incurs a lot of overhead since it requires storing the key names in the index. It would be important to test this for performance on a representative data set before going into production.

B.1.7 *Transactions*

MongoDB doesn't provide ACID guarantees over a series of operations, and no equivalent of RDBMSs' BEGIN, COMMIT, and ROLLBACK semantics exists. When you need these features, use a different database (either for the data that needs proper transactions or for the application as a whole). Still MongoDB supports atomic, durable updates on individual documents and consistent reads, and these features, though primitive, can be used to implement transaction-like behavior in an application.

You saw an extended example of this in chapter 6's treatments of order authorization and inventory management. And the worker queue implementation earlier in this appendix could easily be modified to support rollback. In both cases, the foundation for transaction-like behavior is the ever-versatile findAndModify command, which is used to atomically manipulate a state field on one or more documents.

The transactional strategy used in all these cases can be described as *compensation-driven*.[3] The compensation process in abstract works like this:

1 Atomically modify a document's state.
2 Perform some unit of work, which may include atomically modifying other documents.
3 Ensure that the system as a whole (all documents involved) is in a valid state. If so, mark the transaction complete; otherwise, revert each document to its pre-transaction state.

It's worth noting that the compensation-driven strategy is all but necessary for long-running and multistep transactions. The whole process of authorizing, shipping, and canceling an order is just one example. For these cases, even an RDBMS with full transactional semantics must implement a similar strategy.

There may be no getting around certain applications' requirements for multi-object ACID transactions. But with the right patterns, MongoDB can pull some transactional weight and might support the transactional semantic your application needs.

B.1.8 *Locality and precomputation*

MongoDB is frequently billed as an analytics database, and plenty of users store analytics data in MongoDB. A combination of atomic increments and rich documents seems to work best. For example, here's a document representing total page views for each day of the month along with the total for the month as a whole. For brevity, the following document contains totals only for the first five days of the month:

```
{ base: "org.mongodb", path: "/",
  total: 99234,
  days: {
    "1": 4500,
    "2": 4324,
    "3": 2700,
    "4": 2300,
    "5": 0
  }
}
```

You can update the totals for the day and month with a simple targeted update using the $inc operator:

```
use stats-2011
db.sites-nov.update({ base: "org.mongodb", path: "/" },
  $inc: {total: 1, "days.5": 1 });
```

Take a moment to notice the collection and database names. The collection, sites-nov, is scoped to a given month, and the database, stats-2011, to a particular year.

---

[3] Two pieces of literature covering compensation-driven transactions are worth studying. The original is Garcia-Molina and Salem's "Sagas" paper (http://mng.bz/73is). The less formal but no less interesting "Your Coffee Shop Doesn't Use Two-Phase Commit" by Gregor Hohpe (http://mng.bz/kpAq) is also a great read.

This gives the application good locality. When you query for recent visits, you're always querying a single collection that's relatively small compared with the overall analytics history. If you need to delete data, you can drop a time-scoped collection rather than removing some subset of documents from a larger collection. That latter operation may result in on-disk fragmentation.

The other principle at work here is *precomputation*. Sometime near the beginning of the month, you insert a template document with zeroed values for each day of the month. As a result, the document will never change size as you increment the counters therein because you'll never actually be adding fields; you'll only be changing their values in-place. This is important because it keeps the document from being relocated on disk as you write to it. Relocation is slow and often results in fragmentation.

B.2   Anti-patterns

MongoDB lacks constraints, which can lead to poorly organized data. Here are a few issues commonly found in problematic production deployments.

B.2.1   Careless indexing

When users experience performance problems, it's not unusual to discover a whole slew of unused or inefficient indexes. The most efficient set of indexes for an application will always be based on an analysis of the queries being run. Be disciplined about the optimization methods presented in chapter 7.

B.2.2   Motley types

Ensure that keys of the same name within a collection all share the same type. If you store a phone number, for instance, then store it consistently, either as a string or an integer (but not as both). The mixing of types in a single key's value makes the application logic complex, and makes BSON documents difficult to parse in certain strongly typed languages.

B.2.3   Bucket collections

Collections should be used for one type of entity only; don't put products and users in the same collection. Because collections are cheap, each type within your application should get its own collection.

B.2.4   Large, deeply nested documents

There are two misunderstandings about MongoDB's document data model. One is that you should never build relationships between collections, but rather represent all relationships in the same document. This frequently degenerates into a mess, but users nevertheless sometimes try it. The second misunderstanding stems from an overly literal interpretation of the word *document*. A document, these users reason, is a single entity just like a real-life document. This leads to large documents that are difficult to query and update, let alone comprehend.

The bottom line here is that you should keep documents small (well under 100 KB per document unless you're storing raw binary data) and that you shouldn't nest more than a few levels deep. A smaller size makes document updates cheaper because, in the case where a document needs to be rewritten on disk completely, there's less to rewrite. The other advantage is that the documents remain comprehensible, which makes life easier for developers needing to understand the data model.

B.2.5   *One collection per user*

It's rarely a good idea to build out one collection per user. One problem with this is that the namespaces (indexes plus collections) max out at 24,000 by default. Once you grow beyond that, you have to allocate a new database. In addition, each collection and its indexes introduce extra overhead, making this strategy a waste of space.

B.2.6   *Unshardable collections*

If you expect a collection to grow large enough to merit sharding, be sure that you can eventually shard it. A collection is shardable if you can define an efficient shard key for that collection. Review the tips in chapter 9 on choosing a shard key.

Binary data and GridFS

For storing images, thumbnails, audio, and other binary files, many applications rely on the file system only. Although file systems provide fast access to files, file system storage can also can lead to organizational chaos. Consider that most file systems limit the number of files per directory. If you have millions of files to keep track of, then you need to devise a strategy for organizing files into multiple directories. Another difficulty involves metadata. Since the file metadata is still stored in a database, performing an accurate backup of the files and their metadata can be incredibly complicated.

For certain use cases, it may make sense to store files in the database itself because it simplifies file organization and backup. In MongoDB, you can use the BSON binary type to store any kind of binary data. This data type corresponds to the RDBMS *BLOB (binary large object)* type, and it's the basis for two flavors of binary object storage provided by MongoDB.

The first uses one document per file and is best for smaller binary objects. If you need to catalog a large number of thumbnails or MD5s, then using single-document binary storage can make life much easier. On the other hand, you might want to store large images or audio files. In this case, GridFS, a Mongo DB API for storing binary objects of any size, would be a better choice. In the next two sections, you'll see complete examples of both storage techniques.

C.1 Simple binary storage

BSON includes a first-class type for binary data. You can use this type to store binary objects directly inside MongoDB documents. The only limit on object size is the document size limit itself, which is 16 MB as of MongoDB v2.0. Because large documents like this can tax system resources, you're encouraged to use GridFS for any binary objects you want to store that are larger than 1 MB.

We'll look at two reasonable uses of binary object storage in single documents. First, you'll see how to store an image thumbnail. Then, you'll see how to store the accompanying MD5.

C.1.1 Storing a thumbnail

Imagine you need to store a collection of image thumbnails. The code is straightforward. First, you get the image's filename, `canyon-thumb.jpg`, and then read the data into a local variable. Next, you wrap the raw binary data as a BSON binary object using the Ruby driver's BSON::Binary constructor:

```
require 'rubygems'
require 'mongo'

image_filename = File.join(File.dirname(__FILE__), "canyon-thumb.jpg")
image_data = File.open(image_filename).read

bson_image_data = BSON::Binary.new(image_data)
```

All that remains is to build a simple document to contain the binary data and then insert it into the database:

```
doc = {"name" => "monument-thumb.jpg",
       "data" => bson_image_data }

@con = Mongo::Connection.new
@thumbnails = @con['images']['thumbnails']
@image_id = @thumbnails.insert(doc)
```

To extract the binary data, fetch the document. In Ruby, the to_s method unpacks the data into a binary string, and you can use this to compare the saved data to the original:

```
doc = @thumbnails.find_one({"_id" => @image_id})
if image_data == doc["data"].to_s
  puts "Stored image is equal to the original file!"
end
```

If you run the preceding script, you'll see a message indicating that the two files are indeed the same.

C.1.2 *Storing an MD5*

It's common to store a checksum as binary data, and this marks another potential use of the BSON binary type. Here's how you can generate an MD5 of the thumbnail and add it to the document just stored:

```
require 'md5'
md5 = Digest::MD5.file(image_filename).digest
bson_md5 = BSON::Binary.new(md5, BSON::Binary::SUBTYPE_MD5)

@thumbnails.update({:_id => @image_id}, {"$set" => {:md5 => bson_md5}})
```

Note that when creating the BSON binary object, you tag the data with SUBTYPE_MD5. The subtype is an extra field on the BSON binary type that indicates what kind of binary data is being stored. However, this field is entirely optional and has no effect on how the database stores or interprets the data.[1]

It's easy to query for the document just stored, but do notice that you exclude the data field to keep the return document small and readable:

---

[1] This wasn't always technically true. The deprecated default subtype of 2 indicated that the attached binary data also included four extra bytes to indicate the size, and this did affect a few database commands. The current default subtype is 0, and all subtypes now store the binary payload the same way. Subtype can therefore be seen as a kind of lightweight tag to be optionally used by application developers.

```
> use images
> db.thumbnails.findOne({}, {data: 0})
{
  "_id" : ObjectId("4d608614238d3b4ade000001"),
  "md5" : BinData(5,"K1ud3EUjT49wdMdkOGjbDg=="),
  "name" : "monument-thumb.jpg"
}
```

See that the MD5 field is clearly marked as binary data, with the subtype and raw payload.

C.2   *GridFS*

GridFS is a convention for storing files of arbitrary size in MongoDB. The GridFS specification is implemented by all of the official drivers and by MongoDB's `mongofiles` tool, ensuring consistent access across platforms. GridFS is useful for storing large binary objects in the database. It's frequently fast enough to serve these object as well, and the storage method is conducive to streaming.

The term *GridFS* frequently leads to confusion, so two clarifications are worth making right off the bat. The first is that GridFS isn't an intrinsic feature of MongoDB. As mentioned, it's a *convention* that all the official drivers (and some tools) use to manage large binary objects in the database. Second, it's important to clarify that GridFS doesn't have the rich semantics of bona fide file systems. For instance, there's no protocol for locking and concurrency, and this limits the GridFS interface to simple put, get, and delete operations. This means that if you want to update a file, you need to delete it and then put the new version.

GridFS works by dividing a large file into small, 256 KB chunks and then storing each chunk as a separate document. By default, these chunks are stored in a collection called `fs.chunks`. Once the chunks are written, the file's metadata is stored in a single document in another collection called `fs.files`. Figure C.1 contains a simplistic illustration of this process applied to a theoretical 1 MB file called `canyon.jpg`.

That should be enough theory to use GridFS. Next we'll see GridFS in practice through the Ruby GridFS API and the `mongofiles` utility.

C.2.1   *GridFS in Ruby*

Earlier you stored a small image thumbnail. The thumbnail took up only 10 KB and was thus ideal for keeping in a single document. The original image is almost 2 MB in size, and is therefore much more appropriate for GridFS storage. Here you'll store the original using Ruby's GridFS API. First, you connect to the database and then initialize a `Grid` object, which takes a reference to the database where the GridFS file will be stored.

Next, you open the original image file, `canyon.jpg`, for reading. The most basic GridFS interface uses methods to put and get a file. Here you use the `Grid#put` method, which takes either a string of binary data or an `IO` object, such as a file pointer. You pass in the file pointer and the data is written to the database.

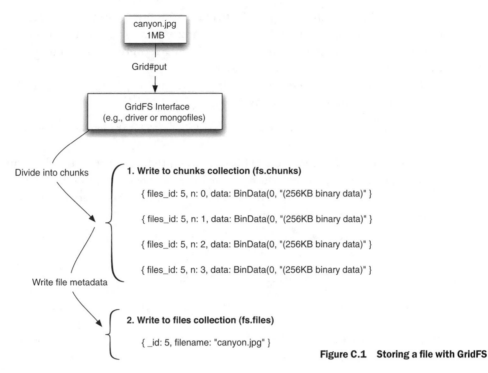

Figure C.1   Storing a file with GridFS

The method returns the file's unique object ID:

```
@con  = Mongo::Connection.new
@db   = @con["images"]

@grid = Mongo::Grid.new(@db)

filename = File.join(File.dirname(__FILE__), "canyon.jpg")
file = File.open(filename, "r")

file_id = @grid.put(file, :filename => "canyon.jpg")
```

As stated, GridFS uses two collections for storing file data. The first, normally called `fs.files`, keeps each file's metadata. The second collection, `fs.chunks`, stores one or more chunks of binary data for each file. Let's briefly examine these from the shell.

Switch to the `images` database, and query for the first entry in the `fs.files` collection. You'll see the metadata for the file you just stored:

```
> use images
> db.fs.files.findOne()
{
  "_id" : ObjectId("4d606588238d3b4471000001"),
  "filename" : "canyon.jpg",
  "contentType" : "binary/octet-stream",
  "length" : 2004828,
  "chunkSize" : 262144,
  "uploadDate" : ISODate("2011-02-20T00:51:21.191Z"),
  "md5" : "9725ad463b646ccbd287be87cb9b1f6e"
}
```

These are the minimum required attributes for every GridFS file. Most are self-explanatory. You can see that this file is about 2 MB and is divided into chunks 256 KB in size. You'll also notice an MD5. The GridFS spec requires a checksum to ensure that the stored file is the same as the original.

Each chunk stores the object ID of its file in a field called `files_id`. Thus you can easily count the number of chunks this file uses:

```
> db.fs.chunks.count({"files_id" : ObjectId("4d606588238d3b4471000001")})
8
```

Given the chunk size and the total file size, eight chunks is exactly what you should expect. The contents of the chunks themselves is easy to see, too. Like earlier, you'll want to exclude the *data* to keep the output readable. This query returns the first of the eight chunks, as indicated by the value of *n*:

```
> db.fs.chunks.findOne({files_id: ObjectId("4d606588238d3b4471000001")},
          {data: 0})
{
  "_id" : ObjectId("4d606588238d3b4471000002"),
  "n" : 0,
  "files_id" : ObjectId("4d606588238d3b4471000001")
}
```

Reading GridFS files is as easy as writing them. In the following example, you use `Grid#get` to return an `IO`-like `GridIO` object representing the file. You can then stream the GridFS file back to the file system. Here, you read 256 KB at a time to write a copy of the original file:

```
image_io = @grid.get(file_id)

copy_filename = File.join(File.dirname(__FILE__), "canyon-copy.jpg")
copy = File.open(copy_filename, "w")

while !image_io.eof? do
  copy.write(image_io.read(256 * 1024))
end

copy.close
```

You can then verify for yourself that both files are the same:[2]

```
$ diff -s canyon.jpg canyon-copy.jpg
Files canyon.jpg and canyon-copy.jpg are identical
```

That's the basics of reading and writing GridFS files from a driver. The various GridFS APIs vary slightly, but with the foregoing examples and the basic knowledge of how GridFS works, you should have no trouble making sense of your driver's docs.

---

[2] This code assumes that you have the `diff` utility installed.

C.2.2   *GridFS with mongofiles*

The MongoDB distribution includes a handy utility called `mongofiles` for listing, putting, getting, and deleting GridFS files using the command line. For example, you can list the GridFS files in the `images` database:

```
$ mongofiles -d images list
connected to: 127.0.0.1
canyon.jpg  2004828
```

You can also easily add files. Here's how you can add the copy of the image that you wrote with the Ruby script:

```
$ mongofiles -d images put canyon-copy.jpg
connected to: 127.0.0.1
added file: { _id: ObjectId('4d61783326758d4e6727228f'),
              filename: "canyon-copy.jpg",
              chunkSize: 262144, uploadDate: new Date(1298233395296),
              md5: "9725ad463b646ccbd287be87cb9b1f6e", length: 2004828 }
```

You can again list the files to verify that the copy was written:

```
$ mongofiles -d images list
connected to: 127.0.0.1
canyon.jpg  2004828
canyon-copy.jpg  2004828
```

`mongofiles` supports a number of options, and you can view them with the `--help` parameter:

```
$ mongofiles --help
```

appendix D
MongoDB in PHP, Java, and C++

This book has presented MongoDB through the lenses of JavaScript and Ruby. But there are plenty of other ways to communicate with MongoDB, and this appendix presents three that span the gamut. I'll start with PHP because it's a popular scripting language. I include Java because it's still arguably the language of the enterprise and thus important to a lot of readers of this book. Plus, the Java driver's API diverges significantly from that of most scripting languages. Finally, I'll present the C++ driver because it's a core part of MongoDB's codebase, and it's likely to be useful to developers wanting to build high-performance standalone applications.

Each language section describes how to construct documents and make connections, and then ends with a complete program that inserts, updates, queries, and deletes a sample document. All of the programs perform the same operations and produce the same output, so they're easy to compare. The document in each program is an example of what a simple web crawler might store; for reference, here it is in JSON:

```
{ url: "org.mongodb",
  tags: ["database", "open-source"],
  attrs: { "last-visit" : ISODate("2011-02-22T05:18:28.740Z"),
         "pingtime" : 20
       }
}
```

D.1 PHP

The PHP community has embraced MongoDB with zeal, thanks in no small part to the quality of the driver. The sample code should feel roughly isomorphic to the equivalent Ruby code.

D.1.1 Documents

PHP arrays are implemented as ordered dictionaries. They therefore map nicely to BSON documents. You can create a simple document using PHP array literals:

```
$basic = array( "username" => "jones", "zip" => 10011 );
```

PHP arrays can also be nested. This complex document contains an array of tags and a sub-document with a `last_access` date and integer `pingtime`. Note you must use the special `MongoDate` class to represent a date:

```php
$doc = array( "url"   => "org.mongodb",
              "tags"  => array( "database", "open-source"),
              "attrs" => array( "last_access" => new MongoDate(),
                                "pingtime" => 20
                              )
            );
```

D.1.2   Connections

You can connect to a single node with the `Mongo` constructor:

```php
$conn = new Mongo( "localhost", 27017 );
```

To connect to a replica set, pass a MongoDB connection URI to the `Mongo` constructor. You must also specify `array( "replicaSet" => true )`:

```php
$repl_conn = new Mongo( "mongo://localhost:30000,localhost:30001",
            array( "replicaSet" => true ));
```

> **MONGODB CONNECTION URIS**   The MongoDB connection URI is a standard way to specify connection options across drivers. Most of the drivers will accept a connection URI, and this can simplify configuration for a system that talks to a MongoDB server across environments. See the official online MongoDB docs for the latest URI specification.

PHP applications often run much more efficiently with persistent connections. If you use them, be sure always to specify `array( "persistent" => "x" )`, where "x" represents a unique identifier for the persistent connection being created:

```php
$conn = new Mongo( "localhost", 27017, array( "persist" => "x" ) );
```

D.1.3   Sample program

The following PHP program shows how to insert, update, query, and delete a document. It also includes several PHP BSON document representations.

Listing D.1   Sample PHP driver usage

```php
<?php
  $m = new Mongo( "localhost", 27017 );
  $db = $m->crawler;
  $coll = $db->sites;

  $doc = array( "url"   => "org.mongodb",
                "tags"  => array( "database", "open-source"),
                "attrs" => array( "last_access" => new MongoDate(),
                                  "pingtime" => 20
                                )
              );

  $coll->insert( $doc );
```

```
    print "Initial document:n";
    print print_r( $doc );

    print "Updating pingtime...n";
    $coll->update(
      array( "_id"  => $doc["_id"] ),
      array( '$set' => array( 'attrs.pingtime' => 30 ) )
    );

    print "After update:n";
    $cursor = $coll->find();
    print print_r( $cursor->getNext() );

    print "nNumber of site documents: " . $coll->count() . "n";

    print "Removing documents...n";
    $coll->remove();
?>
```

D.2   *Java*

Among MongoDB drivers, the Java driver may be the one most frequently used in production. In addition to backing pure Java apps, the Java driver also forms the basis for the drivers powering JVM languages like Scala, Clojure, and JRuby. Java's lack of a dictionary literal makes the building of BSON documents more verbose, but the driver on the whole is still easy to use.

D.2.1   *Documents*

To construct a BSON document, you can initialize a `BasicBSONObject`, which implements the `Map` interface to provide a simple API centered around `get()` and `put()` operations.

The `BasicBSONObject` constructor takes an optional initial key-value pair for convenience. Using that, you can build a simple document like so:

```
DBObject simple = new BasicDBObject( "username", "Jones" );
simple.put( "zip", 10011 );
```

Adding a sub-document means creating an extra `BasicBSONObject`. The array can be a normal Java array:

```
DBObject doc = new BasicDBObject();
String[] tags = { "database", "open-source" };

doc.put("url", "org.mongodb");
doc.put("tags", tags);

DBObject attrs = new BasicDBObject();
attrs.put( "lastAccess", new Date() );
attrs.put( "pingtime", 20 );

doc.put( "attrs", attrs );

System.out.println( doc.toString() );
```

Finally, note that you can inspect a document using its `toString()` method.

D.2.2 *Connections*

Creating a single-node connection is easy as long as you remember to wrap the call in a try block:

```
try {
  Mongo conn = new Mongo("localhost", 27017);
} catch (Exception e) {
  throw new RuntimeException(e);
}
```

To connect to a replica set, first build a list of ServerAddress objects. Then pass that list to the Mongo constructor:

```
List servers = new ArrayList();
servers.add( new ServerAddress( "localhost" , 30000 ) );
servers.add( new ServerAddress( "localhost" , 30001 ) );

try {
  Mongo replConn = new Mongo( servers );
} catch (Exception e) {
  throw new RuntimeException(e);
```

The Java driver includes flexible support for write concern. You can specify a different write concern on the Mongo, DB, and DBCollection objects, as well as on any of DBCollection's write methods. Here we specify a global write concern on the connection using the WriteConcern configuration class:

```
WriteConcern w = new WriteConcern( 1, 2000 );
conn.setWriteConcern( w );
```

D.2.3 *Sample program*

This Java program is a direct translation of the previous PHP program, and it should be self-explanatory:

```
import com.mongodb.Mongo;
import com.mongodb.DB;
import com.mongodb.DBCollection;
import com.mongodb.BasicDBObject;
import com.mongodb.DBObject;
import com.mongodb.DBCursor;
import com.mongodb.WriteConcern;
import java.util.Date;

public class Sample {

  public static void main(String[] args) {

    Mongo conn;
    try {
      conn = new Mongo("localhost", 27017);
    } catch (Exception e) {
      throw new RuntimeException(e);
    }

    WriteConcern w = new WriteConcern( 1, 2000 );
```

```
conn.setWriteConcern( w );

DB db = conn.getDB( "crawler" );
DBCollection coll = db.getCollection( "sites" );

DBObject doc = new BasicDBObject();
String[] tags = { "database", "open-source" };

doc.put("url", "org.mongodb");
doc.put("tags", tags);

DBObject attrs = new BasicDBObject();
attrs.put( "lastAccess", new Date() );
attrs.put( "pingtime", 20 );

doc.put( "attrs", attrs );

coll.insert(doc);

System.out.println( "Initial document:n" );
System.out.println( doc.toString() );

System.out.println( "Updating pingtime...n" );
coll.update( new BasicDBObject( "_id", doc.get("_id") ),
    new BasicDBObject( "$set", new BasicDBObject( "pingtime", 30 ) ) );

DBCursor cursor = coll.find();

System.out.println( "After updaten" );
System.out.println( cursor.next().toString() );

System.out.println( "Number of site documents: " + coll.count() );

System.out.println( "Removing documents...n" );
coll.remove( new BasicDBObject() );
  }
}
```

D.3   C++

Reasons to recommend the C++ driver include its speed and its closeness to the core server. You'd be hard pressed to find a faster driver, and if you're interested in MongoDB's internals, then learning the C++ driver makes for a good entry point into the source code. The C++ driver isn't so much a standalone driver as an integral internal MongoDB API that's intermingled with the core code base. That said, facilities exist for using this code as an independent library.

D.3.1   Documents

There are two ways to create BSON documents in C++. You can use the somewhat verbose BSONObjBuilder, or you can use the BSON macros that wrap it. I'll show both methods for each example document.

Let's start with a simple document:

```
BSONObjBuilder simple;
simple.genOID().append("username", "Jones").append( "zip", 10011 );
BSONObj doc = simple.obj();

cout << doc.jsonString();
```

Note that you explicitly generate the object ID using the genOID() function. C++ BSON objects are static, which means that the insert function can't modify them like it does in other drivers. If you want a handle on the object id after insert, then you need to generate it yourself.

Note also that you must convert the BSONObjBuilder into a BSONObj before it can be used. You do this by calling the BSONObjBuilder's obj() method.

Now let's generate the same document using the helper macros. BSON and GENOID will save some typing:

```
BSONObj o = BSON( GENOID << "username" << "Jones" << "zip" << 10011 );
cout << o.jsonString();
```

Constructing the more complex document will be reminiscent of Java, where you have to build each sub-object separately. Note that you build the array with the standard BSONObjBuilder, only you use numeric string indexes 0 and 1. This is in fact how arrays are stored in BSON:

```
BSONObjBuilder site;
site.genOID().append("url", "org.mongodb");
BSONObjBuilder tags;
tags.append("0", "database");
tags.append("1", "open-source");
site.appendArray( "tags", tags.obj() );

BSONObjBuilder attrs;
time_t now = time(0);
attrs.appendTimeT( "lastVisited", now );
attrs.append( "pingtime", 20 );
site.append( "attrs", attrs.obj() );

BSONObj site_obj = site.obj();
```

Like before, you'll appreciate the macros for conciseness. Pay special attention to the BSON_ARRAY and DATENOW macros, and note what constructs they replace in the BSONObjBuilder version of the document:

```
BSONObj site_concise = BSON( GENOID << "url" << "org.mongodb"
  << "tags" << BSON_ARRAY( "database" << "open-source" )
  << "attrs" << BSON( "lastVisited" << DATENOW << "pingtime" << 20 ) );
```

Unique to C++ is the requirement that you explicitly mark BSON documents that will be used as query selectors. One way to do this is with the Query() constructor:

```
BSONObj selector = BSON( "_id" << 1 );
Query * q1 = new Query( selector );
cout << q1->toString() << "n";
```

Again, the handy QUERY macro will usually be preferable:

```
Query q2 = QUERY( "pingtime" << LT << 20 );
cout << q2.toString() << "n";
```

D.3.2   *Connections*

You can easily create single-node connections by instantiating a `DBClientConnection`. Always wrap this in a `try` block:

```
DBClientConnection conn;

try {
  conn.connect("localhost:27017");
}
catch( DBException &e ) {
    cout << "caught " << e.what() << endl;
}
```

Connecting to a replica set first requires that you build a vector containing `HostAnd-Port` objects. You then pass the name of the replica set and the vector to the `DBClientReplicaSet` constructor. You can check the contents of the object by calling `toString()`:

```
std::vector<HostAndPort> seeds (2);
seeds.push_back( HostAndPort( "localhost", 30000 ) );
seeds.push_back( HostAndPort( "localhost", 30001 ) );

DBClientReplicaSet repl_conn( "myset", seeds );
try {
  repl_conn.connect();
catch( DBException &e ) {
    cout << "caught " << e.what() << endl;
}

cout << repl_conn.toString();
```

D.3.3   *Sample program*

The main thing to notice in the C++ code sample is that there are no explicit classes for abstracting databases and collections. All inserts, updates, queries, and deletes go through the connection object itself. You specify the database and collection as the first argument to these methods in the form of a namespace (`crawler.sites`):

```
#include <iostream>
#include <ctime>
#include "client/dbclient.h"

using namespace mongo;

int main() {
    DBClientConnection conn;

    try {
      conn.connect("localhost:27017");
    }
    catch( DBException &e ) {
        cout << "caught " << e.what() << endl;
    }

    BSONObj doc = BSON( GENOID << "url" << "org.mongodb"
      << "tags" << BSON_ARRAY( "database" << "open-source" )
```

```
      << "attrs" << BSON( "lastVisited" << DATENOW << "pingtime" << 20 ) );

cout << "Initial document:n" << doc.jsonString() << "n";
conn.insert( "crawler.sites", doc );

cout << "Updating pingtime...n";
BSONObj update = BSON( "$set" << BSON( "attrs.pingtime" << 30) );
conn.update( "crawler.sites", QUERY("_id" << doc["_id"]), update);

cout << "After update:n";
auto_ptr<DBClientCursor> cursor;
cursor = conn.query( "crawler.sites", QUERY( "_id" << doc["_id"]) );
cout << cursor->next().jsonString() << "n";

cout << "Number of site documents: " <<
  conn.count( "crawler.sites" ) << "n";

cout << "Removing documents...n";
conn.remove( "crawler.sites", BSONObj() );

return 0;
}
```

With the proliferation of smart mobile devices, the demand for location-based services has been increasing steadily. To build these location-dependent applications requires a database capable of indexing and querying spatial data. This feature was added to the MongoDB road map fairly early on, and MongoDB's spatial indexing, though not as fully featured as, say, PostGIS, nevertheless now powers the location queries for a number of popular sites.[1]

As the name implies, spatial indexes are optimized for data representing locations. In the case of MongoDB, this data is typically represented as longitude and latitude on the geographic coordinate system. A spatial index on the data can then permit queries based on a user's location. For example, you might have a collection containing menu data and coordinates for every restaurant in New York City. With an index on those restaurant locations, you can query the database for the closest restaurant to the Brooklyn Bridge serving caviar.

What's more, the indexer is generic enough to work outside the terrestrial. This means that you can even use it to index locations on two-dimensional coordinate planes or on the planet Mars.[2] Regardless of your use case, spatial indexes are relatively easy to build and query on. Here I'll describe how to build these indexes, the range of queries possible, and a few internal design specs.

E.1 Spatial indexing basics

We'll use a US ZIP code database to demonstrate MongoDB's spatial indexes. The data is available at http://mng.bz/dOpd. When you unzip the archive, you'll get a JSON file that you can import using `mongoimport`, like so:

```
$ mongoimport -d geo -c zips zips.json
```

Let's first look at a ZIP code document. If you followed the import instructions, you should be able to fetch a document like so:

```
> use geo
```

---

[1] The most prominent of these is Foursquare (http://foursquare.com). You can learn more about Foursquare's MongoDB usage at http://mng.bz/rh4n.

[2] A great example of the former is WordSquared (http://wordsquared.com), a Scrabble-like game that uses MongoDB's spatial indexing for queries against the tiles on its game board.

```
> db.zips.findOne({zip: 10011})
{
"_id" : ObjectId("4d291187888cec7267e55d24"),
"city" : "New York City",
"loc" : {
  "lon" : -73.9996
  "lat" : 40.7402,
},
"state" : "New York",
"zip" : 10011
}
```

In addition to the expected city, state, and ZIP fields, you'll see a fourth field, loc, that stores the coordinates for the geographic center of the given ZIP code. This is the field you'll want to index and query on. Only fields containing coordinate values can be spatially indexed. But note that the form of the fields isn't too strict. You could just as easily use different keys to represent these coordinates:

```
{ "loc" : { "x" : -73.9996, "y" : 40.7402 } }
```

Or you might use a simple array pair:

```
{ "loc" : [ -73.9996, 40.7402  ] }
```

As long as you use a sub-document or an array, each of which contains two values, the field can be spatially indexed.

Now, to create the index itself, you specify 2d as the index type:

```
> use geo
> db.zips.ensureIndex({loc: '2d'})
```

This builds a spatial index on the loc field. Only those documents containing a properly formatted coordinate pair will be indexed; thus spatial indexes are always sparse. By default, the minimum and maximum coordinate values will be -180 and 180, respectively. This is the proper range for geographic coordinates, but if you happen to be indexing for a different domain, then you can set the min and max values as follows:

```
> use games
> db.moves.ensureIndex({loc: '2d'}, {min: 0, max: 64})
```

Once you've built a spatial index, you can perform spatial queries.[3] The simplest and most common type of spatial query is known as the $near query. When used in conjunction with a limit, a $near query allows you to find the *n* nearest locations to a given coordinate. For example, to find the three ZIP codes closest to Grand Central Station, you can issue the following query:

```
> db.zips.find({'loc': {$near: [ -73.977842, 40.752315 ]}}).limit(3)
{ "_id" : ObjectId("4d291187888cec7267e55d8d"), "city" : "New York City",
  "loc" : { "lon" : -73.9768, "lat" : 40.7519 },
  "state" : "New York", "zip" : 10168 }
{ "_id" : ObjectId("4d291187888cec7267e55d97"), "city" : "New York City",
```

---

[3] Note that this contrasts with non-spatial queries, which can be issued with or without a supporting index.

```
     "loc" : { "lon" : -73.9785, "lat" : 40.7514 },
     "state" : "New York", "zip" : 10178 }
{ "_id" : ObjectId("4d291187888cec7267e55d8a"), "city" : "New York City",
  "loc" : { "lon" : -73.9791, "lat" : 40.7524 },
  "state" : "New York", "zip" : 10165 }
```

Specifying a reasonable limit will ensure the fastest query response times. If no limit is given, then the limit will automatically be set to 100 to keep the query from returning the entire data set. If you require more than 100 results, specify the number as a limit:

```
> db.zips.find({'loc': {$near: [ -73.977842, 40.752315 ]}}).limit(500)
```

E.2   *Advanced queries*

Although $near queries are good for a lot of use cases, a few more advanced query techniques are also available. Instead of querying, you can run a special command called geoNear that returns the distances for each nearby object and several stats about the query itself:

```
> db.runCommand({'geoNear': 'zips', near: [-73.977842, 40.752315], num: 2})
{
  "ns" : "geo.zips",
  "near" : "0110000111011010011111010110010011001111111011011100",
  "results" : [
    {
      "dis" : 0.001121663764459287,
      "obj" : {
        "_id" : ObjectId("4d291187888cec7267e55d8d"),
        "city" : "New York City",
        "loc" : {
          "lon" : -73.9768,
          "lat" : 40.7519
        },
        "state" : "New York",
        "zip" : 10168
      }
    },
    {
      "dis" : 0.001126847051610947,
      "obj" : {
        "_id" : ObjectId("4d291187888cec7267e55d97"),
        "city" : "New York City",
        "loc" : {
          "lon" : -73.9785,
          "lat" : 40.7514
        },
        "state" : "New York",
        "zip" : 10178
      }
    }
  ],
  "stats" : {
    "time" : 0,
    "btreelocs" : 4,
```

```
    "nscanned" : 3,
    "objectsLoaded" : 2,
    "avgDistance" : 0.001124255408035117,
    "maxDistance" : 0.001126847051610947
  },
  "ok" : 1
}
```

The dist field that accompanies each document is a measure of that item's distance from the center point. In this case, the distance is measured in degrees.

Another slightly more advanced query allows searches within certain boundaries using the $within query operator. So, for example, to find all ZIP codes within 0.011 degrees of Grand Central Station, you can issue the following $center query:

```
> center = [-73.977842, 40.752315]
> radius = 0.011
> db.zips.find({loc: {$within: {$center: [ center, radius ] }}}).count()
26
```

This is theoretically equivalent to running a $near query with the optional $max-Distance parameter. Both queries return all results with the specified distance from the center point.

```
> db.zips.find({'loc': {$near: [-73.977842, 40.752315],
  $maxDistance: 0.011}}).count()
26
```

In addition to the $center operation, you can use the $box operator to return results lying inside a particular bounding box. So, for example, to return all ZIP codes lying within the box bounded by Grand Central Station and LaGuardia Airport, you could issue the following:

```
> lower_left = [-73.977842, 40.752315]
> upper_right = [-73.923649, 40.762925]
> db.zips.find({loc: {$within:
  {$box: [ lower_left, upper_right ] }}}).count()
15
```

Take note that the $box operator requires a two-element array, with the first element being the lower-left coordinate and the second element being the upper-right coordinate of the desired bounding box.

E.3 *Compound spatial indexes*

It's possible to create compound spatial indexes, but only if the coordinate key comes first. You might use a compound spatial index to enable queries on a location in addition to some type of metadata. For instance, imagine that the gardening store introduced earlier in the book has retail locations and that different locations provide different services. A couple of location documents might, in part, look like these:

```
{loc: [-74.2, 40.3], services: ['nursery', 'rentals']}
{loc: [-75.2, 39.3], services: ['rentals']}
```

So to query efficiently on both location and services, you'd create the following compound index:

```
> db.locations.ensureIndex({loc: '2d', services: 1})
```

This makes finding all retail stores with a nursery pretty trivial:

```
> db.locations.find({loc: [-73.977842, 40.752315], services: 'nursery'})
```

There's not much more to compound spatial indexes than that. If you're ever in doubt about whether they're effective for your application, be sure to try running `explain()` on the relevant queries.

E.4   *Spherical geometry*

All of the spatial queries I've described thus far use a flat-earth model for distance computations. In particular, the database uses Euclidean distance to determine the distance between points.[4] For a lot of use cases, including finding the closest n locations to a given point, this is perfectly acceptable, and the simplicity of the math ensures the fastest query result.

But the reality is that the earth is roughly spherical.[5] This means that the Euclidean distance calculations become less and less accurate as the distance between points increases. For this reason, MongoDB also supports distance calculations based on a two-dimensional spherical model. These queries yield more accurate distance results at only a slight performance cost.

To use spherical geometry, you need only make sure that all coordinates are stored in longitude-latitude order and that any distances are expressed in radians. You can then deploy most of the queries expressed earlier in their spherical forms. For example, $nearSphere is the spherical equivalent of $near and is expressed as follows:

```
> db.zips.find({'loc': {$nearSphere: [ -73.977842, 40.752315 ]}}).limit(3)
```

The `geoNear` command also supports spherical calculations with the addition of the { spherical: true } option:

```
> db.runCommand({'geoNear': 'zips',
    near: [-73.977842, 40.752315], num: 2, spherical: true})
```

Finally, you can use $centerSphere to query within a circle using spherical distances. Just be sure that when specifying the radius, you use radians:

```
center = [-73.977842, 40.752315]
radius_in_degrees = 0.11
radius_in_radians = radius_in_degrees * (Math.PI / 180);
db.zips.find({loc: {$within:
  {$centerSphere: [center, radius_in_radians ] }}})
```

---

[4] http://en.wikipedia.org/wiki/Euclidean_distance
[5] Roughly speaking because it's technically an oblate spheroid, which means that it bulges at the equator.

index

MORE TITLES FROM MANNING

Hadoop in Action
by Chuck Lam

    ISBN: 978-1-935182-19-1
    336 pages
    $44.99
    December 2010

Mahout in Action
by Sean Owen, Robin Anil, Ted Dunning,
  and Ellen Friedman

    ISBN: 978-1-935182-68-9
    416 pages
    $44.99
    October 2011

For ordering information go to www.manning.com

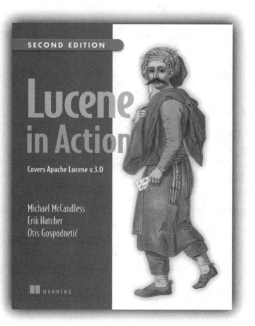

Lucene in Action, Second Edition
by Michael McCandless, Erik Hatcher,
and Otis Gospodnetić

ISBN: 978-1-933988-17-7
532 pages
$49.99
July 2010

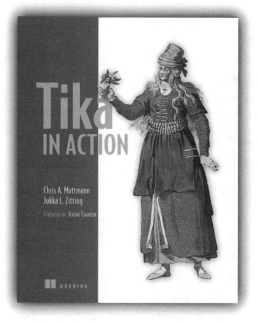

Tika in Action
by Chris A. Mattmann and Jukka L. Zitting

ISBN: 978-1-935182-85-6
225 pages
$44.99
November 2011

For ordering information go to www.manning.com

MORE TITLES FROM MANNING

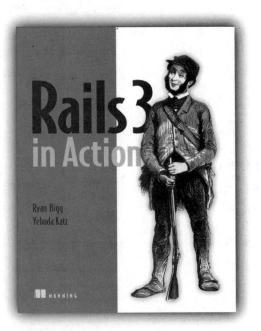

Rails 3 in Action
by Ryan Bigg and Yehuda Katz

ISBN: 978-1-935182-27-6
592 pages
$49.99
September 2011

R in Action
Data Analysis and Graphics with R
by Robert I. Kabacoff

ISBN: 978-1-935182-39-9
472 pages
$59.99
August 2011

For ordering information go to www.manning.com